BALANCING BOUNTIFUL

Caitlin Press Inc.
8100 Alderwood Road,
Halfmoon Bay, BC V0N 1Y1
www.caitlin-press.com

Text and cover design by Vici Johnstone
Cover photo and photo on page 4-5 by Loretta Naylor
Edited by Ruth Daniell

Caitlin Press Inc. acknowledges financial support from the Government of Canada and the Canada Council for the Arts, and the Province of British Columbia through the British Columbia Arts Council and the Book Publisher's Tax Credit.

Library and Archives Canada Cataloguing in Publication

Balancing Bountiful : what I learned about feminism
from my polygamist grandmothers / by Mary Jayne Blackmore.
Blackmore, Mary Jayne, 1983- author.

Canadiana 20200224743 | ISBN 9781773860046 (softcover)
LCSH: Blackmore, Mary Jayne, 1983- | LCSH: Mormon women—British Columbia—Bountiful—Biography. | LCSH: Mormon fundamentalism—British Columbia—Bountiful. | LCSH: Polygamy—British Columbia—Bountiful. | LCSH: Life change events—British Columbia—Bountiful.
LCC BX8680.M58 B53 2020 | DDC 289.3/34092—dc23

BALANCING BOUNTIFUL

What I Learned about Feminism
from My Polygamist Grandmothers

MARY JAYNE BLACKMORE

CAITLIN PRESS 2020

For Kristi

CONTENTS

PROLOGUE *Spring 2020* — 8

1   CHILDHOOD 1989–2000 — 13

THE OLD BARN — 14
SEVENTH BIRTHDAY — 19
THE FIRE — 26
MARY HAD A LITTLE LAMB — 28
THE CEMETERY — 38
BAPTISM — 42
GRANDPA'S HOUSE — 44
THE OLD CHICKEN COOP — 47
MILKING — 50
PERVERTS — 54
PANCAKES AT THE POND — 57
GRANDMA — 63
A BOOK OF RUTH — 68
WHEN I GROW UP — 72
CHICKENS — 77
CHRISTMAS — 84
WEEDING THE CORN PATCH — 89
HARVEST FESTIVAL — 92
KEEP SWEET — 99
THE MOTHERS — 103
HIGH SCHOOL — 110
SUMMER AT THE POST MILL — 118
TEN WEDDINGS — 121
CLEANING UP AFTER BOYS — 127
SWIMMING IN DRESSES — 130
BRIGHT EYES — 134
SWEET SIXTEEN — 139
BANANA PEEL — 142
INSPIRATION — 144
AWAITING PLACEMENT MARRIAGE — 147
THE END IS NEAR — 151

2	MARRIAGE 2000–2011	153
	MARRIAGE	154
	TWO PINK LINES	158
	GOD GIVES LIFE (AND TAKES IT AWAY)	161
	JUDGMENT DAY	164
	BACK TO THE FOLD	167
	DESPITE OUR FASTING AND PRAYERS	172
	A ROUND BELLY AND A TROUBLED HEART	177
	COMING HOME	180
	FEMINIST AND POLYGAMIST	187
	FEMINIST FIRE	197
	DAD'S ARREST	203
	MOMMA BEARS	207
	CALLING CONTRADICTIONS	209
	A BIRD IN A POPCORN POPPER	213
	GOODBYE, GRAMS	217
	WHY, GOD?	221
	DECAY	223
	"I'M BROKEN"	226
3	WANDERING BUT NOT LOST 2011–2018	233
	GOD SITS WITH ME	234
	BARREL OF MONKEYS	240
	NEW ZEALAND	248
	DOUKHOBOR MUSEUM	261
	BURNING MAN	265
	ARRESTED AGAIN	268
	WOMEN'S BODIES	274
	MY THIRTY-FOURTH BIRTHDAY	280
	PEACE IS NOT PASSIVE	285
	FAMILIES, NOT FELONS	289
	CHILD BRIDES	292
	I AM NOT A MORMON	298
	PROTECTING THE SACRED	303
	EPILOGUE	308
	ACKNOWLEDGEMENTS	318
	ABOUT THE AUTHOR	320

PROLOGUE
Spring 2020

I'm planting sunflowers along my fence as the sun finally slants over the towering cliffs of the Skimmerhorn mountains. The early green of the meadow lines the familiar creek that runs behind the Old Barn where I played as a kid. This morning only the cows and ponies keep me company. It's mid-April 2020, a few weeks until my thirty-seventh birthday, and the world is facing a global pandemic.

I've spent the past two weeks in absolute quarantine since returning from a month of travel in India. During the last five days of our trip, the country was shutting down. My cousin Linda, my sister Katie and I watched daily in apprehension as flights around the world were being cancelled. When we boarded our on-time Air Canada direct flight from Delhi to Vancouver, I finally exhaled. Masked travellers with worried eyes reflected what I imagine is being felt deeply in our global collective consciousness. COVID-19 is now part of dinner-table conversations around the world. No large gatherings. No touching. Stay home. Neighbours are policing neighbours. Public shaming is a normal and acceptable way of punishing dissidence. People are hoarding limited supplies. Grown adults are lying and sneaking to get out of their houses for a walk in the sunshine. Community evolves as it naturally does in times of crisis and collectively we fall a little more in love with one another, noticing the heroes of vital professions we previously took for granted. The best and the worst of humanity come out in these challenging times.

Lives and livelihoods are in danger and the world as we know it is transitioning around us. Each day on the news we hear more about areas being hit hard: Italy, Spain, New York City. People are dying.

This eerie apocalyptic scramble feels familiar to me: the preparation for the End of Times, the panic, the anxious waiting for benevolent guidance from unseen, all-knowing leadership. It activates traumatic memories I thought no longer held a vise on me. I feel as if I've already lived through this.

Twenty years ago, prophecies of the millennial End of Times and the Great Destruction promised that the world would be cleansed with fire and the wicked would be wiped off the face of the earth. This narrative shadowed my formative years and crippled my family and community in fear. The terror of being seen outside of the directive of the Prophet, even in the smallest ways, was as real as the fear of getting any virus. The Mormon religion defines death of this physical body as only a temporary separation from loved ones. Succumbing to the temptations of the devil and losing faith in the Prophet, who is the lifeline to God, however, will bring about eternal death and an eternity of loneliness in the fiery inferno of hell. I grew up fearing that hell and preparing for the End of Times. I also grew up surrounded by family and the beauty of these mountains.

I look up at the cliffs of the Skimmerhorn again and shake my head when I realize I've lived in the Cabin down at the Old Barn for ten years now. My dad was born here. My mother's family also lived in the Cabin when they first moved to the ranch from Alberta when Mom was a baby sixty-three years ago. My dad and mom were childhood playmates and grew up exploring along the creek and climbing the hay bales in the Old Barn. They married when they were both only eighteen, and this meadow was filled with the voices of the next generation of children riding ponies and tending farm critters. By the time my children came along, the great Old Barn no longer housed new lambs or a litter of piglets nestled in the fresh hay, but the top of the Old Barn with the smooth wooden floors was busy with the thumping of sneakers as the neighbourhood kids played floor hockey and basketball each afternoon and evening.

I smile and pick at the earnest leaves of comfrey that push their bright green into the light. They say that when Grandpa Ray fell ill with leukemia, the old aunts brought comfrey starts from Alberta to plant beside the Cabin so Grandpa could drink tea made from this healing plant. I've spent most of my ten years here digging this prolific legacy from my grass and flower beds. You cut one plant and it grows back as five. Suddenly the parallels between my grandfather's posterity and this comfrey that was intended to save his life feel significant.

I am Mary Jayne Blackmore, the 5th child of my father's 150 children. He is the 13th child of his father's 31 children. My father is a polygamist, as was his father before him.

I grew up in the glory days of Bountiful. I was raised with a passel of cousins who worked hard and played harder. As kids, we tried not to worry about the End of Times and shared in the dream of the greater good of "the community." I became an adult just as this dream of the greater good was shattering around me. I went to university to become a teacher, carrying the same dream that I imagine motivated my grandmothers: a vision of community. I was twenty-one and already the mother of the two most perfect babies. It seemed unfair to raise them in a box in a city. With the fear of the millennial end of days gone, I wanted to help rebuild the sense of togetherness that was the best part of my own childhood. My grandmothers devoted their lives to children, education and community. I want to do the same thing, my way, with what I have learned about feminism and the world both in and outside of Bountiful.

✿

I have respect for the ways that the women of Bountiful before me worked to put their families and their community first. Grandma Anna Mae (Grams) was Grandpa Ray's first wife. They had twelve living children. When she passed almost ten years ago, we counted over one thousand of her posterity. My grandfather's posterity is multitudes beyond that. This history is my history too. My grandfather converted to fundamentalist Mormonism in the 1940s. On a mission for the Mormon Church in New Zealand, Grandpa Ray found himself spreading the good word to an old Mormon polygamist Maori elder. Young Ray Blackmore tried to explain that God had instructed the leaders of the church to give up the sacred principle of plural and celestial marriage so Utah could become one of the United States of America. He said this elder preached him a sermon he would never forget. Ray took to studying the scripture for himself, and God gave him a testimony of this principle that would set his life on an altogether different path. Upon marriage to his second wife, Grandpa Ray left Alberta and bought the Lyons Ranch in Lister, BC.

My grandmother described first coming to the Creston Valley as if it were the real promised land: "Fruit was ripening on the trees and the cows stood deep in tall grass blowing in the meadows." After Alberta winters, Creston was so mild that children rarely needed to wear shoes. Grandpa bought some dairy cows and quota and raised a herd of well-fed, hard-working farm kids. These kids grew up strong in the faith and strong in body. Ray Blackmore's children raised families whose commitment to community and their Mormon faith bonded them together and to God. There were hard years when they barely made their payments and they lived mostly from food they'd harvested and stored away in their root cellars. There were years of great prosperity and co-operation, and the Blackmores knew to give their thanks to God. For five decades, they thrived. They built businesses, built houses, built a school and raised families, carrying on the vision and legacy of their father. When I think about the sheer work of supporting those families, I'm amazed at the strength of my ancestors, but especially of the women. My grandmothers worked on the farm, in the fields and in the school and gave birth to so many cherished babies, trusting they were raising the chosen believers, those destined to help rebuild Zion. The Blackmores' devotion to community and to live God's word made them resilient in times of trouble.

What had made the Mormon community strong, however, was also what divided it. In 2002, when I was nineteen years old and a new mother, conflict over church leadership split apart the stout-hearted people of Bountiful and their Mormon brothers and sisters in Utah. Somehow, they let someone tell them they were no longer a family and community. They built walls shutting each other out and they stopped working together. As the Bible put it, they sold their birthright for a mess of pottage. In a short time, they forgot the legacy of their ancestors. Working together had made them strong, and their passion to serve God had brought them to this beautiful place, which is where I still live and plant my sunflowers.

I was a witness to the conflict within the community I had been raised in and loved my whole life, and that conflict—along with so much love and tenderness and surprise and beauty—helped to shape who I am.

In 2009 our community was tested again, this time when my father was arrested for polygamy, and we were once again forced to examine under a public eye the legality of ours not being the "right" kind of family.

My personal journey has not followed any course young Mary could have ever imagined. My youthful faith and devotion to serve God and the spiritual guidance of my father held strong through my church-assigned marriage four days before my seventeenth birthday, until my husband and I decided to separate when I was twenty-seven years old. That day, I knew I could no longer fit my life into the box. Broken and divorced, I needed a way of looking at the world that wouldn't leave my only choices to be miserable or to be burning in hell for eternity. Mormon culture has many valuable constructs to support family and community, and I think—with a wary eye to check abuse—religion deserves a place in helping us describe our experiences of the world and of God. But the Mormon narrative is much too narrow for the way I now know God. I no longer call myself a Mormon.

The pleasant April sun warms my back as I pick the tips of the bright comfrey and dandelion leaves from my grass and go inside to put the big tea kettle on. Granny Elene, Grandpa Ray's youngest sister, is on my mind. She and her husband also left Alberta and joined Grandpa and

Grams and the other polygamists in BC. My grandmothers were full of wisdom and good sense. "Make a tea with the first greens of spring to get the nutrients," Grams would say, and "Clean colon, clean lungs. If you get a cough, do a cleanse." Granny taught school until she was ninety-four, getting up every day to help her daughter and granddaughter teach the kindergarten and grade-one class. She'd be seen chewing dandelion flowers as she watched the students swinging on the playground. When asked what the secret of her youth and beauty was, she'd say with a smile, "Eat seven dandelion heads a day and always have a reason to get up in the morning."

I drink my comfrey-dandelion tea and think about my grandmothers. It takes a village to raise a child; this my grandmothers knew well. Our children are our legacy, and it is in the lives of our children that we will know the truth of how we have lived. While my own babies are almost adults, I feel humbled to share a village of children. I don't know if my grandparents imagined a utopia when they purchased the Lyons Ranch in Lister seventy years ago. But I do know the hard work, year after year, that went into creating community to raise children the way they believed was best.

Writing this book has never felt optional. Claiming this narrative has been an essential part of my healing and growth and stepping into my own story as a woman on the planet. This book is about me. It's my story and I speak only for myself, but my motivation in writing it has never been about me. I wrote this book for the ones who don't remember the story and may know about their father and grandfather only from media stereotypes that do not do justice to the hearts of the men and women who put their souls into their families and community. My commitment to the youth of this community has kept me writing and motivated me to turn on my computer day after day. Writing this book has been an act of love and devotion for those dearest loves in my life, especially the beautiful, powerful young women who come through this proud legacy of mothers and grandmothers, our daughters and our great-granddaughters. Empowering my own feminist voice and adding to the collective voice for women has compelled me to keep asking the big questions of womanhood and humanity: What is the right kind of woman, the right kind of family and the right kind of feminist?

1

CHILDHOOD

1989–2000

THE OLD BARN

It's 1989 and I am six years old. I squint up into the bright summer sun. A pigeon swoops in big circles and perches in one of the tiny houses framed on top of the big Old Barn. Miriam and I have apples, picked from the Big Tree out in the cow pasture, weighing down the hidden pockets of our dresses. Mir's blue eyes and freckles are framed with straw-coloured hair hanging in a thick braid to her waist. My own brown hair is parted down the middle with top and bottom braids. Our mothers keep our hair this way so it never gets too messy and we don't look like orphan children. Last year's school dresses are our summer play clothes as they collect dandelion stains and fade from washing and sunshine. Our brown feet and arms are a contrast to the faded ruffles of our skirts.

This day, we are planning which animals we will need to add to our growing little farm. My brother Pete is helping me buy one of Uncle Kev's bummer lambs, and Mir has chickens over at Uncle Guy's place. When we grow up, we will go into business together, like our dads, we say. Our houses will be right next to each other or we will marry the same guy and be sister-wives. We will raise good sons and daughters who will help us on the farm before they get to go play in the Old Barn. Mir and I talk about being ready to take our kids and be pioneers to go help rebuild the New Jerusalem on the American continent. We will be farmers and mothers in God's kingdom after the Great Destruction and Jesus comes again.

We pick up a rock and each bust a hunk off the block of blue cow salt out in the cow pen. The cows have licked deep crevices that I trace with my tongue, as smooth as rocks in the creek bed. I take a bite of apple, lick the salt, then rub it back and forth across the bitten part until the white flesh of the apple is lathered and shiny smooth with the salty juice and take another bite.

The Old Barn is cool after the hot afternoon sun. To the right, the old milk room is at the front with three stalls built along the side wall. This dark, dusty room smells of musty hay and isn't used for much anymore except as a little stall where the boys put a new calf or pony on cold winter nights. We climb the wall ladder to the second layer of the barn. Old dairy equipment lies forgotten and half buried under musty hay and years of dust, reminders of the old days when Grandpa Ray and his kids hand milked the cows before they built the new dairy on the hill.

Nearly a hundred acres of rocky hills and pine trees interrupted with green meadows and scattered with about two dozen dwellings nestle against the towering Skimmerhorn mountains standing guardian over my childhood paradise. A thick marshy forest lines the back of the property against the mountain. Two abundant mountain springs feed a creek that laughs through green meadows. Contented dairy cows chew their cuds in the afternoon shade of a big apple tree. And there stands the big Old Barn.

Daddy talks about when he and his brothers in their bare feet would be fetching the cows for milking. When frost covered the ground, he jumped from one steaming cow-pie to the next to keep his toes warm. He told us he liked to poke holes through horse buns, light one end on fire, suck the smoke through in long draws and try to make smoke rings. Mormons don't smoke and Dad tells us, "If you're gonna suck smoke from something, it might as well be a horse bun; a cigarette doesn't look any cooler than that either."

This middle level of the barn has a low ceiling and extends for only half of the building. When Dad was a kid, the big ranch house burned down. Grandpa and Grandma Aloha converted the chicken coop into a small cabin and put up some bunk beds on this level of the barn for the older boys' bunkhouse.

A big window with sagging shutters looks out over the barnyard. A few old boards are nailed between the narrow strip of wall and the twenty-foot drop to the barn floor. I push up through the square hole and pull myself up, belly sliding on the satin-smooth wood of the hayloft. I keep one hand on the rough, weathered door frame for support as I inch my toes to the edge of the window, far above the dusty barnyard. I lean forward just enough to feel the flutter in my stomach; shivers run up my spine. The chickens look like little bugs bobbing around. The back of the loft is half full of second-cut hay, which has already been stacked to feed the cows during the winter.

Summer is a busy time for us farmers. My brothers and cousins drive tractors, cutting and turning the sweet-smelling hay to dry. Watching them unload a semi-truck of hay is almost like watching a line of ants carrying food back to their anthill. Two of them pull the bales off the trailer and bump them end to end on the complaining chain teeth that take them up and up to the big third-storey window. At the top, two of the big boys or girls wait, stand facing each other and alternate grabbing the bales from the elevator and packing them across the polished floor to stack in the back of the barn for winter.

I can drag a hay bale if I really put my mind to it and with a couple of us girls on a bale we can feed the critters in the stalls or build shacks, but a farmer our size is better at filling water jugs or helping the mothers bring lunch.

A big knotted-together rope is tied to the third beam that spans the width of the open side of the barn. In winter, the barn is full of hay and usually full of kids as well. The big boys drag bales around to make levels to swing from. "Just don't break the bales" is the only rule in the Old Barn, but sometimes it happens by accident and then we can make a big fluffy pile to jump into and then fluff it up again for the next kid. The big kids make tunnels and mazes through the stacks of hay bales that lead into secret hidden rooms. Sometimes they are terrifyingly dark and elaborate.

John Wayne and Louis L'Amour are the great narrators of our childhood games in the Old Barn, which can go on for days. The boys are the brave riders of the Pony Express or cowboys in the Old West. We girls are the daughters and wives who get kidnapped, die tragically in childbirth or are abandoned to raise their children while the men go on some great mission. I prefer to be Sacagawea, who got to take her baby with her and didn't have to miss out on all the fun.

Occasionally, we split into a full-on feud and cousin rivalry. All the kids join one group or the other for some standoff for territory. Sticks become guns and horses; a few of the older boys have their own hand-carved wooden weapons. There is yelling, wrestling, shrieking and prisoners being taken by one group or the other. There is lots of "Bam, you're dead" with no clear rules.

If the games start getting out of hand, the older girls Nancy and Donna usually start yelling at everyone to go home or someone runs to call one of the mothers from Uncle Karl's telephone in the little white two-storey farmhouse across the barnyard.

It's during these wild and reckless gatherings in the Old Barn that our best family history lessons are debated among a pack of us cousins, each with our own authority and God-given right to claim our history.

"Great-Grandpa William Morrish Blackmore was kidnapped by pirates when he was twelve years old and he grew up a cabin boy on a ship," Walter asserts. He grins widely. Two years older than me, he and Dan are the ringleaders of the boys. He whoops and jumps from a beam, swinging through the air to balance successfully on the hay bales.

"He was not kidnapped. His family were so poor that they had to have him go work on the ships because they couldn't afford to feed all their kids," Aunt Margy's girl Michelle argues with him.

"Nah-uh," our older cousin Nancy chimes in with authority. "He actually ran away because he knew his parents couldn't afford to take care of him, so he became a servant on the ship as a cabin boy. The captain taught him all about being a sailor and even taught him how to read and write, and he had to stay on the ship for seven years to serve his contract." Nancy is one of the oldest of our age group of cousins. She's good at bossing the boys around and organizing games and clubs for us kids.

"He was so tough, he could climb overhand up the masts and could carry two five-gallon buckets of water straight out to the side. That's how he escaped from the pirates: he dove overboard and swam three or four miles to shore." Walt swings to a perch on top of the haystack and then jumps with a whoop into the pile of hay.

"Yeah, but if he hadn't he wouldn't have become a Mormon and then we wouldn't be here," Donna continues. "He met the Mormon missionaries on a ship he was working on. They were travelling from America to teach the gospel. They gave him a Book of Mormon, which he read cover to cover. Then they taught him about Joseph Smith and the work the Mormons were doing in Utah. Great-Grandpa decided to be baptized and went back to England to marry a girl he was promised to. Her father was a drinker and he told Great-Grandpa, 'No daughter of mine will marry a man who can't sit down and have a drink with me.' So Grandpa William went to Idaho and that's where he married Great-Grandmother, Mary Christina Ada Horn Blackmore."

No one is keen to polish up the details of our favourite legends of Great-Grandfather William Morrish Blackmore, a descendant of the wild clansmen of the nomadic tribes from the "black moors" of England. He lives on in the boundless imaginations of his burgeoning posterity.

"Great-Grandpa was on the boat that killed the great whale Moby Dick," Dan joins in. "It's true," he continues. "In England, there is a big sign talking about Moby Dick and listing all the sailors; his name is on it." For a bunch of kids who could barely find England on a map, somehow our British Loyalist heritage still held strong.

Beyond the legends, and for three generations, the Blackmore name has stood for a stubborn strong will, a righteous conviction to strictly follow God's word no matter the hardship, the bond and kinship of family and the brotherhood of working together.

In the Old Barn, my daredevil cousins walk the beams, which span the open side of the barn and are only about five inches wide, maybe twenty-five feet above the hay-strewn concrete below. When the barn is almost full of hay, Mir and I also walk the beams. It's easy but I pretend it's dangerous and my muscles tighten with the thrill.

Dust particles dance in the sun slanting through the big open doorway and making a square of light on the wood floor polished from decades of bales stacked there by our grandpa, our dads and brothers and the scurry of feet enraptured in the games of pure childhood imagination.

On this hot summer day, the barn is quiet except for the shuffle of the old sow and her fat piglets in the lean-to at the back of the barn. The ponies stand content in the shade of the farthest corner of the meadow, sending a clear message to any potential riders that a ride will be earned only by lots of chasing and a bucket full of grain.

SEVENTH BIRTHDAY

"Happy birthday, sweetheart." It's May 3 and I'm seven years old. Mother smooths the sleep scraggles from my forehead with her cool hand, bends to kiss me lightly above my eyes. I stretch, snuggling a little deeper next to Susie in our double bed. Mother's eyes sparkle with her own anticipation. She is petite and feminine with olive skin and dark hair she wears in waves and a thick braid hanging down her back. Her eyes are often stern and her brows furrowed in thought. But when she smiles and sings I think my mother is the most beautiful woman in the world.

After seven years of marriage and four children with my mother, Dad married Mother Christina. She had her first son six months after I was born, my little brother Don. Daddy also married her sister, Mother Mary Ann, four years later. The only world I knew was full of mothers, grandmas, aunts, big boys, babies and sisters gathered around the long dining table. There is something special about each of my father's wives— Mother, Mother Mary Ann and Mother Christina—but nothing beats the comfort of my own mother.

Mother always tells me how lucky she felt when I was born and she got to have her two little girls. "You were *so* cute," she tells me. My birthday must be particularly special to her too, her cute baby turning seven. She laughs cheerily, and I notice she's hiding something behind her back. Giggling, she turns so I can't see it.

I knew she was working on something for me because for the past few days she would tell me to run and play when she sat down at her sewing machine. She holds up a pink velour skating dress with white furry trim around the bottom of the skirt, sleeves and a little cape. I had seen the cloth in her sewing box. It is as soft as kitten's fur and is a perfect fit. I put it on and twirl, imagining the way I will look, come next winter, floating across the icy pond, learning spins and twirls. The best is still to come: she holds up my Strawberry Shortcake doll wearing an exact tiny replica of my dress with the white trim and cape. I throw my arms around her neck and squeeze tight before running upstairs to show Daddy.

My father sits in his usual seat at the head of the table, his back to the big window that looks out to the front hill driveway, and the beige-coloured phone with the extra-long, tightly coiled cord near his right arm. He's the bishop and spends a lot of time on the phone. If he gets through a bowl of porridge without the phone ringing, he says it's one of God's miracles, like sending manna from heaven.

I twirl with my doll into the dining room onto my father's lap. He holds the sides of my face, squishing my cheeks out as he does so, and kisses me on the forehead. He bounces me on his knee and I sing along while he croons the chorus of his favourite song:

> *You are my sunshine, my only sunshine.*
> *You make me happy when skies are grey.*
> *You'll never know, dear, how much I love you.*
> *Please don't take my sunshine away.*

My brother Pete and I share birthdays. He is eleven today. He's four years older and a little extra nice to me. He tells me I'm his favourite birthday present. Mother's four older children are Jacob, Hyrum, Peter and Sue, then me. Joey is her baby boy.

Daddy playfully puts me over his knee and lays out my birthday spankings, one for each year. Then he stands me up with a pinch to grow an inch and a pat to grow fat. Next he digs into his pocket and pulls out a crisp five-dollar bill and two loonies, my long-awaited birthday money. I'll squirrel it away for the farm Mir and I plan to have. Each year our birthday money goes up a dollar.

Daddy continues singing as I climb onto a chair next to my little sister Niki, who is sitting next to him with our Sunday morning treat of cornflakes.

My father has the wide shoulders, powerful arms and barrel chest they say made Great-Grandfather Blackmore such a good sailor. When Dad and his brothers were young, they did their share of slinging hay bales and other hard work around the farm, but now Daddy drives a semi-truck; they haul logs, hay, cows and whatever else is needed for the farm and logging business. Dad also spends days in his office, where he organizes church and school stuff. Along with fresh bread and Sunday dinners, all that sitting in the semi-truck is showing in Dad's belly. "Too many mashed potatoes and gravy and Grandma's fresh bread," Dad says, patting his stomach. "There never was a Blackmore who was too thin."

In the corner by the little table, Mother Mary Ann is combing Katie's hair using a tail comb, dipping it into a cup of water. Katie complains that she is pulling too hard and little droplets of water run down the sides of her face each time Mother Mary Ann dips the comb to wet the hair.

Her fingers fly, neatly parting Katie's hair and securing it into a wave with a clip and two braids. Katie looks fresh as a shiny new penny and ready to face the day, and before anyone else can get in line, I ask Mother Mary Ann to comb my hair for my birthday and for church.

Our three mothers bustle about to mobilize the small army that is our family, making preparations for the big dinner served at our house after church each Sunday with easily fifty to eighty extended family members showing up for mashed potatoes and gravy with all the fixin's.

Susie clears the breakfast dishes. Mother Christina asks me to help our chubby little sister Nesta down from the high chair where she's thrown her spoon and is eating her porridge with her hands. Vicki, Mother Mary Ann's baby, is only three months younger. Not yet two, they keep our house full of smiles and curls.

Milking pails clang against the opening door; my brothers come in from doing the morning chores. Hyrum quickly strains the two buckets of steamy, frothy milk and Peter has a bucket of poopy chicken eggs that need washing.

We turn and smile as Pete walks into the dining room and shakes Dad's hand to say good morning. Dad hugs all of us but the boys shake his hand and we girls kiss him on the cheek. When he comes to breakfast, he has changed into a white shirt and black pants with his shirttails tucked in, church ready. Dad does the birthday ritual all over again, slapping a ten and a five onto the table with exaggerated despair.

"Now I'm broke! And I'll let ya earn the other four bucks off of me on a business deal."

We all laugh. Ours is a frugal household, with parents who have never heard of allowances and would never dream of paying us to do chores. We have what we need and we rarely ask for or receive extra anything, so birthday money is a highlight of the year.

The chicken roasting in the oven fills the whole house with the aroma of Sunday. Grams stands at the kitchen sink, looking out the long window, peeling potatoes to fill the heavy steel pot, happy, she says, that she is hard of hearing and doesn't have to listen to the chaos of the running, hollering kids.

The bright May sun shines through the open door as people go in and out. Joey is walking around with one shoe on.

"Hurry, bud, we gotta get going," Daddy scolds him.

The mothers are gathering up babies, checking on things in the kitchen and running back and forth to get something forgotten. Niki doesn't have her hair combed so Mother Christina runs back to grab a comb. Daddy tells Danny and Dave, his younger brothers who live with us, to take his truck and drive Grams to church. Joey and Don ask to ride in the back of the pickup and Daddy lifts Joey into the box as Don climbs over the tailgate.

I'm busy admiring the way my skirt flares out to the fluffy white trim. When I twirl, it goes up almost in a perfect circle, showing my white slip and my lacy bloomers. I keep the skirt down with my hands so no one will scold me to act more like a lady and not show my underwear.

Daddy steps out the kitchen door and I'm the only one who appears ready to go to church.

"Walk with me, sweets." He takes my hand and we head up the hill. I skip a bit to keep up with him so he starts to sing, "Skip, skip, skip to my Lou, skip to my Lou, my darling."

I sing along, thrilled I get my daddy to myself. At the top of the hill, we turn onto the New Road. It's been a couple of years since they made it and the dirt is mostly packed down smooth, but the name stuck.

Daddy and I turn up the trail to the new school, where we have church in the big room, instead of sticking to the long, windy road. I walk ahead of him because the trail is wide enough for only one. I'm stepping carefully so as not to get dirt on my shiny black shoes. Daddy stops. He lowers down on his heels and says in a soft voice, "Look at this, love." I turn. He points to a little hollow beneath a large fallen tree. I wouldn't have seen it if he weren't pointing, though it's but a foot from the trail where I walk every day to school. I count four eggs, as blue as a summer sky, carefully hidden there by their momma.

We smile at each other. If you touch a bird's eggs, when she returns to the nest she will smell you on her eggs and will roll them out of her nest. We both love birds. Daddy's the bishop and in church he tells the boys not to shoot the birds with their slingshots. Daddy and I decide we will keep it our little secret so no mean boys will break the eggs.

Daddy starts singing while we prop some branches to block the view from the trail:

> *I know where there's a robin's nest, a robin's nest, a robin's nest.*
> *I know where there's a robin's nest, but I'm not telling you where.*

We sing together walking up the hill in the fresh May sunshine.

You might frighten the birds away, birds away, birds away.
You might frighten the birds away, so I'm not telling you
where.

❦

Mashed potatoes and gravy, bread dressing, canned corn and green beans to go on the side and then cake with strawberries and whipped cream or Jell-O salad for dessert. The best reason to go to church is to come home to all that food. Mother pulls a big chocolate cake from the oven, spreads a white baking sheet over it and sets it in the dining room out of the way to cool. It will be my brother's and my shared birthday cake, which has been the tradition since our first birthday together.

"A family just doesn't need two cakes in one day," Mother says. Pete and I sit together on the long bench on the far side of the table; our siblings and cousins who came over after church squeeze in close. Jake helps Mother light the candles and someone switches off the lights. Our voices fill the room with harmonies of "Happy Birthday to You" that even the von Trapp family would envy. Mother pulls out her camera and winds the film for a few snapshots of us blowing out the candles in unison. Another birthday celebration checked off the to-do list.

❦

In the early days on the Lyons Ranch, everyone looked out for everyone the best they could. It was a community that worked together to raise the children, as much out of sheer survival as out of idealism. Those were some lean years but nobody had more than anyone else so the family barely noticed. A lot needed to be done just to keep food on the table and a roof over their heads. The dairy farm where my father and his brothers worked was the main source of income. The gardens, eggs, milk from the dairy and meat from the chickens and a cow butchered in the fall, as well as the deer the boys shot, were staples of their diet. There weren't many trips to the grocery store.

Just one year before my parents married, Grandpa Ray lost his battle with leukemia. He was only fifty-seven years old. He left a startled half-grown family and four wives. My parents, the young couple, moved into the big house with Grams. Sharing the cooking and cleaning of the busy, full household with her mother-in-law and her sister-wives, Mother became operations manager of a home that was also the centre of community life. The house was always filled to overflowing with church visitors or boys who needed to "work off some steam" on the farm, people in transition after a house fire or newlywed couples figuring out a place to live. She took on the practicality and efficient personality of someone who has always had too much to do. Uncle Mac summed it up one day, telling a big roomful of company, "Jane runs a tight ship."

Mealtimes clamour with cousins and uncles, sharing stories, songs and generally not the best manners. On any given night, there are easily a dozen extra people at the family dinner table. It's simple food, usually soup and fresh bread, but it's hot and delicious and there is always plenty in the big cooking pot. "Never send a child home hungry" is a rule Grams lives by and says often. The mothers and girls cook the meals and do the dishes and, mostly, the boys do the farm chores. That's just how it is.

After the dishes are done, the children put on their nightclothes and the family starts to gather in the living room. Mother sits in the middle of the big couch with one of our favourite Thornton W. Burgess books, *The Adventures of Reddy Fox*. We kids snuggle in close to hear the adventures of the animals on Farmer Brown's farm as we wait for the family to circle on the brown shag carpet on the living room floor. Daddy offers a prayer to our dear Heavenly Father for the blessing in our lives, and for the sacred principle and for babies to be born into celestial marriage. After the prayer, Daddy grabs his guitar from behind the big rocking chair where Grams rocks gently. The harmonies of the guitar strings croon like childhood lullabies. Daddy says he wrote this familiar tune when his first son was born and his heart was bursting with joy. I sing along, even as my eyes are closing. The arm of the plush brown couch with the little log cabins on the fabric cradles my head. My bare feet are wedged down the side of the cushion. I wiggle in closer to my mother's warmth while the fireplace crackles below us in the basement. Dad sings:

> *When I wake up in the morning then I thank him.*
> *I thank him for the light of a beautiful day,*
> *And I thank him for my friends and for my neighbours*
> *And for the chance I have of improving myself some way.*
>
> *And for the air I breathe, the cows I feed, the fields that I walk through.*
> *For my children and my family and for everything you do,*

While on my knees, my father dear,
I thank you for my start, and I thank him from the bottom of
my heart.

In the middle of the day again I thank him.
I thank him for the plan of eternity,
I thank him for the man who represents him,
And that this man was known so well by me.

When my day is done beside my bed down on my knees,
I thank him for the blessings of this day,
For health, for strength, for life and for his charity
And for the father, hallowed be thy name.

THE FIRE

A few weeks ago I was eating birthday cake with my family and playing up at the Three-Layered Shack in the trees on the hill above the Old Barn. Today is one of the days when all the kids show up at the same time. Jolene, her brother Johnny and I make a horse corral with sticks tied to the trees with orange baling twine. Each of us has a really good stick horse notched with a string tied around it. Nancy and Donna get all the kids organized so we are all a part of the Pony Express riders, or sometimes we play Wild West games with all of the capturing and shooting and running away, hunting and stealing one another's stick horses. All Mormons learn the Articles of Faith by heart before getting baptized. I've been working to learn them all before Don does.

At bedtime I ask Mother Mary Ann if I can sleep in her bed with her. We get all snuggled in and I'm feeling cozy and safe when someone comes running down the hill, hollering, "Uncle Marvin's house is on fire!" Mother Mary Ann jumps out of bed. I hear her talking to Daddy and then they both leave. I'm scared. Only grey light is visible outside. I bury down in the covers waiting but I can already tell something really bad is happening.

After a bit Mother Mary Ann comes back in carrying my little cousin Tammy and puts her in bed with me. Aunt Marlene stays in my daddy's bedroom with her baby, and the boys sleep on the couch. People are coming and going. Trucks pull up to the house and leave again. I can hear sirens in the distance and can see the red lights go flashing up the road past our house. There is a bright red glow above the trees. Tammy and I stand on the bed together looking out the window, then we huddle together, barely whispering in the dark.

※

In the morning they say Daddy is in the hospital. Mother says I can go with her to see him. He has oxygen in a tube going into his nose and he keeps coughing. He talks really rough and quietly. He says the doctors said it was like he smoked a thousand cigarettes at one time and burned his lungs. I stand beside his bed and hold on to his hand, looking at all the tubes and listening to the hissing sound of the breathing machine. Big tears fall on my cheeks. The doctors say he is lucky and he could have even died. He lies back on his bed, his body racked with coughing, wincing with pain.

"I'm going to be okay, love. I'll be home soon," he says. I believe him but I'm still scared.

Daddy says he rushed up when Aunt Debbie called him about the fire. She had her children loaded in the station wagon but she said one of them was missing. Daddy told us his terror imagining her little Tim—who is the same age as my brother Pete—sleeping in his bed while the flames engulfed the house. Daddy went running into the blackness and billowing smoke. He went from room to room feeling in the beds and under the beds, finding nothing, and finally was forced out of the house in agony that he was leaving the boy behind.

Miraculously the boy was somehow in the back of the station wagon the whole time and had been missed.

It will be a long time before Daddy doesn't have to hold on to something when he coughs. In the meantime there are other things to think about: after the fire that night, Aunt Debbie leaves. Some say she flew off the handle. To me it feels as if she just vanishes, taking my cousins away forever. One day I am making shacks in the forest with my cousin Jolene and the next they are gone. Just like that, in one night, the fire burned up the house that had been always bursting over with kids.

I can't think of anything scarier than the fire. I know that the fire was a bad thing but I don't understand why Aunt Debbie had to leave. I remember the way my stomach twisted inside me when I heard the sirens outside the window. Maybe Aunt Debbie did fly off the handle. I hope my cousins like their new house.

MARY HAD A LITTLE LAMB

I'm late to school today. This morning my breakfast job was to wash dishes. Whenever it's my turn to wash the dishes, I can never leave on time. I'm not supposed to leave until it's done and my little brother was taking forever to get all the dishes gathered up. Some of the babies were still eating. Finally, Grandma said I could just go and she would finish for me. Susie just had to sweep the floor, which took her only five minutes, and then she was out the door. I'll be on floor tomorrow.

The gust of warm air and the bright lights of Bountiful Elementary-Secondary School are inviting after my run up the hill through the trees to school on this snowy February morning. I'm late and my frosty cheeks hide my blush when our principal, Uncle Merrill, starts singing, "Mares eat oats and does eat oats and little lambs eat ivy." When I come into the school, everyone looks at me as I carry my snowy winter boots to my locker. Grandma Della smiles brightly from her door of the resource room as I pass. I hate being late. But that doesn't spoil my mood. I'm bursting to tell my friends. I've waited my whole life for this and finally, now that I'm in grade three, I am going to be the real Mary-had-a-little-lamb.

Late February and March is lambing season and if I can get away with it I go almost every day after school to see the lambs at Uncle Kevin's. I love the feel of their tight-knit curly wool after the mother has licked the birthing goo from them. I love their soft little tongues as they lick my hand or coat, looking for their momma's milk.

I've been saving up and now I have the money to buy my own little bummer lamb. Last night Pete told me one of Uncle Kev's ewes gave birth to twins and one of them was a bummer lamb. It makes me a little bit heartsick thinking how any mom could choose one of her babies to live and kick away the other one to get sick and die.

"It's part of nature," my uncle tried to explain to me. "It's how God designed it. The mother knows she cannot feed both of her babies and if she didn't kick away one of them, there is a chance both of them would die." The mean moms just kick at the bummer, not letting it suck until finally it gives up. If the farmer didn't bottle-feed them, the bummers would die.

One time, my cousin Daisy and I decided it was just too mean. We were going to make one of those old girls give the bummer lamb a suck.

We caught her up against the fence. Daisy had her arms wrapped around the ewe's neck and her whole body weight pressing her into the wooden panels. I leaned up against her middle and held her back leg. The lamb, not quite understanding that we were giving her lunch, took her sweet time. Finally she got the idea and tried to suckle. The ewe was having none of it. She kicked her back leg and wriggled out of Daisy's grasp. I held on a little too long. All I got for trying to solve injustices in the world was sitting in the dirt with poop smeared down my dress.

Having my own little bummer lamb would somehow help me set the world a bit more right. I would love that lamb and bottle-feed her and then maybe she would let me ride her. We would be the very best friends.

One of the big boys in high school says an opening prayer. His head is bowed so low and he speaks so fast that I catch only the "Dear Heavenly Father, in the name of Jesus Christ, amen." We all say "Amen," sending our prayers to God along with whatever it was he said.

After assembly we file into class. When I tell my class about the lamb I'm getting after school, my cousins Lorin and Kenneth, who are the mean boys in my class and like to tease the girls with worms and bugs, start singing a taunting rhyme. "Mary had a little lamb, her daddy shot it dead. Now it goes to school with her, between two slices of bread." The kids laugh and I crinkle my nose at them. Today, even this hardly bothers me.

After school I'll have to figure out where my lamb will live. It is still February with snow on the ground. Without a mother to snuggle up to, a newborn lamb could never sleep outside in this weather. The Old Barn would be too far away for bottle-feeding four times a day. I have a plan but I'm not sure how Momma will feel about it.

❧

Daddy's truck is just pulling out of the school parking lot, leaving from his other job as superintendent of the school and community wiggly tooth puller. Don and I crash through the front doors of the school, hollering for him to wait. Two of my cousins, Andy and Vance, pile in; they holler, "Uncle Wink, will you drop us off at our corner?"

He drops us off and leans out the window as he's pulling away. "Don, haul ten pieces of firewood for the Bottom House fire. Bye, loves!" Don is just six months younger than me, but he is a grade lower. His teachers send his work home with me so he doesn't lose it.

I spot a sled half buried under the snow. "Hey, Don, if you pull me halfway, I'll pull you the rest of the way." He starts pulling me like crazy and makes me do a jump. He's running to keep ahead of the sled. The sled hits a hidden rock and I go sprawling in the snow.

While I'm gathering myself together, my brother plasters me with a snowball. I wipe the handful of wet snow all over his face, filling his mouth and eyes. He leaps at me, knocking me back into the snow, surprisingly strong and fast. He is ruthless as he sits on my chest and smears handful after handful of snow into my nose and mouth. I push him off and I'm mad. My skin stings from the snow burn. I start bawling and yell at him. My pride is hurt more than anything. Boys are mean.

The last part of the hill is steep, down into our driveway.

"Jump on," he coaxes.

I quickly forget my anger and soon we are picking up speed. He flops onto his knees on the back of the sled, clutching my coat. We speed forward. Thrown off by his momentum, we career off the steep bank and narrowly miss a tree. We are left breathless and laughing in a tangled mess of coats and gloves.

"I'll come help you haul firewood at the Bottom House and you can come help me at the Top House to make a lamb pen."

Our family is getting big now. Our whole family used to live in the Bottom House. Last year Daddy married two sisters from Utah, Mother Sharon and Mother Midge, his fifth and sixth wives. Our family became too big for the Bottom House. Uncle Guy's family moved out of their house, which is just up the hill from ours. Mother and her kids moved up there along with Mother Sharon and Grams. Don's mother, Mother Christina, Mother Midge and Mother Mary Ann live at the Bottom House now, which is where our family eats all of the main family meals. It's exciting having the new mothers. Mother Midge combs my hair over and over, making fancy braids, and tells me I look so cute in yellow dresses.

With Mother's children now old enough for her to leave at home to be tended by the other mothers, she decided it was time to fulfill the calling of her patriarchal blessing. Her blessing told her that she would be called to take care of the sick in the last days. She told Daddy that she felt she needed to get some training if this was to be her calling. She attended the nursing program at Selkirk College and then started working at the Creston hospital.

✤

Don and I use the sled to drag pieces of firewood from the woodpile to the bottom door. I load several pieces onto Don's outstretched arms. "One more," he pants, directing me to load him with three big pieces. They clunk against the back of the woodbox.

My plan is to have the junk room cleaned up and the fire going when Mother gets home, and then to ask her if I can clean out the closet in the back of the junk room for my lamb to live in until the weather warms up. I'll put down lots of cardboard on the concrete floor and get a piece of old plywood from behind the house to finish off a nice little pen for my lamb.

There is a big office downstairs we call Uncle Rulon's Room. Uncle Rulon is the Prophet of God. He comes up from Utah a couple of times a year to see the people, and he stays in our house. I can already imagine someone arguing that a lamb pen shouldn't be in the same house the Prophet stays in when he comes to Canada, but the lamb has got to live somewhere.

My teenage brothers Jacob, Hyrum and Peter work in Kitchener after school making fence posts at the post mill with the other big boys. They will be bringing my lamb on their way home from work. They usually get home just after dark.

The back closet of the junk room has collected all kinds of old boots and coats and ski gear. Don and I find a basket and a box and start filling it with the good stuff that will never be thrown away, old work boots and leather gloves. I even find some figure skates that will probably fit me next year. I hang them on a hook so I'll be able to find them.

An old blanket makes a nice bed in the corner. Don helps me make a slot for the milk bottle to slide through. Momma's not home yet but someone calls to the Top House that dinner is ready. My stomach has been telling me that for a while. We run ravenously to the Bottom House for a bowl of hot chicken and potato soup and a slice of fresh bread with lots of butter and homemade raspberry jam. The house is bright and warm and clamours with life. Mother Christina's baby, Chelsea, sits in the high chair and my older sister Susie feeds her little bites of mashed-up potatoes out of the soup. The little girls all sit at a small table in the corner. Daddy and Uncle Dean sit at the end of the table by the window. He's not really my uncle but he's an elder visiting from Utah. Mother Sharon and Mother Midge sit next to them, laughing about something from "down home."

As if a spell were set over the room, everyone freezes, heads bowed, eyes closed, while Daddy offers a prayer of thanks and blessing over the food. I peek during the prayer and see Joey with his eyes tightly closed, sneaking little bites of his bread. Daddy tells us that if you eat before the prayer, you will have to hold your mouth open during the prayer so God can bless that food too.

I'm only a few bites into my soup when the boys burst through the front door. I jump out of my chair and run to meet them. "My lamb, my lamb, my lamb!"

There is a huge box on the porch and in it is the dearest, scrawniest lamb I have ever seen. It stands in the corner of the box, wobbling on spindly legs. It's a girl, they tell me. A girl! I'm overjoyed. I really hoped it would be a girl, not just because girls are smarter but because then she wouldn't have to go to market. I could keep her to breed and then she could have babies. I will become a regular little sheep farmer. Just one look at this pathetic little creature and I am in love. Oh, what fun we will have together! The boys bring in a bucket of milk replacer to feed her and a big white bottle with a large orange nipple on it for her to drink from.

Mother gets home in the middle of the kerfuffle. She stands in the doorway, still wearing her nursing dress uniform. "Well, it sure is a skinny little thing, isn't it?" she remarks.

All the children have forgotten dinner and are gathered around me, stroking the lamb's back and legs. I lower her down so my little three-year-old sisters, Nesta and Vicki, can hold her together. I clutch her to me, willing her to know I will keep her safe and loved. Her bewildered black eyes blink.

I stay up late sitting in the corner of her pen, petting her while she sleeps. I make her a bottle and sing to her while she sucks. She wiggles her little tail as the warm milk drips from the corner of her mouth. "I love you, little lamb," I whisper. "Your mother didn't know what she was doing when she didn't pick you."

Mother calls that it's time to go for prayers. Daddy is sitting on the edge of the big chair playing his guitar while the little girls sing along. Our one-year-old babies, Amos, Joni and Chelsea, toddle around dancing to the music, making us all smile. Nesta and Vicki hold their hands and play for a few minutes as we wait for the family to gather.

Since my dad married Mother Sharon and Mother Midge, we now have six little kids under school age. There is lots of happy noise whenever we all gather under one roof, as we do for main meals and for prayer.

The couches fill up as more of the Blackmore clan trickles in. Those who have made it to the first round of showers are wearing bathrobes; a few have wet hair wrapped up in towels, looking steamy fresh.

"Move over for your mother," Daddy instructs. The younger kids move to cushions on the floor. We all move from the furniture onto our knees in a big, concentric circle–like gathering on the brown shag carpet. "Run, see if Mother Midge is coming," Daddy tells Don. He starts into a snippet of a Bible story as he pulls a dental floss dispenser from his pocket, takes some floss and passes it around the room. As our knees weary in the waiting for Mother Midge, who reported she just needed to dress the baby, the familiar gentle click of my family's good oral hygiene is soothing.

Our youngest sister, Hanna, her hair in wet ringlets, is just learning to walk. She giggles and puts her arms out when she sees our father. Her feet already moving as they touch the carpet, she makes us all laugh as she toddles, lands softly on her padded diapered bum, gets to her feet and is scooped into Daddy's strong arms, which whisk her up to give her twenty kisses on her face and neck.

"A man's got to have the patience of Job just to get his family together to thank the Lord," Dad sighs in exaggerated frustration. He winks, teasing Mother Midge, who playfully rolls her eyes and says, "Well, next time you bathe the baby and I'll be on time for prayers." Daddy sits Hanna on his knee and helps her to fold her arms. There is lots of shushing as he finally offers a prayer of thanks, expressing our gratitude for our life, health and strength, asking for safety for those on the highways and working in the mountains and for the sick and the afflicted to be healed. "Humbly we ask for forgiveness of our sins and transgressions, thanking the Lord God in the name of Jesus Christ, amen."

The youngest race to Daddy for their good-night kisses. He is plastered with kisses and hugs. We bigger kids hang back. The girls give Dad a kiss on the cheek. We hug the mothers and kiss and hug the babies and one another, going around the room. The big boys shake everyone's hands good night. The bedtime kisses and hugs last a few minutes and people slip off to bed, or settle back onto the couch to talk quietly or read.

I go to bed, dreaming of lambs and spring.

🐑

Daddy walks into the Top House junk room, where I'm sitting next to the lamb, reading my favourite *Little House on the Prairie* book, *Farmer Boy*, oblivious to any offensive smells.

"I'm going to name your lamb Flower," he announces. "She smells like Flower, the skunk." Flower seems to suit her just fine. She wiggles her tail when I tell her the news. Flower is her name.

Flower is settling into her new home just fine after a week in her pen in the boot closet. I take her outside every day.

"Daddy, can I take Flower to school for show and tell?" I ask at breakfast time.

He laughs and sings cheerfully, "It followed her to school one day, school one day, school one day, it followed her to school one day, which was against the rule."

"I don't know of a rule that says I can't take a lamb to school. I've never even heard of that rule at our school," I reason.

"What does your teacher think?" Daddy asks, amused.

Mother Mary Ann is just sitting down at the table to her breakfast. I look to her with pleading eyes. She raises an eyebrow. "You'll have to ask Uncle Merrill," she answers. "It's fine with me."

Daddy helps me get him on the phone. I turn to the window, my back to the room to block out the laughs and giggles from my family. I stretch the long coil cord as far as I can to the corner. Uncle Merrill laughs too but gives me permission.

At school, they all want to touch her, pick her up and feed her the bottle. Mother Mary Ann quiets the room and gives me a chance to tell them about her and what I do for her and that she can't have the bottle until recess. It's so exciting having my lamb at school. No one wants to do math. We try to listen. Teacher is standing at the board giving us a lesson.

"Ew!" several students shout together.

Flower has peed a perfectly round puddle in the middle of the carpet floor. "Run, grab paper towel from the bathroom, Mary," my teacher directs me. I get some of them wet with a bit of soap. This is a disaster! The kids are laughing and holding their noses. It really doesn't smell that bad. Just some lamb pee. I take her home at lunch so we can get our work done.

⚜

After I've been her new mom for only three weeks, my dear little Flower starts getting sick. I've seen it before in the lambs and the calves. Runny yellow poop that just squirts all over the place. It's time to make her a new home. I decide to move her out of the Top House junk room, where I made her first pen, and out to a shed. It's small but cozy and I hope she will be happy and healthier there.

After a week of her living in the shed, Flower and I have a routine. I'm heading out to visit her before I have my breakfast. It's still dark outside. The spicy fragrance of the pumpkin pudding Mother has made for breakfast wafts through the house. My stomach complains like a whiny child begging for candy. Mother's made the hot pudding with cream skimmed off the top of yesterday's milk.

The light of my flashlight glistens off the lightly falling flakes and I kick up funny little points of snow on the toe of my boots as I walk up the hill in the three fresh inches that have fallen over yesterday's packed snow.

I have a little stick hidden under the corner of the shed, which I use to turn the little wooden lever that holds the door shut. I push up on one side with the stick, since I'm not quite tall enough to reach it yet. My mind is so busy planning the events of the day that I don't notice the unusual silence within. It's dark in the shed, but warm and dry. Odd, Flower isn't pushing against the door as usual and I don't see her as I look into the blackness. The door had been securely fastened. She couldn't have got away. Worry creeps up my back and across the top of my head. I flash my light around the four brown walls. A little giggle of relief floods through me: silly lamb, she's sleeping. There she is in the corner on a pile of straw, but she looks funny.

I crouch beside her and put my small hand on her stiff neck. Realization, like cold water, comes into my veins and straight to my heart. I've seen death before on the farm. The flashlight and warm bottle drop with a thud on the straw-strewn floor, breakfast forgotten. I scoop straw and my dead lamb's stiff little body into my lap and crumple onto her manger. Guilt and grief consume me, more questions than my eight-year-old mind can even try to answer. Why, God? Why? I shouldn't have put her into this dumb old shed. I shouldn't have taken her away from the other sheep. How did I think I could be a lamb's mother? Was I feeding her too much? Or was I not feeding her enough? Maybe she needed to go for more walks. I shouldn't have gone to my friend's house the other day instead of coming to spend time with her.

My mother is a nurse and she will know what to do. I awkwardly place the stiff body into a bed of straw, her legs so straight I wonder if she died standing and then just plopped over onto the straw. Slip-sliding, I run, blinded by tears and snowflakes. I fling open the Bottom House door, which hits the wall with a smack. Tears flood anew as my alarmed mother turns, ready to scold. Sobs choke in my throat.

Her tactic changes to comfort. "What is it, sweetheart?" The genuine concern in her voice shatters me. I bury my face into the soft sweet smell of my mother, who always makes the world right for me. Her arms and body envelop me. I don't even try to move as I let the anguished and confused tears wet the front of her apron.

"What is it, sweetheart?" she asks again, gently smoothing my dishevelled hair off my forehead and wiping my cheek with her thumb.

"My lamb," I choke. "My lamb is dead."

"Oh, sweetie." She holds me in the middle of the kitchen, the door still open and potatoes frying on the stove. She doesn't try to fix it. She just lets me cry. My heart feels as if it might break. The children at the table, busily getting full on fried potatoes and pumpkin pudding, just stare.

Finally, I pull away. "Momma, come see her," I say, even though I know a nurse can't do much for a dead lamb.

A little string of kids follow us up the hill and crowd in the doorway in the now greying light of dawn. They each take a minute to look, touch or nudge the dead lamb. Katie gives me a hug in an attempt to comfort me. My practical mother takes charge. "Well, come have some breakfast."

Four-year-old Niki is trudging through the snow ahead of me in too-big boots. I shuffle out the door and let it slam shut behind me. She hits a spot of ice under the fresh snow and slips on her bottom. I pull her to her feet and help her brush off the snow. She looks up at me, her thick glasses a little to one side. "I'm sorry Flower died."

I squat down in front of her and say, "Jump on." She puts her arms around my neck for a piggyback ride and I carry her down to the Bottom House for breakfast.

✖

I've never buried something as big as a lamb, nor anything I loved as much as Flower. Making sure our many dead pets are given a dignified final resting place is important to us kids. Our little animal cemetery holds many dead birds, kittens, fish and even rabbits.

Daddy is in the kitchen when we come in the door. I walk to him. He puts an arm around my neck and I lean onto his big chest.

"Not long after the house burned ..." he begins and tells a story about a dog he had loved that had been his best and devout companion. The dog had been badly hurt by coyotes while it was trying to protect some of the new calves out in the west meadow. My daddy was good at tending animals, even sewing up the bad cuts and helping calves being born, but this poor dog had made the ultimate sacrifice. Dad decided he didn't want to see his dog suffer any more and took him out to the back of the field and shot him.

"There is an animal heaven," Daddy says. "And those good animals have safe and happy places they can go. They lived good lives of service and don't have a wicked bone in their bodies. Little Flower will be better off there. She didn't want to live here away from others, without a mother. She has gone to a better place."

I guess he does know how I feel. Dad and I are a lot alike.

I think about some of my favourite family times in the evenings when we pull out paper and pencils at the big kitchen table. We're all pretty proud of the way Daddy can add double-digit numbers in his head as fast as we can write them down. He shows us how he groups the numbers. While the big boys are stressing through their math homework, the little kids draw or colour and tape their pictures all over the fridge. Don works on the math drills I bring home. Dad and I are poets. Dad and I make poetry about critters and God and being farmers. He reads them out in his animated voice, reading my poems with as much flair as he reads his own. "Won't we be famous someday?" he adds.

Today I don't care much about being famous. But I think that maybe someday I'll write about the real Mary-had-a-little-lamb and the little bummer lamb named Flower.

THE CEMETERY

I try not to wonder what it would have been like this spring if Flower, my sweet lamb, had lived through the winter. Nothing says spring like the smell of burning leaves and freshly overturned dirt for planting gardens. Few things are more satisfying than burning dead grass and watching the fresh tips of green poke through. Mother keeps us busy after school raking the yard. We are working to chop and burn all the dog burr up by the old chicken coop to make a play yard. Watching the tongues of flame gobble the skeleton stacks of dog burr brings satisfaction to my young farmer's heart. Every family in our community plants a big garden and all my friends are busy after school getting seed in the ground and flower gardens and fruit trees pruned.

Each spring, raking the cemetery just below the Top House is a big project. Mother buys a stack of chocolate bunnies when they go on sale and chops them into three chunks each as treats for those of us who help rake the cemetery. She and Mother Mary Ann spend a few long afternoons organizing the neighbourhood kids, our cousins, who come by on horses or bikes to help rake and burn the branches and pine cones and pick rocks and sticks. The cemetery is a treed area about the size of a baseball field across the road from our Bottom House.

"I don't plan on it soon," Uncle Mac's boy Matt, who is Pete's age, says matter-of-factly, tying his horse to a fence post so he can help for a bit, "but one of these days, I'll go into the ground here too."

A little shadow of sadness passes over us kids and we look in the direction of the fresh mound on the far side of the field. Last summer Uncle Mac had been working in the bush with some of his big kids. The brakes went off on the old skidder and Lydia was killed. She was sixteen, just a year older than Jake. She died innocent and perfect and went to heaven to live with the angels. For a minute I imagine my lamb running around meadows in heaven with my beautiful cousin Lydia.

An afternoon of work for a chunk of chocolate was a fair trade for us kids. It would usually take us most of the week during the spring break from school with a good crew of about a dozen kids and some of the mothers, and then Mom would buy hot dogs and marshmallows and have a community barbecue.

As she rakes around Grandpa Ray's headstone, Nancy tells us a story we all know about Grandpa and his third wife, Grandma Nesta. "She died in childbirth and her baby Joey died a few months later. He was buried beside her." We work while Nancy relates her story.

Grandma Mem has told us all this story many times in Sunday school. I almost feel that I remember this bookwormish younger sister of Grandma Aloha who had married Grandpa Ray. Grandma Mem teaches us the importance of learning the stories of our grandparents and having pride in our strong pioneer heritage. Their stories, she says, are also our stories, as they give us strength and courage to press forward in the work. Our forefathers left Europe to gather with the Saints in America to build the kingdom of God. If we fail in our work of building Zion, the New Jerusalem, all their sacrifice is for nothing. We are God's chosen people to come onto this earth in these last days, and we have a very important sacred work to do to help prepare a people who are pure of heart and worthy to stand before the Saviour in the Second Coming. Each Sunday, I renew my determination to be among those people.

I rake around the marble headstone engraved with her name. Grams says Grandma Nesta was cheerful and pretty. I imagine she will stay like that forever. She made the ultimate sacrifice to give life to her child. The baby screamed his whole time on this earth, Grams says. "Something was wrong with his insides but mostly he needed to go be with his momma."

Grandma says Joey was in the Cranbrook hospital for a couple of months. The whole family was praying he would pull through. Grandma says Nesta came to her in a dream and was singing this song:

> There's a lonely, little robin in the tree by my door,
> Who waits for his mate to return evermore.
> Oh, remember, yes remember that I'm lonely too.
> Like the lonely little robin, I'm waiting for you.

It was so longing and sweet, and she knew they must stop praying for Joey to live and that he was to go be with his mother who was missing him. She called to Cranbrook and told the family, and Joey died the next day.

As I continue working, I think of the grave that is missing in the cemetery. I wonder why Grandma Joanne wasn't buried here. It was Mother's fifth birthday the day her mother passed away. Grandma Joanne was only twenty-six years old and she left three small children. Aunt Debbie was seven and Uncle Ken only three. Grandma had a heart condition and never fully recovered after her son was born. Mother remembers the last time she saw her she was waving from the hospital window a month before she died, as they wouldn't let the children in to see her. The prayers of her loved ones were not enough to heal her and she went to heaven.

✒

The house is warm and wafting with the alluring scent from the hot hamburger and potato soup bubbling on the stove. Coming in from the chilly afternoon air, the hot water is welcome as we wash for supper.

"Mary, come and I'll help you with your piano practice," Mother encourages. My belly is full of soup and pumpkin pudding and I feel a bit sleepy. I slide onto the smooth piano bench, feeling her warmth next to me. Grandma Mem has been my piano teacher since I was five. My favourite moments with Grandma Mem are when she tells me I look so much like Grandma Joanne. I hear this often from the older aunts and uncles who remember my beautiful grandmother when she was a girl.

Last week Grandma Mem brought me the sheet music for "Greensleeves." She tells me Grandma Joanne could play the piano masterfully and loved this song. She says the slow eerie notes of "Greensleeves" always remind her of her beautiful, gentle sister-wife.

I play through the top hand of the music, with Mother helping me with some of the more challenging timing as I play. Once through, I ask Mother if she will play it for me.

The house has settled into the evening hush as people shuffle with their preparations for bed. I lay my head against my mother's arm and drift into the beautiful black and white photo of my young grandmother with her stylish curled bob and silky complexion in her well-fitted graduation gown. She would have loved flowers and long, sunny Sunday walks with Mother and us kids. She would have listened to our stories and sung with us to the river. Secretly, I've decided I would have been her favourite.

Being God's chosen people and being born into the gospel is a blessing in my life greater than all the gold and earthly wealth I could acquire in this life. Having a testimony of the truthfulness of the gospel and the one living Prophet is my most valued possession. We know the innocent who die are greeted by loving family members who have gone on before, and I feel so blessed to have the faith and knowledge that if we prepare our lives to be worthy of meeting Jesus Christ, our families can be together forever.

When I finish my practice through the song, I snuggle in one of

Grandma's patchwork quilts on the couch as mother continues to play her mother's song. The longing notes of "Greensleeves" fill the dim living room as our full house falls asleep.

BAPTISM

It's a hot sunny Sunday in July. Directly after church the congregation walks down to the pond where kids have been baptized since Dad was a kid. I'm wearing the new white dress Mother sewed for me. "Now don't pick any dandelions today. They will stain your dress," Mother instructs me as she finishes my second tight braid, fastening a bobble to hold it. A plain white dress isn't very practical for a farm girl except to be baptized in or to wear to church, since it can get stained easily.

Don looks like a basket of fresh laundry and even his hair is combed with only his turkeys standing on end. Mother Christina takes a photo of me and Don together sharing our baptism day. Today we will both become members of the Church of Jesus Christ of Latter Day Saints. Don will eventually become ordained a deacon, then a priest, then an elder who holds the holy Melchizedek Priesthood and do sacred work and blessings for the church. I will marry a good priesthood man in the church to be a jewel in his crown and be a mother in Zion.

Mormons are taught that parents are accountable for the actions of their children as long as the child could stand before God and say truthfully, "My parents never taught me." My parents have always taught me, so I won't be able to say that. I sit every Sunday and listen carefully to the elders preach and to Daddy's sermons and teachings of the words of Christ. I sit up tall and straight when Uncle Charlie Quinton, the patriarch, gives his dead cat sermon, thumping on the pulpit and waving his fist in the air. I always pay attention when Grandma Mem teaches us lessons about sharing and kindness in Sunday school.

In grade two, I stole a little bag of chips out of Shalina's desk. I knew it was wrong, but I wanted those chips so badly. I'm not going to steal anymore. Never again, I resolve. If I get a fresh start, there is no way I'm going to mess this up. "Don't sell your birthright for a mess of pottage as Esau did in the Bible," Daddy reminds us in church. Now I'm eight years old. I'm getting baptized. I know right from wrong. So, now I will become a member of the Church of Jesus Christ of Latter Day Saints. I will be responsible for my own salvation and making decisions for my life.

By grade three, all the children have memorized all the Articles of Faith that Joseph Smith laid out as the basis of the Mormon Church. I've memorized all the Beatitudes of Christ and I'm ready and eager to have my sins washed away and to finally become a member of the Church of Jesus Christ.

🕉

Our families sit along the grass beside the swimming hole, a few people on chairs, some standing. The grandmothers fan themselves in the stifling heat; the children gaze longingly at the cool crispness of the rushing water. Uncle Duane blesses the water and my mind wanders to cooling myself. No one swims on Sunday as it is breaking the Sabbath and they say it is the day God has given Satan power over the waters. But come Monday, as we jump and splash off the raft, we joke that we are swimming in everyone's sins. Each year, when everyone starts asking about the baptisms, Daddy talks about building a baptismal font for a dedicated place to perform this sacred covenant. Maybe by next year, he says.

I remind myself to stay focused as this is one of the most important days of my life and one of the biggest decisions I will make. I'm committing my life as a member of the Church of Jesus Christ of Latter Day Saints. Katie and Joey sit neatly in their Sunday clothes. In two years they will join us as members of the church.

The strength of our community is our security against the outside world. Our families work together, harvest together, serve one another. Baptism is a protection for the soul. The worst thing we can imagine is to be a family alone. We have one another, safe together banded against the outside world. Peter 5:8 in the Bible reminds us to stay alert! "Watch out for your great enemy, the devil. He prowls around like a roaring lion, looking for someone to devour. Stand firm against him, and be strong in your faith."

My older cousin, Big John, takes my hand, my father repeats my whole name to him so he will get it right and we walk into the water until it's up past my waist. He repeats the exact words of the prayer. I plug my nose with one hand and cross the other across my chest. He dips me backwards so I'm completely submerged and stands me back up in the water. Water pours from my clothing, face and hair. I walk to shore, sputtering and smiling. Mother wraps me in a big towel. I sit on the waiting chair. The men put their hands on my head and Daddy gives me a blessing. I open my eyes. Uncle Charlie extends his hand to me. "Welcome into the church, sister."

GRANDPA'S HOUSE

Summer ends too quickly and suddenly it's fall. Grandpa Oler's family invites the whole community to a Halloween party down at the Big House. Grandma Mem calls around the community and tells everyone she will drive the big yellow school bus around to pick everyone up. Grandma Mem is my father's oldest sister; she married Grandpa Oler at sixteen and became his second wife. When Grandma Joanne died on Mother's fifth birthday and left her three children behind, Grandma Mem raised her stepchildren along with her own fifteen.

Our house is a flurry of preparation. The mothers put together homemade costumes for everyone. I wear my brand new Sunday dress with yellow overlay lace patterns. My brothers call it my chicken wire dress because the lace looks like the wire off the chicken run made into ruffles. Mother pins a piece of silver garland in my hair for a fairy crown and glues some to the end of a stick for a wand. The mothers scramble to gather up the cakes and cookies and an elk roast cooked in onions. The smells make my mouth water. We load on the bus, giddy with excitement, to drive down through Canyon around the winding switchbacks to the Big House above the Goat River.

Grandpa Oler has the biggest family probably in all of Canada. He has six wives and one of them just had a baby boy making forty-seven children. The Big House was designed and built to be the perfect place for kids to grow up.

We pile out of the school bus. The mothers carry the goodies into the kitchen to help set up the food and we kids scurry into the corners to find our friends. Amy and Mandy are Grandpa's girls and are a year younger than me. My friends have cute animal costumes with little ears and black noses drawn on.

A room just inside the main entrance is called the nursery. Four crib beds are built into the wall, and the bathroom has a really small tub built at waist height with a little ladder so the mothers don't have to bend over when they are bathing the babies. There is even a toilet for washing out cloth diapers. I guess they used a lot of diapers when all of those kids were babies.

Upstairs we are free of adults. We chase in stealth mode down the long hallway. At each end are the stairwells; one goes down to the kitchen and the other to the entrance. We slither up the other stairs to run down the hallway again. We walk quietly through the kitchen and sneak through the nursery, not attracting too much attention so we aren't told to go outside. The mothers barely notice us.

There are about fifteen big bedrooms and lots of bathrooms on three storeys. The upstairs has a great, long, wide hall with brown shag carpet and dark brown-lined panelling on the walls. Grandma Mem's collage of photos runs the whole length of the house on both sides, wrapping around into the piano room. Her wall photo album is loosely organized by time, starting about when Daddy was a teenager, making a wallpaper of the smiling familiar faces of our community protected with a layer of Mactac.

Just at the top of the stairs to the right is a large sewing room with at least eight sewing workstations. There are bins and shelves of fabric in a long cupboard and a big cutting table in the middle of the room. Grandma Mem sewed my favourite stuffed lamb for my birthday here. A window looks out over the play yard out back to make it easy to keep an eye on the kids. The piano room is halfway down the hall and filled with large, overstuffed animals Mother's sisters sew.

There are two wood stoves for heat as well as a big boiler, which heats hot water that runs all through the house to keep it warm. Grandpa is an inventor and a mechanic and can build anything. All his vehicles are jimmy-rigged old beaters. He uses a screwdriver to start his pickup truck and they have a short yellow bus with some letters peeled off called the Cool Bus. It's always packed full of kids going to weed strawberries, heading to school or going camping at the lake. He has an old boat he gets going every summer to take us camping across the lake. Grandpa's motto as he's loading the bus or the boat or even kids onto horses is "There is always room for one more." Then he laughs and adds, "As long as it's one at a time." He'd never say no to any kid coming along. Mother got that from him.

The long tables are heaped with food and are lined against the wall opening up the big dining room. Mostly cowboys and pioneers fill their plates with the fresh buns and salads and treats. Uncle Al and Aunt Robin are dressed as Raggedy Ann and Raggedy Andy and Grandma Mem is the fairy godmother. Grandpa Oler is an Indigenous chief wearing a feather headdress. Everyone gathers in concentric circles, leaning against the walls, children seated on the floors. Grandpa offers a prayer of thanks for this gathering, for the food and for the gospel. He leads the group in a few songs of gratitude and thanks to God. Grandma Mem says a poem. Grandpa thrills us all when he announces he will perform the harvest dance dressed in his chief's regalia. While his heritage is British and Scottish, he always speaks with respect for Indigenous traditions. His dance is as much a dance of thanks as it is of entertainment for his family.

The back of the house has a long, covered, smooth plywood deck painted green. We kids are as eager to get outside into the crisp October air as we were for the dessert. We race for the big tricycle and squabble over the wheeled toys to ride on. I dig in the wooden box of brown leather roller skates and find a matching pair my size and lace them on. The smooth wood rumbles under the wide rubber wheels. A trampoline is partly sunken in the backyard and another is on the deck. There is a tricky bar that goes from the deck out to the big trampoline in the backyard and there is a giant twirly slide Grandpa fabricated himself. It kicks me out into the sandbox and I decide to be more careful with my Sunday fairy dress. The backyard has a playhouse and lots of junk and things for kids to play with.

Our time at Grandpa's never feels long enough. Mother is telling the kids to find our shoes and socks and get ready to go home. Just in time, Grandpa comes out of the back entrance off the kitchen and announces the ice cream is finally frozen. Grandpa got the machine at an auction and keeps tinkering to keep it running. We make ice cream pretty much any time we go down to the Big House. Because they have lots of milk from their cows, it doesn't matter how much ice cream we make. One of the big girls mixes up an ice cream mix. Sometimes they just blend a jar of canned peaches, mix it into a bucket of milk and dump it into the machine and in twenty or thirty minutes it is ready. We can heap our bowls as much as we like and we say it is better even than Dairy Queen.

The mothers pack up all the kids back onto the school bus and we drive back home out to Lister by the mountain.

THE OLD CHICKEN COOP

Spring comes again. Mir turned ten and on my birthday in a few weeks I'll be nine. This year it feels like the rain will never stop. Down at the old chicken coop between Mir's house and the hay shed is a mud bog bigger than any I've ever seen. The tractor slogs through it each day taking hay to the critters, working it into a heavy soup. Mir and I drag planks of raw-cut lumber from beside the coop and make a sort of boardwalk out over the mud bog. The mud reaches the tops of our gumboots and we giggle over the slurp and sucking each step makes. We play that it's quicksand and lava and that we have to heroically rescue each other or we will fall to a certain death.

"Do you think fire from heaven will be lava?" I ask Mir. We don't really talk about the Great Destruction much but it can be really scary when you just stop and think about it. "So what would happen if you got stuck outside when God decided to protect your family in their house?" Mir and I are the same size and share each other's clothes even though she is a year older, but it seems as if she always has smart things to say about stuff like this.

Mir is standing on the plank over the mire and turns to look at me. "If we get and keep the spirit of God on us, we won't have to worry about that, will we? God said even the faith of a child could move mountains. So I don't think we need to worry about that." She is so confident in her answer that I have no doubt that is just what I am going to do. Our dads are faithful, hard-working men. Their priesthood will protect our families in the End of Times.

The lava turns back into mud and we concoct a plan to make our older sisters wade out into the mire. As they pass the coop on the way up to the house, we get into the middle and start shouting, "We're stuck, we're stuck! Help us."

When they come to rescue us, we will run out of the mud and our sisters will be left standing in the middle of it. How clever. After some coaxing, they decide we really are stuck and venture in. On cue, we try to run, but after standing still for so long, the slurping clay holds tight to our boots. My foot comes out of my boot and I sink to my knee in sticky grey goo. Mir is cemented beside me.

I grab my boot to yank it loose and the mud suddenly releases the boot. I totter, then smack onto my rear end. I shriek and Mir drags me to my feet beside her. I knock her off balance and we topple sidelong into the soppy soup.

"Help us," we beg our sisters, who are already working their way out of the bog.

"Not a chance," they call over their shoulders, disgust clear in their voices.

"Mother's gonna be so mad if you guys tromp mud into the house," Susie yells at me. She's right. Mir's house will be our best bet.

We make the most of it, trying bellyflops and bum busters off our plank walk and throwing mud balls at each other, which get into our hair. We smear mud on our cheeks like war paint and make terrific faces at each other.

Finally, the ice-cold mud gets the best of us. With frozen, claw-like hands we work our boots free, then clutch them beneath our arms as we run past the hay shed to Mir's house. Mother Rose, Mir's second mother, sprays us off with freezing-cold water from the garden hose before bringing us a mop bucket of warm water to clean up before we are allowed in the house to have a hot bath.

✺

Summer arrives and finally we are free. Summer is long, warm afternoons riding horses, swimming in the pond, making shacks in the trees, playing in the Old Barn, picking green apples and weeding gardens.

There isn't too much work to do until the end of summer, when canning season starts, and then there's a lot of work to do—picking and pickling cucumbers, canning raspberries, freezing green beans—but mostly we are done each day by noon. Mother gives us a list of jobs the night before and we can get up as early as we want and get it done as fast as we can so we have hours to swim and ride our horses. My cousin Vilate thinks we are like wild children since we just roam free when our work is done. As long as we get our jobs done and are home when Mother gets off work at seven, we get to do what we like.

My days are full of work but they are also carefree and joyous. My heart is full—full of love for my family and this life we live together, full of sunshine and the smells of cut grass, freshly swathed hay and raspberry jam bubbling on the stove, getting ready to be scooped out and put into cans. The taste of summer will grace our toasts all year long.

Sometimes I worry about the things I hear in church: the End of Times is coming and soon we will all face the Judgment Day. When I notice the bees pollinating the flowers, see the eggs in the chicken coop or the wild birds that Daddy and I like so much, or look at my baby brothers and sisters I think how little they are and wonder how old they will get to be before the day of the Great Destruction. I remember Flower, my precious lamb, who couldn't live without a mother who loved her.

I push aside my worry and rush through my chores so I can meet my friends at the pond. I'm blessed to be a member of the true church of God. Daddy teaches us that if we get and keep the sweet spirit of God on us at all times, and prepare our hearts to meet Jesus Christ when he comes back to the earth, then we will be saved. Unlike my poor lamb, I have many mothers who love me. Besides, Daddy reminds us of the promise God gave to old Father Noah after the flood: "God promised that in every year that you see a rainbow, there will be a seed time and harvest." In this year of constant rain, I've seen a rainbow almost every day.

MILKING

Fall is crisp in the air. The smell of woodsmoke rises from chimneys. Already the nights are darkening earlier, so the big boys don't have enough daylight to finish their chores if they don't get an early start.

"Mary, come hold the flashlight for me and help me with the milking," Hyrum coaxes. Mother quickly rinses the milking tins in scalding hot water and fills a small bucket with warm water and a clean rag for washing the cow's teats. I jam my feet into a pair of tall black gumboots sitting by the door. My toes curl but I will manage. I scurry to keep up to my brother as we walk up the hill to the small cow barn past Uncle Rich's house in the already greying light.

We have two really good Jersey cows we share with four other families. Since we milk morning and night, each family does the milking and keeps the milk once every other day. The cows give three and a half gallons per milking.

While there is still some light left, I climb to the cozy loft of the cow barn to throw some loose hay down to the milk cows and fill the grain bucket from a large barrel.

It is darker in the barn and my brother flips on a single electric bulb, which shines a timid ball of light above the straw-scattered barn floor. The two milkers, Old Gertie and Butter Cup, are already pushing against the gate, anxious to get in to be relieved of the pressure in their udders. We dump the grain into the wooden troughs and the cows walk calmly in, put their heads through the stall and chew contentedly while my brother latches the metal contraption to hold their heads firmly until the milking is done. He washes Old Gertie quickly with the warm water and lets me start on her while he milks Butter Cup. Her calf has just been taken off of her so she is kind of feisty, and she has a bad teat on the far side. But Old Gertie is as gentle as a kitten and lets down her milk without any coaxing. She'll never move a muscle, so I just set the bucket on the ground beneath her so I can lean forward on the stool and get both hands around her teats.

Already I can hear the singing of milk hitting tin in a steady rhythm almost like a tambourine, until the ring is drowned out in the soft foam of the warm milk. I try to keep time with my brother's milking. My smaller hands aren't nearly as strong or skilful as his and before too long my muscles ache from the open, lift, squeeze and pull motion. Each time, I feel the lowering of milk into her udder and down into my hands. Her bag is soft, supple and leathery. I like the warm smell of her with my face so close to her round belly.

My aunts were as fast as their brothers at hand milking. "Just keep practising," my brother tells me. "Your muscles will get stronger every time." By the time he is done with Butter Cup and has turned her back into the pen, I still have only about half of my pail filled. He settles in to finish, with strong, swishing jets that quickly fill the bucket to the frothy top.

"Gotta get it all out," he reminds me. If you don't milk a cow right out every time, she will slowly start producing less and less and can get mastitis infection. All the good cream comes at the end and we have to get that cream to go on our canned raspberries with toast for breakfast.

Hyrum carries two steaming, full tin pails home, while I carry the flashlight and the wash bucket. I'm impressed with how strong he is. We follow the little beam of light down the path, side by side, listening to the sounds of the dark.

We walk past the silent shadow of the house where Aunt Debbie lived before the fire. It is nice to see some lights on in the downstairs after it being empty for so long. The guys fixed up the downstairs, which mostly had smoke damage, and Uncle Rich's family lives there now. The upstairs has been all gutted and cleaned out but still smells dank with some charred scarring, like a blackened skeleton of a bat cave.

Some kids like to play hide-and-seek up there but I don't. It still makes me shiver to remember the night of the fire. For me the house is still filled with the haunting stories of the fire that changed so many lives in one night. I feel as if my Aunt Debbie and her children moved into a book and now I just hear little pieces about their life, but somehow it doesn't seem real. They left everything real and drove away in an old brown station wagon. Mother says they have moved a lot. Now they live in the city in a house they rent. They go to a public school and probably have new friends.

I walk past the house where they used to live, here, on the land with our family, and I think about the one time I went to visit them in their new house. On a trip to Alberta to see my great-grandparents, Mother asked me if I wanted to take the Greyhound with Grandma Alaire, one of Grandpa Dalmon's wives, to go see Jolene. I was excited to see her and we hugged and played, but everything felt strange. Aunt Debbie had her hair all cut off like a boy's and put a lot of dark makeup around her eyes, and she and my cousins all wore pants. Her kids loved the movie *E.T.* so I watched it with them. The show gave me the creeps and I cried during the night because I had a bad dream about clammy aliens coming to take me to a strange place. Mem, Aunt Debbie's oldest daughter, let me sleep in her bed.

My cousins even talked differently. They had a lot of new toys, wore T-shirts with big Ninja Turtles and Smurfs on them and talked a lot about the movies they watched. We got to watch cartoons for almost a whole day. I had fun seeing Jolene. She wore my dresses and I tried on her sweaters and combed my hair into a top ponytail. I was really happy when it was time to go home.

These days it makes me feel sad when I hear about Aunt Debbie telling the reporters a lot of bad things about the people in our community and our religion. She says she had to get away so her children would be safe. She says a lot of bad things happened to her when she lived in our community. We get lots of reporters coming around asking questions to write a story. I see pictures of Daddy in a newspaper that somebody brings to school, and there are not very nice things Aunt Debbie says about him. But it makes me mad when kids make up rude little songs about her and laugh and say she is crazy, and some parents say she "flew off the handle."

When I ask my mother why Aunt Debbie would say all those things, she sighs and says, "Aunt Debbie has had a hard life."

They talk on the phone sometimes for a really long time. "I just don't see what good it is going to do," my mother says into the phone. After she hangs up, Mother walks around with her forehead wrinkled and sighs a lot.

Daddy discusses with us the importance of not telling the media information about our family's personal life. Polygamy has been illegal in Canada for a long time, since Mormons first moved to Canada when Utah was making polygamy illegal. No one has ever been arrested or charged on anything polygamy-related in Canada because Canada is a free country that embraces many cultures. Still, Daddy feels it is best if we don't tell the media information like how many wives our fathers have.

"Besides," he says, "it is just nobody's business."

Just after Christmas last year, Aunt Debbie and the cousins came to visit for Grandpa Dalmon's birthday party. I had a small gift for Jolene, since I missed her birthday, and, excited, I ran in to see her. She was running and playing with some other kids I didn't know very well and she took a minute to say hi, then ran giggling and screeching down the long deck. Her hair was cut into a short bob above her shoulders with thick bangs in the front. Her eyes looked the same but when she didn't remember what special friends we were, I thought maybe aliens did take her to a different planet and she forgot all about me.

Walking beside my brother, I reach out and hold on to his arm. I shiver in the dark. The clammy face of E.T. is still vivid in my mind with his gross rubbery skin and long fingers. I'm glad I'm home with my family and our farm and our cows. I step along closer to my brother, so I bump into his bucket of milk. Aliens.

PERVERTS

As on almost every other Sunday morning in my life, Aunt Marlene shows up to our house at nine thirty sharp to comb Grams's hair. Aunt Marlene runs a sewing and mending business and is a well-known person around town. She volunteers with emergency social services and helps a lot of people with their papers and stuff. She always has lively stories and she and her mother share tidbits of gossip while she fluffs and combs her hair into a regal updo plastered down with hair spray and finished with a bright cluster of flowers pinned in the back. Both are generous with treats, which they keep tucked away in their Blue Bag Lady bags. I'm ten, so naturally lounging on Grandma's bed catching juicy snippets is where I want to spend my Sunday morning. Aunt Mar brings a new copy of *Time* magazine with a pleasant-looking picture of the Queen on it.

"Isn't she looking good?" Grandma says as she opens the magazine. Since she is the same age as the Queen Mother, she takes a keen interest in her life and, I think, secretly feels she looks just as well as the Queen. Especially with a fine updo, Grandma looks a lot like her.

Grandma wears white or pastel flowy dresses, with a drapey apron over them. She takes special care of her appearance when she goes out in public. She has her designated cushioned chair in the front row in church and her grandchildren wait eagerly to sit beside her. She is Grandma to hundreds of children and must get a thousand hugs every Sunday. She has made being "Grams" her profession and takes care to welcome all with intentional cheer.

❧

After church my aunts talk together in hushed voices with Mother in our living room after the Sunday dinner dishes have all been taken care of. The hush tells me their conversation is not meant for little ears. Two of them work at the school and when they come into the kitchen they are talking about one of the girls at school.

"She has really changed," one aunt says. "She just stares off into space and will barely listen when I'm trying to help her with her work. I feel something is wrong with her." I get a crawling feeling inside me but I know it isn't my business to ask.

The next few weeks feel weird at school. We are used to having the health nurse come to school to give us our shots and teach us how to wash and clean our teeth, but there seem to be more of them now and they come to all the classrooms and give us papers with pictures of a cartoon rabbit wearing a bikini talking about good touching and bad touching. They talk about our privates and not letting people touch us, and about how we should tell our parents if anyone tries to and how we shouldn't keep secrets like that if someone tells us to.

I feel embarrassed hearing them talk like this and it makes my stomach crawl again. I learned all this when I was five. I know to cover my special body and not to look at other people's nakedness. Baby boys and girls can bathe together and it's okay for little girls to bathe together and little boys to bathe together until they are about eight. Once we are old enough to get baptized, our mothers say we probably should bathe by ourselves. The little kids get spankings if they get caught playing with their pants off.

I can't imagine why the nurses are telling this to kids in grade five. It feels strange and the women are very serious about it.

Over the next while, we hear that one of the older cousins who is almost grown up had to go to jail because he was being a pervert with his little sister. The parents don't talk about it and we kids just whisper about what we heard. We knew it was really bad. All the children in their family had to talk to social services. Some kids said all of their children might even get taken away from their parents and be given to foster care.

At school, no one knows what to say to them so we just pretend everything is normal and try to be a little extra nice.

🔞

The sun is shining outside, which makes the long hallway feel dark, and from the classroom window I can see kids running, shouting and playing one of our favourite games of dungeon tag on the playground.

In the hallway, alone, one of the younger sisters from the family is sitting in the bottom of her locker, which is mounted to the wall. She can just fit so her back is to the back of the white wood and her skinny legs dangle. She is one grade lower than me and usually she is ready and looking for a game or fun. She just sits, silent, staring at the brown janitor room door. The hall is quiet.

I think about my big brothers and how much I love them. I know I would be really sad if one of my big brothers were a pervert and had to go to jail, and I don't know how to ask her if social services is going to take her to live in a foster home.

Digging in the brown lunch bag in my locker, I get the red licorice and dangle it back and forth in front of her staring eyes, like a clock going tick-tock, tick-tock, tick-tock. Ever so slowly, the corners of her mouth curl up.

"I have two. Do you want it?" She smiles and takes the licorice. We take big bites. I hold my hand out to her. She takes it and I give her a fast pull that makes her fly off the locker shelf.

"Last one to the playground is a rotten egg," she says, giggling. There isn't a teacher in sight down the long hall, so we run around the corner and out the door, our shoes squeaking on the polished floor.

PANCAKES AT THE POND

It's summer again and our family has grown a lot in the last couple of years. I'm much better at milking cows. Finally, when Joey was eight and I was ten, Mother gathered her kids around her one night and told us she was expecting a baby. We were overjoyed imagining our own little baby, a baby girl. We thought we'd died and gone to heaven having Mother home and our darling baby sister, Brittany, to fuss over. When Brittany was six months old Mother went back to work, but Susie is thirteen and I just turned eleven so we are plenty old enough to tend Brittany during the days we don't have school.

Life feels full and happy at our house. Mother is always keen to enrich our lives with a summer road trip, to stop at sites and museums and to stay with our great-grandparents in Alberta for a week. On occasions we go to town to visit Mother's nurse friends or to go to the dentist. Mother ensures we are dressed up in our nicest new dresses and our hair is neatly braided with waves, matching clips and bobbles, or she'll even go to all the work of putting our hair in curlers. Most often, these visits are to see my very favourite town person, my dentist, Dr. Catheral.

⁂

We know she will ask Mother Sharon how we did when she gets home but we like tending our little sister and having the responsibility anyway. Our family has lots of babies now. All of Daddy's seven wives had babies the same year except one. But it's different having Brittany. She's our baby. We can take her with us and dress her up and take her photo. Susie and I have a pretty good system worked out to get our jobs done and tend Britty, ride our ponies and still hang out with our friends. Mother leaves us a list of jobs every day that must be done before she gets home at seven in the evening. She doesn't care when or how we do them.

We get up early to get all the hoeing and weeding done before Britty wakes up and it gets too hot. Because the garden isn't overgrown with weeds, we weed our seven rows and take only an hour or so. After that we do our inside jobs. Mother always has us practise six piano songs, do each of our Highland dances once and read for thirty minutes. We are off lessons for the summer but she reminds us about the importance of keeping our practice up. There is always a bit of housework each day.

Today I must clean the fridge, vacuum the stairs and hall and clean the downstairs bathroom. Susie has the upstairs bathroom, plus she sweeps and mops the kitchen.

Our goal is to be done by noon. We pull a handful of fresh hot radishes out of the garden, wash them and slice them up on bread with Miracle Whip for lunch with a cup of milk. I feed Britty a bowl of applesauce and make a couple of honey sandwiches to put in her diaper bag to bring for later.

Sue and I saved up a couple of hundred bucks to buy a horse, Sassy, from one of Mother's nurse friends, and our horse Shorty has been in the family since our oldest brother, Jake, was a kid. Shorty is a really good kid's horse but Sassy is a little wild as she hadn't been ridden much when we got her.

Last fall, Mother helped us make a horse pen in the trees up behind our house. We found two big old fence posts in the swamp and dragged them home with our ponies. We pulled and pounded three rows of wire up around the trees and put a gate between two trees at the front. We picket our ponies around the cemetery in the summer so they can eat the fresh grass and we don't have to feed them hay. Our saddles are in the shed just outside the top door. It takes us only a few minutes to have our horses saddled and ready to go.

Whoever rides Shorty takes the baby and the one on Sassy takes the diaper bag. Britty loves the horses and she loves riding. I hold her in front of me in the saddle. She can hold the saddle horn or I give her the reins and she clucks at the horse to make him go faster. She'll be two in a few months and I can't believe how smart she is. She says so many words and is our little Highland dancing star. Mother made her a little costume out of some extra fabric and when we turn on the bagpipe music, she puts up her hands and dances.

We ride around a bit, stopping at our friends' houses to see if they are finished their chores and can join us for a swim at the pond. Everyone ends up at the pond eventually on these hot days. Our last stop before the pond is at Aunt Leona's to get Mir and Fara to come swimming. We take off the horses' bridles and hang them on the saddle horns. We loosen the saddles and tie the horses up to Aunt Leona's white picket fence where they can reach lots of tall grass.

Fara is making bread and says she will come over later for a minute, but her mother is helping her sew a dress for the afternoon. Mir is stirring a big pot of soup she made for the kids for lunch. Aunt Leona rolls out some of the bread dough on the table. Then with a knife she cuts two slices across each way, like tic-tac-toe, and quickly sets the diamond-shaped pieces in sizzling hot oil. They puff up quickly and turn a golden brown. She turns them and pulls them out with tongs to drip on a cloth. "Take one," she says.

The little kids crowd onto the bench behind the table. We join them. There is some squabbling over who gets to say the prayer and who said it last time. "We will all say it together," Aunt Leona works out. Six of them fold their arms and squeeze their eyes tight.

"Dear Heavenly Father, thank you for the food." They repeat the lines after her. "We ask you to bless it so it will nourish and strengthen our bodies and do us the good we need." The older kids quickly reach across the table to grab the sizzling hot dough babies from the plate and drizzle them in honey to eat with a bowl of hot soup.

Brittany plays contentedly with her cousins on the floor while Susie and I help with the dishes. Aunt Leona tells Mir to take the little kids over to the pond and she will walk over to get them in a while. Then Mir can swim with us.

Sue and I get the horses ready and we load them up with our little cousins. They are eager to play and swim and are pleased to be riding the horses. Sue piggybacks Britty and we get them all singing, "Horsey, Horsey, on our way, we've been together for many a day." The older ones, Jeff and Linda, and my little sisters Vicki and Nesta, who had a sleepover at Aunt Leona's, decide to come and walk along with us.

The creek from the Old Barn winds though a thickly forested draw to fill a deep, long, S-shaped reservoir, which was built forever ago to hold water for irrigation and has long since grown in with willows and a few shady pine trees.

I smell the pond before I can see it. On a hot August day, it's a cool earthy smell. Aunt Margy's girls, AJ and Michelle, arrive just after us, wearing their bright pink and floral culottes, and riding bikes. Their brown bare feet and muddy knees tell the tale of their morning working in their garden.

The best part of summer happens at the pond. Cousins show up all afternoon. Some wear homemade swim dresses and some of the boys wear jeans cut off below the knee, but mostly our swim clothes are the dirty ones from working in the garden. Some people come for a quick dip and hurry off but most swim away the day. The raft is pulled in close to shore so the kids can play on it and jump off the side into the shallow water.

It is an ongoing race each day to be the first one completely submerged in the chilly water. The five of us run down the sandy hill into the water and dunk, swimming a few laps under the water.

The little kids use shovels, buckets and jars that have been abandoned on the beach and carry water up to make waterfalls and try to dam it up. We talk and laugh on the raft close to shore so we can watch the kids until the mothers get there.

We take turns giving them alligator rides where they sit on our backs and we crawl around in the shallow water.

Linda and Vicki are learning how to swim, so I show them how to make a bubble with their skirts to help them float. "When you are waist-deep in water, grab the bottom of your skirt and pull the front out of the water so it gets full of air. Gather the edges together in front of you to hold the air in and it will hold you until the air leaks out."

There is an old canoe someone left on the far side of the pond. It is half full of water and has a bullet hole in the side of it. Michelle and I pull it out to dump the water.

We paddle back around the corner as explorers looking for lost lands. We often play that we are Indigenous princesses captured by white explorers to show them through our homeland. We know all the secrets of the woods; we pride ourselves on our fire-making skills and knowledge of edible plants. We paddle through the bog at the back of the pond where the creek runs in.

"Imagine being the first people to come into this valley," Michelle says. "That's where I would have built my cabin. Just on that grassy hill, with a good view of the Skimmerhorn. I love the way it reflects in the water." We paddle back around the bend. Bikes are piling up against the fence. Our horses are tethered out of the way and are munching calmly on grass, used to this daily ritual. Aunt Margy's blue Chevy is parked on the hill. She is unloading stuff onto the picnic table beside the big griddle.

"Looks like Mother is frying pancakes for supper," Michelle says. Nothing is better and there is always enough for all the kids.

Aunt Marlene and Aunt Susie show up, pushing strollers. They bring butter and fresh strawberry jam to go with the pancakes. When Aunt Leona arrives, she has a gallon bucket of peeled and sliced carrot sticks for everyone to munch. Aunt Margy sends some of the little boys up to Uncle Brandon's to get some firewood and she gets a crackling fire blazing while she cleans off the griddle. It was taken off an old stove and stacked on cinder blocks. It weighs a ton. Once the fire is just right, she ladles pancake dough from the bucket, making lines of even, round pancakes that sizzle in the bubbling grease. Kids line up around the fire, teeth chattering, dripping from head to toe.

There are pancakes for everyone. Little kids are served first. I grab one quickly and put a smear of jam on it for Brittany to eat. She is grubby with sand around her mouth as if she has been eating it the whole time. I use my wet skirt to wipe her face as I have seen the mothers do a thousand times. She is pleased with the hot sticky treat and gets jam all over her hands and face.

"She looks as happy as a pig in mud," Aunt Marlene says.

Aunt Mar helps kids who are learning how to swim. We have a rule that the little kids can't get on the raft until they can swim across the pond without help. Aunt Mar swims with them shorter distances until they get their confidence up to decide to do the big swim across the pond. Then they are allowed to join the ranks on the raft and are fair game to be tossed off it.

Uncle Bran's girls finally get released from their duties and join us on the raft. With eight to ten people on board, the weight must be evenly distributed or it will tip up on its side and dump everyone into the water. When we want to jump off the diving board, we have everyone get to the far side to make it high out of the water, or on the near side to lower it closer to the water. We girls practise synchronized dives and swim routines and make up moves we call dolphin dives and Mary Poppins dives.

"Girls can stay in the water so long because they have an extra layer of fat under their skin," the boys tease us.

"You boys are just jealous because girls are tougher than boys. Boys are wimps and are afraid of the cold." Whichever of us is right, we girls could spend hours swimming in the chilly water, which we always swear is as warm as bathwater even when our teeth are rattling inside our skulls.

I press close to the fire so the steam rises from the wet fabric plastered against my skin and I can feel the warmth seeping through. My aunt flips a pancake and extends it to me. "Flapjack?" she offers with a smile. I take it sizzling on my cold stiff fingers, letting the warmth and the crisp morsels crackle on my tongue.

I eat one quickly and get another. I slather it in the fresh strawberry jam. Mir and I head out to the raft. We swim, one hand up in the air. I lower it to take a bite mid-paddle; the jam drips down my arm so I lick up the drips.

"You shouldn't swim while you eat. Isn't that how it goes?" my cousin Shirl says, laughing.

"I think it's 'You shouldn't swim *after* you eat.' So I'm okay." I laugh.

As another batch of pancakes sizzles on the griddle with the hot fire crackling its agreement, my aunts ask Susie to say a prayer to bless this food. We call out to the raft and there is a collective "Shhhhhh" over our gathering of soggy shivering mothers, girls and little kids as each in turn reminds the next to fold arms, bow heads and take a moment of thanks and reflection for the gifts and blessings of our generous God. We ask God to bless our daddies and the big boys who are always gone to work. We ask him to bring them home safely. I pray for my mother too. We all work for the greater good of our whole community and dedicate our earnings and our lives to building up God's work.

Our horses chew grass and a few of the little kids whisper together while our dresses drip and we shiver in the hot afternoon sun. The smell of hot pancakes teases our rumbling stomachs and gratitude fills our hearts, another reminder that we are safe in the promised land, God's chosen people.

GRANDMA

"Sit down, Grams," I instruct her. "I am going to let you soak your feet, then I'll rub lotion on them." School has just started and I'm in grade five. My teacher is my older cousin, and she wants us to call her Mrs. Ilene. I walk into Grandma's room carrying the big square bread pan full of hot water, concentrating on not spilling it. "Oh, you kids spoil me," Grams says, settling into her big chair and grabbing the fabric bag from her night table cupboard, never to sit idle. This is the best way to get her undivided attention and she makes a fuss about what good care we all take of her. I send my brother Joey to the bathroom to get a towel so we don't slop onto the carpet.

Daddy's mother, Grams, has lived in my mother's house since the day my parents were married, their bond as deep as that between Naomi and Ruth in the Bible. My mother's children, she says, feel like her own children. She mixes up our names so often, I know the summons is for me when she calls for Margaret, and it is for Susie when she calls for Marlene. My brother Peter is often Guy. Now our little Britty, with her bright blue eyes and golden curls, is Grandma's joy.

Susie joins us and Grandma shows her how to pick the article apart and then cut the fabric in a circle into a strip about an inch wide. She cuts around and around until it's gone. Then, with a needle, she stitches the next piece to it so she will have one long continuous piece. Joey rolls it into a ball while she cuts and Grandma starts crocheting it round and round into a big hook rug. She takes pride in coordinating the colours so they are just right. This one will be really good, she says. She'll sell it at the Christmas bazaar for about fifty dollars. I gently rub her feet in the hot water, which softens her hard calluses.

"Tell us a story, Grandma, about when you were a little girl," I say. I've heard the stories hundreds of times so sometimes I correct her if she leaves out parts I particularly like, but I never tire of hearing them.

As a little girl, Grandma grew up in the prairies in southern Alberta near Cardston. Her father was a very talented man, a jack of all trades, she says. His skills included stealing and lying. He got put in jail and his wife was left with five children to feed and no way to make any money. This woman, realizing she could not afford to raise her children, with no social assistance in those days, felt she had no option but to give them away.

The Wynders, a successful Mormon farming family, heard of this and decided to open their home to one of the children. When they went to pick up their new daughter, the mother wanted to take the younger girl, Thelma, who was three. The Wynders' teenage daughter Erma would hear none of it. She told her mother they absolutely must take the five-year-old, Anna Mae. Erma got her way, and Anna Mae, delighted, went to live with her new family and became hopelessly devoted to Erma.

"When I was saying goodbye to my mother," Grandma says, "I couldn't understand why she was crying. She had prepared me to be so excited to go live with this new family who would buy me nice things and make me pretty clothes."

Grandma tried especially hard to please Erma, and Erma sewed her new underpants and taught her everything a big sister should: how to cook and sew and have proper manners. When they put her in school, the teachers were all amazed that this little six-year-old could do long division.

I towel off Grandma's warm wet feet, smear a thick layer of lotion over them and start rubbing round and round. When she is coming to a favourite part, I look at her in anticipation. I'm so absorbed in her expressions that my face mimics her lifted eyebrows.

Grandma says that when she was little, she used to lie. She says she couldn't help it and she was such a good liar that even she would start to believe her stories.

Her adopted sister Erma married Jim Blackmore, and as Grandma got older, she came to adore the youngest of his brothers, Ray Blackmore. As a returned missionary, he was the most eligible bachelor in town.

A large black and white picture of him as a young missionary is framed on the wall beside her bed. In the photo, he smiles, showing his perfect line of white teeth, and he has bright clear eyes and smooth dark hair. Grandma's eyes soften and get far away. She's looking at the same picture but has drifted to a place I know only from her stories.

"Gramsey, will you tell us about when you and Grandpa moved to BC and bought the ranch?"

This part always comes next in the story; we just don't want her to stop.

"He had it all. Tall and handsome. He had honest eyes that really looked at you. With his perfect teeth and strong jawline, people said he looked like he should go in the movies. He was a cowboy who could rope and ride with the best. At dances and community gatherings, he would sing, yodel and tell stories or recite poetry that would hold the interest of the crowd."

He served his two-year mission in New Zealand with the Maori people and had learned their language and customs. He could do a *haka*, the tribal war dance of the Maori, and sing many of their songs, and he had baptized many people there into the Mormon faith, which they felt was kindred to their traditions of family and community.

Ray Blackmore was devoted to serving his God with every fibre of his being. He could quote scripture, could discuss principles of doctrine with anyone and was a rousing church speaker.

Grandma prayed to God and promised him that if he would let her marry Ray Blackmore, she would never lie again.

There were many families, including the stake president in the church community around Cardston, Alberta, who were interested in having their daughter marry Ray Blackmore. Ray, on the other hand, knew what he wanted in a wife. He was a farmer so he needed a farm wife, but more than that, she needed to be strong, loyal and faithful to her husband and to God. He picked the Wynders' sixteen-year-old adopted daughter, Anna Mae.

There was a community dance on a Saturday night in late summer. Everyone was going but the hay was down and they needed to get it raked before the Sabbath. Grandma needed to stay home to finish the raking. She was driving the team around the field, pulling the rake, which would turn the long windrows of sweet-smelling hay. Usually she loved the work and driving the horses, but this evening she was feeling sorry for herself, imagining the music and the fun that was going on without her. Most of all, she knew Ray had returned from his mission and would be there. "I started bawling," she says. "I kept getting little blackflies in my eyes and my nose was running, sniffling, round and round the field."

Unexpectedly, Ray showed up to the farm to get her and take her to the dance. She quickly blew her nose and changed her dress and went with him.

I never tire of this story. As she talks about him, I can see her devotion to him has never diminished since that day. To me it is the most romantic story in the world and I imagine the day when I too will meet my tall, dark and handsome cowboy who will come to take me to the dance.

Grandma always adds at the end, "I have never lied again."

✺

"If ever a woman loved another woman," Grandma says, she loved Grandma Aloha, her sister-wife.

Grandma says Aloha had lived and worked with them for a few years. They were all studying the fundamentalist teachings of Joseph Smith and were hopeful they could live this sacred principle and the fullness of the gospel. The two women went to Grandpa with the idea that he should marry Aloha. Grandpa said, "Well, why would we do a thing like that?" On a trip to BC to pick apples, Grandpa took Aloha for his second wife.

The church brethren met them in the orchard where they were married. They finished filling the pickup truck with apples and headed back to Alberta.

They kept the marriage a secret from the rest of his family for several years, until one day Great-Grandmother Blackmore pointed to one of Grandpa Ray's daughters and said, "That little girl looks just like Aloha."

Grandpa told his mother, a staunch Mormon, of his commitment to live a plural marriage. Great-Grandmother went into her room and did not come out for three days. When she did, she told Grandpa Ray that God had shown to her that her youngest son was in fact living God's will.

Grandpa Ray was excommunicated from the mainstream Mormon Church, which meant that no one from his family and community would be allowed to speak to him. He was shunned by many of his family and other members of the church. In order to live the fullness of the gospel as they felt inspired to do, they paid the high price of losing all family and community ties, which required them to build a new life.

When their family was still young, Grandpa was out in the field working with the tractor. He went to step over the spinning power take-off, which grabbed his pant leg and quickly wrapped him in, tearing off all his clothes and almost pulling his leg off as well.

During these dark times, Grandma says, it was Grandma Aloha who ran the farm, doing the work of two men and never complaining. Grams says she worked up until the day before she had the baby, and the day after she had the baby, she was right back at work. Grandma tended the babies, often breastfeeding her own and her sister-wives' babies at the same time.

And then, one night, the big ranch house burned to the ground. Grandpa went to town and bought hot dogs, which the family roasted for dinner over the dying coals of what had been their home.

The boys put up beds in the barn. The big chicken coop was turned into a makeshift dwelling. Grandpa worked alongside his children hand milking the cows and was quick to help a neighbour. Grandpa Ray was unshaken in his faith and family.

My grandfather Joseph Raymond Blackmore died at the age of fifty-seven after a painful fight with leukemia. Grams wrote this poem for him as she watched him struggle in the last days of his fight for his life:

> I'm youth, I'm health, I'm strength
> He said to the man in the glass
> In my heart I had to agree
> But I knew his health was failing
> His spirit would soon be free

I pat Grandma's feet to let her know I'm now done with the pampering. She gets Susie to help her cut her thick toenails. I leap onto Grandma's bed and burrow under her thick blankets. "Oh, what are you doing in there?" she says, laughing. To our surprise, she pulls a Mr. Big out of her cutting bag. She opens it and breaks it into four chunks for each of us. I nibble mine to make this treat last and snuggle deeper, determined to sleep the night right where I am. She laughs. Even when she says it's like sleeping with a windmill, I know she likes the extra snuggles.

A Book of Ruth

It's one of those golden fall days when mornings are crisp but afternoons still feel like summer. Father has gone to Utah for conference with a few carloads of people. This morning Mother Sharon and Mother Mary Ann called Aunt Leona and decided it is a good day to do apple juice.

Mir and I carry a heavy basket between us, running up and down between the long rows of trees, picking up the windfall apples from the ground and whatever is left hanging on the trees. We fill basket after basket and stumble down the row, dragging them to dump in the back of the pickup truck—mostly Macs and Spartans with a few Jonagolds to make a good juice mix.

I pluck a huge Jonagold from the tree and take a big bite. While juice runs down my chin, I blurt out the secret I can't keep a moment longer. "Father is getting two new wives," I say with my mouth half full. I'm dying to tell someone so I confide in Mir in the shadows of the apple grove. When Father returns, we will have two more mothers, two sisters who will marry Father on the same day.

Aunt Leona backs up the pickup. The apple press and chopper are tucked in a corner in the back of her woodshed. The big boys haul out the old equipment and start spraying it off with the garden hose. Mir and I drag the stainless steel vat from the corner where bales of hay have been stacked around it. Everything gets a good scrub down: the chopper, the big press and the little press, the barrels and buckets we will fill with juice and the stainless steel vat for washing the apples.

We unload the apples directly into the washing vat. Two people lift each basket of clean apples and dump it directly into the belly of the chopper Grandpa Oler built. An old motor turns a belt to rotate blunt blades on a spinning shaft. One of the kids stands beside the metal hopper with a clean length of two-by-four, pounding the apples down into the chopper blades. The apples come out in a snowfall of juicy pulp while the old motor roars. I scoop a handful, squeeze it into my mouth and then munch the bits.

The pulp, gleaming with the sugary juice, is packed into the round barrel press made with thin strips of wood riveted to three metal bands. It sits on a metal stand with a thick pole in the middle that is wound with threads like a giant screw. Once it is packed, the juice pours down the seasoned wood where it froths from the spout; a golden waterfall fills a three-gallon milk bucket in a matter of minutes. Wooden blocks are secured inside the cage of the press and a heavy metal head is twisted down the pole with several of the mothers or bigger kids walking round and round pulling on a thick steel rod, squeezing the last of the juice from the hard, dense brick left in the bottom of the press. The juice foams and jumps, a cascade of golden, pure delight.

The children stand ready with their carved apple cups to intercept the flow. You pick a really good apple, cut it flat on top and carve out the core, being careful not to puncture the bottom. After drinking the juice from the hollow in the centre, you eat the cup for dessert.

The forms then come off. A hard, round cake of browning apple bits clings to the pole in the centre. We cut it into wedges with our hands, which hold together pretty well while it goes into the wheelbarrow for its last ride to the pig pen to become pig dinner.

Making apple juice is one of our favourite harvest days. The big boys are needed for all the heavy lifting and it's fun having them around joking and singing while we work. Little kids load buckets from the back of the pickup truck. All of us, little kids and big kids too, eat as many apples and drink as much juice as we can hold. The work of juicing is so engrossing and so fun I discover that I have almost no time to think about my father arriving later today with his two new wives. The smell of apples engulfs me.

At the end of a day like this, the whole crew drag our feet as we pull up to our house. The fleeting fall light has left us. The single brave light bulb above the door lights the porch as we unload more than fifty full gallons of juice in varying pails, bins and containers. We've dropped off buckets of juice to the neighbours and the rest will be strained into two-quart canning jars, boiled for twenty minutes and loaded onto the shelves in the cool dark cellar to become a Sunday dinner treat or to pour over snow to make winter slushies. Already nights are quite cold, so the juice will stay cool on the porch for a few days if needed. We find a sheet of plywood to cover the tops and lift some heavy rocks on them to keep the critters out.

I step into the Bottom House. The living room is filled with dressers, beds and boxes. Our houses have turned into bedroom musical chairs, with people hauling dressers and beds here and there, painting, hanging wallpaper and shampooing the carpets. The mothers who weren't making apple juice with us for the day are rearranging to make room for two more mothers in our already overflowing houses. It is we kids who don't need walls for privacy, they've decided.

Susie and I move our things into the Top House storage room with the deep freezer and the walls lined with jars of canning. "At least we won't starve in here," my sister and I joke.

We decide we will turn our mother's storage shed into a bunkhouse for the summer. We like to sleep out on the veranda or trampoline when it's warm enough anyway. There are nights we have woken with a layer of dew or even frost on our blankets. "I sleep the best under the open sky, breathing fresh air," Susie says casually, as if being a gypsy in your own home is really no bother at all. "Now we don't have a bedroom to clean."

My brothers are moved out of their room as well, making way for these new mothers. Mother, ever the woman of solutions, gets our cousin James to build a wall dividing the big entrance "junk room" with built-in bunk beds at each end of the long narrow room so Pete, Joe and Don will have a bit of privacy and a door to close on their things.

Anticipation fills the air. We hang around waiting for the van to pull into the driveway. I can't wait to see what our new mothers look like. I've heard they are really pretty and sweet.

"They're here. They're here!" The little kids run into the kitchen hollering their arrival.

There is a scramble, new people, boxes and suitcases. "Three new mothers," people are saying. The unexpected third mother is Ruth.

Ruth brought with her a two-year-old son. We stare, surprised, at this little boy. Without so much as a whisper of warning, I got a new mother and a new little brother, Jason. He is the same age as our tiny preemie brother Stevie. At his mother's coaxing, shyly he gives me a hug before running to hide behind her skirt.

After prayers, we serve up tall glasses of fresh apple juice and some of us kids sit around listening to the mothers talking, getting to know one another and sharing their stories of how God had brought them all together to be a family.

Ruth becoming Father's tenth wife had been a total surprise for her and Father both, she tells us. The two sisters he had originally gone to marry were married and packed when the Prophet told Father to go talk to Ruth's father.

Ruth had left the religion with her boyfriend when she was a teenager. She had gotten pregnant. Her man was young and not ready to be a father. She determined that raising her son in the church was the greatest gift she could give him, and she returned to her father's home and was rebaptized into the church. Under the direction of God through the Prophet, she found her place among God's people sealed for time and all eternity to a faithful priesthood man. She committed to raise a family as a faithful servant to help build up Zion, the New Jerusalem, here in the last days. She never would have guessed in a million years, she says, that her calling from God would bring her to the middle of Timbuktu, Canada.

She arrived at our house unannounced and unexpected. Five feet and a few inches tall, she has thick, almost black hair that brushes the floor when she lets down her braids. I watch, mesmerized, as her fingers fly expertly weaving thick sections into two equally weighted braids that reach below her knees. She hooks the braid around her back and arm so she can hold it secure to braid down to the end. She then coils them around the back of her head and pins them securely in place to make a neat braid bun, which is my father's preference for his wives and daughters to wear their hair. It is also a practical thing to do with floor-length hair.

We don't know what to think of Ruth. Besides having had a child out of wedlock, she is loud and funny and a little too sacrilegious for most of our straitlaced Mormon relatives in Canada. She likes to disarm people by playing up the stereotype of being the angelic, demure polygamist woman, then saying inappropriate things or making a dirty joke.

My own hair is almost to my knees and I wear it mostly in a wave and a French braid. Ruth helps me practise my braiding and pinning. She's a whiz of a seamstress and is keen to help us in the sewing room with our projects. I like her. I wonder what else Mother Ruth and I could have in common. I can't imagine ever leaving the church with a boyfriend, even temporarily, or having a child out of wedlock, but I do like her laughing and jokes.

When the house is tidy enough, after we've listened to stories until our eyes won't stay open, Sue and I drag ourselves down to the storage room that is now our glamorous bedroom. It's too cold tonight for me to want to spend the night on the veranda or in our makeshift bunkhouse. If it's cold enough to keep the juice outside, I think, it's cold enough to keep me inside.

When I Grow Up

Peter stands in the back of his little pickup and hands out heavy plastic grocery bags to Susie and me. Loaded down like pack mules, we make the long trek across the wobbly suspension bridge, along the river and past the apple trees to the saggy old ranch house that looks over the Moyie River. With the pumphouse on the north corner next to the river and the garden on the south end, a rail fence lines the boundary of the yard and orchard to keep the grazing critters out. The river is the west boundary. The log arch over the gate has a couple of horseshoes pounded into it and Grandpa Ray's brand, JR, burnt into the wood; the R is turned backward, keeping it authentic. Two wooden wagon wheels hang dutifully on hinges as the gate.

This isn't the original ranch that proudly sported the JR brand. The Blackmores bought the old Ryan's Station Ranch in the late eighties, ran cows out on the range all summer and had work crews living in the ranch house most of the time. They told us that, before that, it had been some kind of reform work ranch for boys who got into trouble with the law.

The Moyie River is one of the warmest rivers in the whole area. Mother brings a load of us kids camping up here in the summer. There was a biffy by the swimming hole and the mothers had the advantage of being able to use the house stove to cook some of the food to feed all us hungry kids. Mostly they cooked on the big grill set up beside the river on cinder blocks with a fire toasting underneath.

Since Pete got his driver's licence, our Sunday afternoon ritual is to take Grandma into town to do her grocery shopping for the crew house for the week, then drive her to Yahk, help her carry her things and the food across the swinging bridge and get everything put away. Often she makes a big puffed wheat cake as the lunch goody for the crew. She always cuts a generous portion for each of us to enjoy on the way home.

Grams has dozens of granddaughters and she doesn't hesitate to ask for help when she needs it. Often Sue or I will stay the night or even a week with her at whichever crew house she is working to clean and set up. She is an efficient manager.

She has no time for talking back or laziness when there is work that needs doing. No one says no to Grandma. She works hard and she expects us to work as long as she does. She teaches us thrift and to see value where others see none.

The second-hand stores save Grandma ballooning garbage bags of clothes they don't want to put out. She glows like Christmas morning when the bags are particularly full of treasures. Its fun to see her feeling as wealthy as the Queen as each item is pulled from the bag to determine if it is in good enough shape to be given and enjoyed by anyone we know, or if the fabric is good enough for making over. "Oh, there's so much good fabric in this," she exhales in delight, holding up a billowing sundress. "Imagine. They were going to throw this out."

Mother is particularly skilled at making over dresses into smaller ones our size, so Grams keeps a sharp eye for the good cotton florals. Worn flannel sheets make excellent tea towels, which are always in high demand. Bright cotton fabrics make good aprons. Two-way stretch knits make sturdy girls' leggings. Fortrel fabrics are saved for cutting into crochet rugs for which Grams is famous. Bags of light denims, corduroys and cotton blends are donated to the school sewing classes, while sweaters are saved for making heavy camping blankets. Buttons and elastics are cut and saved for the sewing classes. We can have whatever we want for crafting and everything else is cut into rags for the uncles out at the shop.

"C-A-Y-G, clean as you go," she always says. "If you put things away as you are finished using them, you don't end up with every countertop cluttered when you are finished."

I am trying to get better at it. She can move quickly when she wants to and she briskly tidies up the kitchen while I carefully stir the gooey mess and slip a gob into my mouth whenever her back is turned. Sue and I whisper and giggle, knowing she can't hear us.

Grams is famous for her bread and her cookies, but no one can do puffed wheat cake the way she can. "The secret," she says, "is to make it soupy with marshmallows and cook it just long enough so it is crisp but not hard."

ᛉ

"When I grow up, I want to be a mother." The song is sung by my little sisters Vicki and Nesta, who are in the line of adorable curly heads singing their hearts out, holding dollies in the air, twirling, their skirts swirling around their legs, then puffing out so they sit on the floor, each inside a lacy ring. Vicki catches my eye as we clap and she waves, grinning from ear to ear. Each has brought her own special dolly from home and I can't imagine how many curlers their mothers had to put in to make all of those curls in their hair.

Each grade gets up to do their Mother's Day performance. Church today is mostly a program with lots of songs. The sermons are really short and are about honouring our mothers. Grades six, seven and eight have been practising a medley of spring and Mother's Day songs, about gardens and flowers and sunshine and walking, all of those things that make me think of my mother. I know she likes the song. We each have a big paper heart with a poem written inside and, after the song, we walk out into the audience and give the hearts to our mothers.

I'm in grade eight and I love my mother very much, but I know life isn't easy for her. Still, I'm too wrapped up in my own life of school and friends and fantasy to think too seriously about what it is really like to be a mother. I want to be a mother someday too but it still seems like something far enough in my future. It's an abstract desire, not one I think about with much attention. I spend more of my days thinking about how I want more time to read my favourite books or ride the ponies over the hills. May is gorgeous in the valley, with the grasses dotted with early spring flowers.

❧

Mother's Day is on the second Sunday of May, but before the first day of May, each day after school I have to meet at the high school to practise the maypole dance with all the girls in the school. First the bigger girls are going to braid up the pole, then we middle-sized girls unbraid the pole, then the small girls come dancing out and hold on to the ribbons as they dance around the pole. We dance and sing, and dance and sing.

The mothers are all sewing us new, coordinated, pastel-coloured dresses so we look like a well-organized basket of flowers. We have been working on the performance for weeks. Aunt LaRee ordered huge bolts of fabric and our mothers have been cutting and sewing for days.

May Day is fun but the grand performance will be performed at the Focus on Youth Festival of the Arts that is put on every year at the public school auditorium. Bountiful School has a reputation for its extravagant performances, costumes and flair. Certainly, the kindergarten girls will do their adorable dolly dance for the festival.

After the second time the little girls sing their song in church, though, Aunt Marlene voices her concern about the upcoming public performance at the youth festival. "I'm sure the media will have a heyday with this. 'Bountiful School is grooming girls as young as kindergarten to have children and be mothers.'"

The teachers are alarmed. They never considered that someone could take offence at this simple children's song. Recently, Aunt Debbie and an anti-polygamy group have been pushing the government to cut funding to our school. They've made accusations in the media about the girls not getting fair access to education. They've said that girls are not allowed to learn the sciences and are taught only to cook and sew. Young girls, they've said, are being indoctrinated to be wives and mothers. After discussing it with other parents, the principal and Daddy, they decide to cut the song from the performance.

Through a swirl of pastel dresses, long curled locks, braided ribbon around a white maypole and songs of spring, the festival is a success. Aunt LaRee glows in the praise of the Creston Valley music teachers and arts world, and the mothers of Bountiful wow the Creston Valley yet again with their skills at the sewing machine and putting curlers into waist-length hair. Whatever the media said about us, we face the world smiling, organized and singing our little hearts out.

Mother told me that in her patriarchal blessing, which was given by her father just before she and my father were married, she was called of God to be in the service of the community and administer for the sick in the last days. She felt that if this was to be her responsibility, she needed to get all the training she could. With six young children and the support of her sister-wives providing child care, Mother went to nursing school to become a registered nurse.

Mother takes on a lot of stress taking care of all the people in the community when they get sick. It seems as if she is always taking more courses by correspondence. Daddy wants her to become a midwife so she can deliver the women's babies at home. Many of the women are immigrating or American citizens and don't have their medical insurance. Daddy talks about a community birthing centre where women can have home births and receive care from family while they recover.

Mother also informally becomes a marriage and family counsellor because women in our community come to her for support and care.

She speaks to Daddy on their behalf when she feels a family needs an intervention, or when women or children are not getting the support they need. When there is a new baby, she organizes support for the mother, whether it is meals for the family or help with child care or housework.

❧

It's dark outside when Mother's car pulls up the hill and into the driveway. Susie, Joey and I jump up from where we have been playing a board game on the living room carpet, with two-year-old Brittany climbing over us, always sure to have someone's attention. I have left a sink half full of dishes. Susie's stacks of laundry sit on the couch and Joey had only pulled the vacuum from the closet when the impromptu game began. We rush to do our chores as Mother walks in.

She takes her time, hangs her coat and purse and sits looking out the window. Even her uniform, the knee-length hem on her nursing dress, looks tired tonight. Her eyes are puffy and red, her brow furrowed. I can tell she has a headache.

We glance at her, working even more industriously to tidy the house and ease some of her burden. Joey fills a plastic cup with water, sets it beside her on the table and rubs her back gently. She smiles her gratitude, then puts her weary head onto her folded arms and lets her tears run over her wrist. Her tears break our hearts. Sue and I go to her and wrap our arms around her, not knowing what pain she carries from that mysterious adult world. Baby Brittany climbs up on her lap and wraps her chubby arms around Mother's neck. She goes for a bath and we take extra care not to argue as we finish up the housework.

Later, I hear her telling Daddy that one of the doctors started yelling at her about a woman from the community who was not in good health and was pregnant yet again.

"You people have no sense having so many children," he had said, exasperated. As she was a polygamist woman herself, with seven children, this man certainly included her in that statement. I was one of those children he was referring to.

CHICKENS

"Chickens on Friday," my teacher reminds us at the end of the day. "It is a school day so if your family isn't getting any chickens to butcher, you need to go help a family that is. It is not just a day off."

It's mid-April and outside of the schoolhouse the farmland is finally truly green; the snow's been melted now for several weeks and the ground that was covered with snow has had time to breathe and grow. I'm in grade six at school and I'm used to the semi-regular interruptions to our usual studies. Four times a year, we get the old chickens from the egg farm down on the flats to butcher for our families. When a line of their birds are getting past their prime laying age, the folks at the chicken farm order new ones and call Uncle Brandon. He has a deal with them that we can take the old hens in trade for cleaning the coop and putting the new birds into cages when they arrive.

School is cancelled for the day so the children can help their families as the labour force for killing, cleaning, cutting and packing three to four thousand chickens. Families call Uncle Bran the night before to tell him how many chickens they want dropped off at their houses. Four or five trucks transport the killing crew of a dozen grade-nine and -ten kids and a few parents. A few of us younger kids come to push the carts. Trucks arrive at the shed at five in the morning and each will take several trips unloading carcasses to each house that has asked for chickens delivered. The trucks leave weighed down with a big, unusually white mound rounded over the top. It looks like it could be snow in April, but puffs of feathers twirl in the wind as the truck pulls onto the highway. Bigger families like ours will take more or fewer depending on how many chickens are available.

An old shopping cart with a piece of plywood on top and a strong pair of bare hands—or, better, gloved ones—are the killing tools. My fifteen-year-old cousin Roy is a strong and skilled chicken-neck stretcher. "It can't feel anything," Roy reassures me as I push the rattling cart behind him.

Each cage compartment holds four hens. He reaches into the hanging cages and grabs a chicken by its legs. Holding the chicken upside down, he puts the other hand around the thin part of the neck, getting a vise hold with his thumb and top fingers. Bracing its body and neck against his thigh, he pulls down quickly with a twist of the wrist, stretching and popping the neck in a quick, painless motion. The life is already gone.

Poop and feathers collect on the shopping cart's wheels, making it a challenge to move. I'm using both hands to hold the plywood sheet down on the shopping cart so the desperate flapping creatures will not escape and get into the poop gutter far below. I force my cart along the narrow concrete walkway, which provides access to the hanging cages for gathering eggs and checking on the feed and water system running to each cage. All the hens do is eat and lay eggs until the time they are brutally pulled feet first from their cages to get their necks stretched. What a reward for all those eggs they laid for somebody's breakfast.

Ammonia from the poop pit below burns my eyes and I adjust the dishtowel I have tied over my face. I move carefully, scaring myself with my imagination as I picture the cart going over the edge of the steep concrete barrier, sending me plummeting into the heaps of chicken poop.

"Twenty," I count, nodding to my cousin. The cart rattles and wobbles, feathers sticking to the wheels down the long concrete of death row. When I finally burst into the fresh, cold morning air, I suck deeply.

At the loading dock, Uncle Bran grabs two chickens at a time, throwing them into the bed of a waiting pickup truck backed in below us and counting out the requested number. "Five hundred." He calls to the driver to pull ahead. These will be for two families, 250 each. He sends them on their way and another truck backs into position.

I try my hand at stretching a neck. My arms aren't long enough and I'm really not strong enough to be effective as a killer. I feel something give in the neck, and I'm sure her neck is longer. I look down. Even at that odd angle she is looking me in the eye. She lets out a deep low cluck. The sound escapes through my fingers pressed onto her windpipe as I twist and pull. The pure white of this lifeless body makes me think of seeing little Flower lying so still on the straw, an innocent life. It crosses my mind to wonder how many chickens there are in heaven. We farm so we can eat, but killing is not the best part of being a farmer.

Eight hundred chickens. The mound of white heaps up against the back window and bulges into a dense, warm mass two feet higher than the top of the sides of the truck. It looks like it could be pillowy soft if I jumped into it, but I know the squishy warm bodies would be anything but welcoming. Only one more load to go, so I jump into the pickup to deliver these eight hundred carcasses to my house.

We pull up to the house.

"We are doing the chickens over at Uncle Guy's," Mother Mary Ann directs us. I'm happy as I will get to work with my cousins all day, and more people to help makes it more fun—but it also means our total chicken count for the day is twelve hundred.

Farther down, two of the mothers set up a workstation for processing: a foldable table, a sheet of plywood set on two barrels, and a wooden feed bin on its side set into a line. One end has the barrels and bins and a garden hose for filling them and cleaning the meat. We unload the eight hundred onto a blue tarp at the other end, where we will start our processing line.

The mothers are eager to get an early start to the day as there are hours of work ahead to clean the meat, and then hours more once we get it into the kitchen to put into jars for canning or into bags for the freezer.

Mother Sharon has a big knife sharpener in a pan and is putting a fresh edge on the big kitchen knives. Smaller kids will lift the chickens from the pile onto the work table. I feel to see if there is an egg in them as most are killed before they lay their morning egg. With a slow pressure above the abdomen, the egg can be laid without it breaking inside the hen. They collect in a large bowl in the middle of the table to be used in baking.

These chickens are small and skinny; they don't make very good roasting hens for the pot for soups and stews and there just isn't room in our freezers for all those carcasses to go in whole, so mostly we will skin off the legs and breasts, cut the meat, then throw the carcasses and giblets to the coyotes.

The processing line fills up as my older sister and brother and my older cousins get into place, aprons tied on, hair tied back. The conversation is cheerful. Cousin Dan the comedian sings loudly, making jokes and witty remarks. While the banter rolls back and forth, hands fly.

I take a sharp knife, showing Nesta what to do so she can cut the chickens Joni and Amos, the five-year-olds, bring to the table. With a quick slice on each side between breast and leg, I leave two holes. I grab the centre skin, pulling up to reveal the shining, bare, thin breast. In two quick movements, I split the skin and pull it off the knuckle of each leg and up its back, and then slide the bird down the line to the next person who will cut the breast meat only, putting the white meat into a large bowl in the centre of the next table.

Depending on what is needed most for the family, we may take the legs off whole—these are then frozen, a bag of legs to be used for baking for dinners, or, most often, they will be packed into jars with some of the breast meat, salt and pepper, cooked in a boiler bath for four hours and then stored in the cellar. Canned chicken can feed many hungry mouths and is a staple for our big families. Often it is pulled out to make cold sandwiches or is mixed with pickles for a spread. The bones and broth are used in soups or gravies and sometimes we kids will sneak a jar and take it to our shacks for a snack.

If the moms don't want the legs for canning or freezing, we cut the meat off right there and leave the bone on the carcass. Meat piles up in huge stainless steel bowls. The family owns three of these multi-purpose containers, used for everything from harvesting fresh fruits or veggies from the garden to holding steaming mountains of mashed potatoes or a Jell-O salad at Sunday dinner.

The leg meat on these laying hens is lean and meagre since they have not moved around much to build up their body mass. We will grind the leg meat into a lean ground meat. Since it doesn't have its own fat, it is much better if it can be added to some pork. Some of the best burger of all is to mix deer, pork and chicken together. The pork fat makes it tasty and, mixed with the chicken, it helps mask the gamy taste of the deer.

The morning plods along with cheerful stories and singing and, ever so slowly, we make a dent in the mountain of dead chickens. The barrels on the other end of the table fill with meat. A few more cousins come to help for a bit since their families are not butchering chickens today. Mother asks if they would like to take a few bags of meat home to throw in their freezer.

Aunt Leona has one of the boys help her carry a full barrel into the house. The mothers inside, who are watching the babies and toddlers and making lunch, will also start the meticulous process of washing and picking over each piece of meat to get any small bits of feather that were missed. A feather sticking out of fried chicken is never appetizing.

There are about fifty brown chickens in the heap. Mother tells Mir and I to skin out about ten of them and gut them. We will throw them in the freezer whole since the brown hens are bigger and fuller than the others.

We pick the ones we want and go to find a five-gallon bucket for the entrails.

✿

Driving up the Long Road is a dark van none of us recognize. It is driving slowly as if not sure where to go. It looks like a service van with darkened back windows. We watch it go up the long hill to the elementary school and sit there for a few minutes. Despite the empty parking lot, a tall, thin man in professional clothes gets out and walks to the door. The school is dark and locked so he gets back into the van and drives back down the hill. It's obviously no one we know.

"Probably reporters," Peter concludes for the rest of us.

Dan gets a dishtowel and ties it around his neck like a napkin, picks up a knife in each hand and bangs the handles on the board table in front of him and hangs his tongue out the side of his mouth with his eyes too wide like the Wile E. Coyote cartoon. "Send more reporters; the last ones were delicious," he chants.

We all laugh at his imitation of this well-known sketch our older cousin Kathy, who is a skilled artist, had made for the local newspaper in response to the recent onslaught of reporters and news stories about the scandal that is polygamy. She drew a cartoon of a cat with a sheepish smile, sitting beside a notebook, pencil and camera, and a word bubble with Dan's catchy line.

The van pulls into the driveway. The team sits for a minute. I imagine them pondering how badly they want a story when they see the heaps of chicken carcasses and the pans of shiny pink meat.

The mothers start to argue, laughing nervously.

"You go talk to them."

"Why do I have to? You do it."

Aunt Leona must have lost because she wipes her hands on her apron and walks over.

They quickly jump out to meet her, the man reaching forward to shake her hand out of habit. She looks down at her apron and laughs.

"It's okay," she assures him. He gratefully stuffs his fingers into his pocket.

"We are from *The Fifth Estate*," he says. "We want to do a follow-up on the story we ran a few months ago. Do you folks mind if we get a few pictures and chat with you for a minute?"

"We are kind of busy," Aunt Leona responds, stating the obvious.

When Aunt Debbie left after the fire, she told social services that she was escaping her polygamy life. After that, police and reporters came asking questions and have become a familiar presence in our community.

"Oh, we were hoping to get the kids in school, but we can see school has been closed for the day and we're not staying around for the weekend. It would really help us out if we could just take a few pictures so we can get back to Vancouver tomorrow."

The mothers look at one another and shrug. These days, doing our chores for national television is becoming part of our daily lives, with a different news crew showing up every few weeks, taking pictures of the kids playing. They've asked if they can go into the school and even into church to take video and pictures.

"Is nothing sacred to these people?" Uncle Mac had roared in frustration.

"I sure don't mind if you take my picture," Dan says. He has his sleeves rolled up well past his elbows and begins flexing his muscles with the big knife still in his hand.

We all roll our eyes at him. "What will the next headline be? Black-more youth threatens reporters with a knife!"

The Fifth Estate camera crew laugh good-naturedly and eagerly set up their cameras as one starts asking the children about what they are doing.

Mir and I have just cut the parson's nose off the chickens we are cleaning and are up to our elbows in the gooey warm entrails. I curl my fingers, working my pointer finger into a small crevice, loosening the organs that are bound there. In one pull, the whole mess slops into the bucket below me with a loud thud and a splash. Something punctures and squirts sideways, getting on the surprised man's shoe.

"Oops," I say, genuinely apologetic. "It's kind of a messy business." A woman with a big camera on her shoulder films our little group. As she works her way closer, she steps carefully over some dead chickens and gets a close-up of Joni and Amos, who immediately decide it is a fine time to make a dead hen give up its last unlaid egg. The two of them show her where to push and, to the woman's surprise, out pops a clean white egg.

Always a social butterfly, seven-year-old Vicki explains to the reporter why we aren't in school today. "This is school," she says with an air of authority. "We are learning how to kill chickens and make them into food. That's why we don't have to go to school."

I roll my eyes and look at Peter.

"Great," he says. "Now we will read in the newspaper that all we do in school is kill chickens."

His comment gets me thinking about the fire and Aunt Debbie.

I wonder if she really does hate Daddy so much that she makes up lies so everyone will think we have bad parents who don't care about us. I don't understand why people in Vancouver would want to watch a video of us butchering chickens or really what is so wrong with girls wanting to grow up to be mothers and have children. I know polygamy is against the law but it seems silly to me that people would think my family is bad. I just can't imagine why Aunt Debbie and everyone are so mad about it.

CHRISTMAS

I remember the excitement of Christmas morning when I was little. We went to bed anticipating the wonder of the presents we knew were hidden in the corner behind the piano. Our parents didn't bother with the fickle story of Santa Claus but planning to wake up to presents and treats was thrill enough. We girls each got a small wooden chest Mother bought from Uncle Brandon, who made them with personalized engraved designs etched into the front. All the kids got stuffed animals Grandma Mem sewed for us and a box of Old Dutch potato chips to ourselves from Grandpa Oler. Mine were salt and vinegar and I pushed them down beside my bed so I could eat them slowly after the other kids had chomped theirs down. Daddy brought home bags of oranges and nuts and we had Fruit Loops for breakfast.

That was a long time ago. Now it's 1995 and these days in church, the brethren remind us that Jesus was born April 6. Christmas Day is actually a pagan holiday that is followed by devil worshippers. The early Christians had decided to celebrate this day in the name of Christ as they did not want to give up their worldly ways and truly turn themselves over to God. The tradition of bringing a burning tree into the house and putting wrapped offerings under it, we are taught, has more to do with spooks and demons than it ever had to do with Jesus Christ, who was the Prince of Peace. And Santa Claus, Daddy explains, doesn't have anything to do with anything except greed. If Christmas should be about anything, it should be about service. "We sure don't need any more stuff," Father says. "For Christmas, we need to go help our neighbours and make sure everyone has firewood."

꒰ꗥ꒱

The hand on the clock ticks closer to three. I've cleaned up my desk and am restlessly waiting for the bell. It's our last dance class before the break for the winter holiday. I hear a horn honk. I hate it when Mother honks for us outside the school. Susie, Mir and I have a half-hour to change and drive into town every Wednesday for our dance lesson. We change quickly into our practice skirts, pinning and tucking each other. Mother has sewn and altered our dance costumes so the full-plaid fabric reaches just below our knees.

On the fifteen-minute drive into town, we lace up our tight leather dance slippers, then slip our toes into our shoes to walk into the dance studio in our dance teacher's basement. If mother isn't working, she joins us for our dance classes. She took lessons when she was a little girl and is thrilled that her daughters are dancers.

Our dance teacher, Lori, grew up a Catholic city girl in Cranbrook. Then she married a cowboy–dairy farmer from Creston. She says they don't go to church except at Christmas and Easter. She told us she promised her husband she would learn to can peaches when he built her a house with a big dance studio in the basement. He built her the house, so she often asks Mother for tips on canning, gardening and preserving meat.

We are amazed at all the work she goes to at Christmastime to decorate her house. She starts Christmas baking a month before Christmas and puts it all in her freezer. She sets up three different trees with lights, and presents are heaped under the tree for her two children. She tells us about their faces on Christmas morning, about them tearing through the wrapping paper and their excitement with their presents.

"I hate all this Santa Claus crap," Lori says dramatically. "I keep that downstairs for the kids; upstairs I keep my nativity and the pretty part of Christmas." She brings out some leftover baking to share with us.

With her fluffy bleach-blond hair and curled bangs, hoop earrings, dark blue eye makeup and tights that accentuate her muscular legs, Lori is the worldliest woman I know. She went to Scotland when she was young to dance in the Highland games world championships. My dance lessons at her house are a peek into how the town people live.

The town girls in my dance classes ride the school bus every day and have their bobbed hair flopping around until Lori tells them to put it into a ponytail. The other girls are tall and wiry and usually polite about our differences. Their thin arms and legs seem weightless in their tank tops and small, tight dance shorts. They talk easily with Lori and at times are sassy and often tell Lori they are too tired, have a headache or just don't want to dance.

❧

The Prophet has instructed that all members of the church who are above the age of accountability to be baptized, eight years old, should wear the sacred long underwear called "the garment." Before this, only people who had made the marriage covenant were required to keep their bodies fully covered as a symbol of their covenant to each other before God.

Modesty has always been an important part of Mormonism. However, in the summers our play clothes usually got shorter—cut-offs and split skirts, our bare brown legs tanning in the summer sun.

"It will certainly never hurt to create a habit of modesty," Grandma Mem affirms matter-of-factly. The Prophet warns us that the sacred long underwear will be the symbol that sets God's people apart when the destroying angel comes in the last days to rid the wicked from the face of the earth. As the End of Times draws near, we must wear them always under our clothing, especially in the final hour of our preparation. We must take them off only to wash and put on clean ones.

Mother never takes these things as seriously as other mothers do. Aunt Leona made Susie and I two pairs each and we wear them as often as they are clean, eager to follow every direction from the Prophet.

Finally, Mother orders a bolt of fabric from one of the old church aunts in Colorado City. Our new underwear is thick and soft, all one piece with snaps in the front, to cover us from our necks to our wrists to our ankles. I love snuggling into a fresh clean pair of underwear on a cold day.

Now that we wear the underwear, the challenge is to keep it covered. It's easy for the boys with their one style of denim pants and button-up shirts. But it takes some creativity to make it all work for the girls. We start wearing leggings to match our dresses as the solution. They are warm, functional and modest. But to look more ladylike at church, we wear pantyhose with our nicer dresses. To cover the thick white underwear at our ankles, we double up the nylon stockings to smooth the wrinkles. The layers are tight and pinchy.

Accommodating the long underwear is even more of a challenge with our Highland dance costumes. Regulation for competition is very specific about length of skirt, plaid socks just below the knees and black panties. The Scottish didn't wear anything under their kilts but the black underwear was added—Lori says with a laugh—to keep it more family-friendly as the deep pleats swing during the dances and reveal a very clear shot of the behind.

"If people are going to be seeing your backside," Mother says, "I think you should have more than black panties on."

Mother and Aunt Leona ponder a solution to our costume dilemma. We wear pantyhose over our underwear and the socks and black underwear over that. It makes for a lot of layers but we feel better that we aren't compromising our values in order to compete.

"I'm sure God will bless you in the competition for doing his will," our cousin Shirl assures us sincerely. We all agree.

❧

During our dance theory classes, we sit at Lori's kitchen table while she makes a tiny pot of soup for her two children. She tells her little kids to pick up the toys and they yell "No!" at her. She yells back and forth with them and the kids go stomping off. I've never seen kids have a yelling fight with their parents, especially ones where the kid wins. I would have gotten one hard thumpin' for talking to a parent like that.

When she says two children are enough for her, I'm startled. Children are the blessings of God. She says it so matter-of-factly. Her kids make her crazy, she says. My adjusting brain rationalizes that this is what it must be like to raise children if you don't have the priesthood in your home.

❧

Even without a bunch of presents, the holidays are still one of the best times of the year. We stay up late and eat good food night after night during our break from school. Uncle Brandon puts big candles in buckets up the sleigh-riding hill so we slide into a blackened hole following the timid dots of light. We have a big bonfire at the top to warm our fingers and toes. We celebrate New Year's and have a winter festival, with a barbecue and a community sleigh-riding party. Uncle Mac gives hayrides, pulling a sleigh behind his big horses. We pull tubes behind the four-wheelers bumping across the snowy fields.

The boys rig up a car top to pull behind the tractor. An old Lincoln has sat dead for years up behind the cow barn; it has the right kind of top, with the front curving down before the windshield starts, and it all comes off in one piece. They rig a rope through the bolt holes and pile it with straw under an old blanket. The kids pile on and the big boys pull us around the field. If we fall off, we jump up and chase across the field to catch them on the next round. Then we flop on top of the other kids, clinging to one another for dear life, as the snow sprays over us and diesel exhaust blows in our faces.

Our mothers help us make stretch candy, either by boiling honey or the kind with vinegar and sugar. We make snow slushies, pouring bottled raspberry juice over fresh snow. Daddy makes an exception to the no-television rule during the holidays and some of the mothers will rent one for the Christmas break. We eat good food and watch *It's a Wonderful*

Life, The Story of Robin Hood and His Merrie Men and *Seven Brides for Seven Brothers* until we are all doing Friar Tuck impressions and singing "Bless Your Beautiful Hide" at the breakfast table.

Daddy has an old film projector and a black and white French movie on reel-to-reel called *The Promised Land*. He rigs it up every year for a family film night. It's dubbed over the French and is challenging to understand. It's about some French-Canadian families in Quebec, cutting trees, clearing land and building a community, a church and then a school. They face hardship but their faith in God and hard work pay off. Daddy loves that old show. His favourite character is the handsome French minstrel playing his guitar and singing in a thick Québécois accent. They celebrate weddings, births and funerals. It's just real life, Daddy says, and it doesn't count as watching a movie. We pop a mountain of popcorn, make milkshakes and lie on the floor and tables, on blankets or couch cushions in the dark dining room, watching the light jump through film roll projected onto the white wall.

With our close friends, we draw names and do a gift exchange. A favourite for the girls is going Christmas carolling with Aunt Marlene. "All year is the season to sing songs about Christ," Aunt Marlene says. She pins garlands in the girls' hair. We hold candles and sit on a hay wagon going around the community, singing to the grandmas and spreading holiday cheer. Father, too, loves singing the Christmas songs of Christ. He announces that our church service will be dedicated to our Lord and Saviour Jesus Christ, regardless of the time of year of his birth. We sing through the section of the old brown church hymn book all the favourite songs about Christ our redeemer, who lives to come again. We remember his birth and sacrifice for mankind, that we might live again.

WEEDING THE CORN PATCH

"In 1953, the police came into the homes and they took all the women and children and loaded them on buses to send to the Flagstaff area. The attorney general was a wicked man who hated the priesthood. He created a plan to put the children into the foster system and the women in safe houses or institutions." Mother Zelpha is visibly agitated by her retelling of this horror that has shadowed her hometown and her childhood. "He predicted to the newspapers that in less than a year, no one would have heard of the town of Short Creek and the polygamists who lived there. The men would be scattered across the States and serve varying sentences for their crime of polygamy."

We are weeding long rows of corn while Mother Zelpha tells her version of this familiar tragedy of the persecution God's people have suffered at the hands of the wicked American government. We've heard the story in Sunday school but it always seems long ago. She brings the story to life. It's been over a year since Mother Zelpha married Father. It's 1996, almost fifty years since the story she tells really happened.

Mother Zelpha pauses and we all work in silence. The images are alive in my mind. Police coming into the houses, children hiding under their beds, mothers being dragged into buses, not knowing where their children were taken. Babies were taken screaming from their mothers.

Her father, Grandpa Marvin, was born while his mother was in government care. His two older siblings were in foster care while their mother was in an institution, where she had the baby. He was taken into the care of the state and was later adopted by relatives but never returned to his mother.

Mother Zelpha continues her story. "The presiding brethren, including the Prophet, Uncle Roy, pledged they would not rest until every child was found and returned to their home. Two years after Uncle Roy was released from prison, he fulfilled his promise and the last of the children were returned to the families.

"We were always afraid of the police." Mother Zelpha's voice changes as she is getting to the moral behind the tragedy. "If there were police driving around, we ran and hid. If anything, the raids made our community stronger because people banded together against the outside world.

In the government reports authorizing the raid, the officials predicted that the sacred law of plural marriage would be eradicated and God's people would be assimilated into mainstream culture."

I'm a teenager now. I don't fear being taken away from my parents. They would never let that happen. I'm not really afraid of the police, either. Daddy is a well-known businessman and talks to the police all the time. We have an officer, Constable Penny, who comes to our school and is really nice to the kids. If something bad happened, I think he would help us.

Even I can feel a difference in how the new mothers talk about the Great Destruction and the lifting up. Mother Zelpha is really scared. She tells stories that give the kids the heebie-jeebies. My little sister Vicki has started waking up in the night crying about a fire and being locked outside and not being able to get back into the house.

"We learned a valuable lesson in the raid," Mother Zelpha concludes. "Little did they know God was using them to remind the people to be more prayerful, united and determined. They taught us not to trust outsiders and not to answer their questions. They are not our friends. In the years that followed, we bonded and worked together. Our people expanded and grew to be a prosperous and thriving community."

"I'm glad we live in Canada," my sister Vicki concludes, her eyes looking worried. "They don't take away kids here."

Daddy has thirteen wives now. He still leads us in evening prayer when he isn't away doing work for the Church, and he finds the time to read my new poems. Mother seems tired much of the time, with her work as a nurse and all the work she does for our community. Her life is service to the greater good.

God said he would have a tried people. I push the fear out of my mind and pull the weeds out of the earth. The corn will reach almost as high as heaven by the time the summer ends.

Reporters are a nuisance but it is ignorance of God's truth that makes the outside world persecute the Saints as they struggle to find meaning in their own lives.

I miss Aunt Debbie and the cousins less now. They've been gone a long time. We rarely see them anymore. I'm happy that they moved out to the old farm in Rosemary, where Aunt Debbie was born, with Great-Grandma. It feels better knowing Jolene is living on a farm raising goats rather than living in a city. They are part of the old Mormon Church, which is good for them, Mother says, because they will have people who will help them. I pray that Aunt Debbie can find peace and not persecute the Saints. In church we are reminded that those who turn away from the gospel will have a troubled mind and heart. I know this is what makes her want to fight the work. It breaks my heart that she has become an enemy of the priesthood.

God blesses my family. I agree with Vicki. I am glad we live in Canada. We are safe here.

HARVEST FESTIVAL

A bright July Sunday afternoon. The petunias in the hanging baskets along the veranda waft the fragrance of sunshine across the group gathered on the concrete pad next to the arbour that leads into my mother's rose garden.

There is a special guest at our house. He's not the Prophet himself but a man as highly revered by most: Uncle Fred. He is the elderly bishop and spiritual leader of the community in Colorado City, Arizona. He speaks slowly and walks slowly, with a man on either side of him for support if needed. This is the first time I ever remember him coming up here to visit us.

The community has planned some special entertainment to welcome him in our Canadian way. We put on a Saturday festival, starting with a parade down the Long Road with two dozen floats representing our community businesses and organizations. There are probably more people in the parade than there are watching it. Uncle Duane's family, who own a sewing business and laundromat, dress their little kids up in aprons with washtubs and an ironing board. We have a Shop Easy Grocery Store float handing out candy, a couple of big logging machines washed and decorated on trailers, semi-trucks polished and a Highland dancing float with some of the younger girls dancing on a flat-deck semi-trailer that has had the hay swept clean. There are decorated tractors and clowns on motorbikes, a farming and gardening float, a Relief Society float and dozens of fancy cowboys all dressed in their finest on gleaming horses. Kids ride unicycles and walk on stilts. Dozens of little girls in flowing pastel dresses are doing a group dance and formations; they look like matching porcelain dolls. Long lines of little boys dressed as mounted police riders on stick horses do a synchronized march, high-stepping their knees and crossing in perfect patterns.

After the parade ends up at the pond, we start with races, games and contests. There is a greased-pig contest: contestants chase the poor animal around the boarded-off pen and flop in the dirt, trying to grasp the slippery critter, while kids hoot and cheer hanging on the rail fence. There's a catch-the-chicken race for little kids and some roping contests with kids running out of the chutes at full speed. They tie bucking ropes around a couple of the smaller steers, ponies and even some sheep and throw some kids on their backs to see if they can ride for up to seven seconds. There are a couple of horse races and a tug-of-war. A Saturday afternoon community barbecue turns into a full-on water war with every one of the dads, and most of the moms, being dragged into the pond by groups of the big boys and girls. As the buckets of water fly, no one is safe. The aunts snatch up babies to use as protection, because not many people will stoop low enough to douse a sleeping baby.

The next day, after Sunday service, my family has prepared an extravagant Sunday feast: turkey dinner with all the trimmings and chocolate cake piled with whipped cream and strawberries to honour this great man in our home.

Mother has been a guest in Uncle Fred's home many times. She has been working with his wife, Aunt Lydia, who is the community midwife and care provider for the town of Colorado City. Uncle Fred and Aunt Lydia have built a birthing centre in their home, which serves most of the women in the rapidly growing town. Mother must do sixty births under the direction of a midwife to become a registered midwife in BC. Uncle Fred and Aunt Lydia have welcomed her.

After the meal, a large group of twenty or thirty people gather in front of Dad's office around our guest to soak up the sun on the pad and hear the conversations. The men have grabbed the office chairs out of Father's office and the missionaries carry stacks of chairs from the dining room where we have just finished eating. The mothers and girls on Sunday dinner duty are finishing up the dishes.

These after-dinner gatherings around Father are a regular Sunday event. Each Sunday, Father invites a family to come dine at our house. There are lots of regulars as well, including a dozen young men who are in the church missionary program. The lot of them are between the ages of fifteen and twenty and are mostly from Utah. These guys usually show up at our house because they have been getting into trouble with alcohol or girls. Their frustrated fathers call Father to see if he can find a spot for them to work for a year or two on the farm or on a post crew. "They're good kids," Father is famous for saying. "Like anyone else, they just need someone to see the good in them. They need something to do, and they want to buy a motorbike and to get a chance to grow up."

Needless to say, the house is never short of boys and I am never short of male attention. Probably as much for practical reasons as for religious reasons, my father is extremely strict about the interactions between boys and girls. No boys should be in or near or around the girls' bedrooms or vice versa. Our mothers are vigilant about keeping an eye on the goings-on when the boys are home. If the boys didn't get up in time to go with the work crews in the morning, Father told the moms they had full church permission to keep them busy with chores around the houses, yards or gardens. Idle hands and idle minds are the devil's playthings, he reminds us, and a good day's work makes food taste better and beds feel softer.

Enjoying the shade outside his office on the porch, Father usually sends for his guitar and sings and tells stories when he needs to entertain a crowd at any time. Whether he is telling a Bible story or tales of growing up on the farm, singing an old cowboy ballad or a heartfelt rendition of "How Great Thou Art," people are drawn to listen to him. There is usually a moral lesson behind each tale. Later on, he starts meetings about work and business with the uncles who come to discuss projects and crews and organizing for the next few weeks.

Today, though, with our crowd of visitors from Utah, the gathering feels more festive and Father wants to showcase the talent in his family to entertain his guest and mentor.

"Run and find your sisters," he tells me. "I want you girls to sing some songs for Uncle Fred." We are a singing family. We will practise parts for church or a community program, or for Father on his birthday. The mothers make us new dresses and the kids learn skits and songs to perform for him. We have been practising harmonies and have some songs that sound pretty good. Don runs to fetch his cello, and Katie and Nesta play duets on their violins. With our Father on his guitar, we put on an impromptu concert for our guest.

In between performances, Uncle Fred asks Mother how her midwifery training is going and they discuss the regulation differences between Canada and the US. My mother mentions that her girls have been taking Highland dancing lessons. Uncle Fred finds this fascinating and asks to see a dance. Father, coordinating the show, without hesitation sends us to get our swords and music for dancing. We lace up our shoes and perform a sword dance, a Highland fling and a lilt. Uncle Fred loves it so much that we change into our costumes and dance a Scottish jig and a sailor's hornpipe.

Delighted, he turns to my mother and tells her she absolutely must bring us down to dance at the Harvest Festival he organizes in Colorado City in October. Breathless, after just shaking my fist as an angry housewife chasing her husband around the kitchen in a very technical Scottish jig, I feel the familiar tension between my mother and father and the knot that forms in my stomach when she wants us to do something and he probably won't let us.

"Well, you will have to talk to Winston about that one." My mother's sentence is loaded with five years of struggle to allow her daughters to take dance lessons from a town lady.

Hesitantly, Father has supported our dancing efforts at times and even came to one of my Highland dancing competitions. He sounded genuinely proud as he realized I was quite a good dancer, even squared up against the other girls at the competition. He clapped loudly and beamed when I won gold and took home the trophy.

Susie, two years older than me, developed early, a beautiful, busty Blackmore girl. Father is noticeably uncomfortable with his daughters dancing in front of large groups of people. She struggles to find a properly fitting, sturdy bra to keep her bosoms in place during the vigorous jumping, leaps and twirls.

Father reminds us to wear loose, modest clothing that doesn't accentuate our curves and blossoming bodies. Uncle Merrill tells us how challenging it is for boys to keep their feelings in check and not have lusty thoughts about girls they like. We girls are reminded often that chaste priesthood women can play an important part in helping our men with their struggle to stay clean and moral.

Father would have preferred that we stop the dance lessons but Mother has her ways of negotiating the system, and occasionally she reverts to asking for forgiveness rather than permission. Because Mother works as a nurse, she had money for dance lessons, which some families could not afford. Mother is always thinking about how to help others and she arranged for us to teach free Highland dance classes to all of the girls in the community. We had impressive dance recitals with close to sixty girls doing Highland flings and lilts and jigs. Since all of our friends danced with us, we spent long hours after school and on weekends choreographing new dances for every community festival or program.

This was all fine with Father; it was taking the lessons in town and having the worldly influence in his family that was the problem. Our taking lessons challenged church teachings to "get out of the world, oh ye my people, and be not partakers of their ways," which made us the target of a few sideways comments and raised eyebrows from our various well-meaning aunts and uncles. "The bishop's daughters and their privilege and worldly ways," they insinuated.

Uncle Mac scolded my mother, "There is more twisting and hopping and butt shaking in that than a bunch of rock and roll." He made it clear that his daughters wouldn't have anything to do with it as girls shouldn't be putting themselves on display and flaunting their bodies.

Uncle Fred turns to my Father in front of the large group gathered next to my mother's rose garden in the shade. "If he values my friendship, he will bring them." He responds to Mother, but the statement is directed at Father.

I can't believe my ears and my heart flutters with excitement.

"We'll be there," my father says with a smile, clapping a hand on his elderly friend's shoulder.

⁺⁰

Our bags are stuffed under the seats of the big grey eighteen-passenger van. For many of the girls, this is their first trip to Colorado City, Arizona, twenty hours away. I have visited before, for fast trips to church conference weekends, in which I'd sit in the car for two dozen hours only to arrive and sit in church for what felt like two dozen more. This time will be different.

The group of us Canadian girls make new matching dresses for the festival. We travel together and feel like celebrities of sorts for our five days in the town. Cottonwood Park in the middle of town is jam-packed with people. Vendors cook up hot spudnuts and big juicy hamburgers and serve ice cream. The festivities go on for two full days. Friday night is a program in the huge church building. We whisper nervously in our seats near the front rows of the congregation, listening to the inspiring melodies from the elaborate pipe organ pointing up to the vaulted ceilings above the choir seats behind the stage. The big meeting hall is full of the spirit of welcome and worship for all of the Saints to gather.

Of course, our priority is to hear the instructions from the Prophet so we can better sculpt our lives in the service of God. At this weekend conference, the Prophet instructs us that we should refer to our priesthood parents only as Mother and Father. We are guided that if we use higher-minded language, we will remember to honour our father's priesthood authority over our lives and honour our mothers who gave us life.

We perform on the Saturday at the outdoor stage at the park. The costumes Susie, Mir and I wear to competitions barely reach our knees, so for church functions our mothers have sewn us another set of dance costumes that match those of the other girls. We've got tufts and ruffles on our blouses and sleek, black, tailored vests with silver trim. Our well-pressed kilts swing smoothly and modestly as we twirl through the broadswords. Aunt LaRee tells us to look like we are cheering in the Scottish jig, rather than like angry housewives chasing husbands around the kitchen, as is the tradition of the dance. "We women must keep sweet," she reminds us with her enthusiastic smile. "We don't need to cuss and chase our priesthood men around the house." The sailor's hornpipe is traditionally danced in a bell-bottomed pantsuit. We designed our own "hornpipe dresses" with a drop-waist A-line bodice, keeping the wide square collar of the sailor's traditional uniform and finishing the skirt with deep permanent pleats all in navy blue. Our white dresses worn for the national dances are the most elegant. The neatly fitted bodice is pointed daintily at the waist, with detail at the neck going into a Victorian lace collar. Puffed sleeves fit into a wide cuff finished with lace, and the gauzy sheer layers of the full circle skirt are finished with narrow lace that reaches the mid-calf. We each wear a matching royal-blue sash pinned over the shoulder that hangs down our backs, and of course our tight black dance slippers and brown nylon stockings.

The bright lights, the big stage and the applause, but mostly the approval, are intoxicating. We meet dozens of new people. We are invited to dinners and parties with pie, ice cream and games. Oh, and there are boys. The second-best thing about church conferences in Utah is seeing so many cute boys who aren't my cousins. In mixed groups with lots of supervision, we pile into four-by-fours to ride out across the desert of the Arizona Strip to where the desert drops off suddenly at the jutting precipice at the Edge of the World. This gash in the earth that drops off to nowhere reminds me that God could literally open up the earth and swallow whole cities just as he did when Moses came off Mount Sinai with the Ten Commandments and found the Israelites worshipping a golden calf. "No man knows the day nor the hour" is a warning always present in my mind. It is my duty to never be out of alignment with the direction of God.

We hike up the Narrows through the staggering red cliffs. Pure fresh water pours from the rocks as if by a miracle and I'm reminded of the stories of the founding fathers of the church who settled Colorado City and this life-giving water that has sustained this community ever since. Uncle Roy, the old and beloved Prophet, had been like a kindly grandfather checking on and caring for the less fortunate and always encouraging those struggling in the faith and bringing new lambs into the fold.

Icicles hang from the seeps in the rocks and ice forms on the little pools in the cracks of the canyon. New friends show us the trails up through the water canyon. As we hike, the fresh October air quickly becomes hot, toasting through the layers of our dresses and undergarments. We wow our Yankee friends with our Canadian bravery of cold water and the outdoors. We show them we are not vain about getting our clothes and hair messy. By their town-folk standards we aren't very ladylike, hiking up our skirts to scramble over fallen trees and plunging from overhanging boulders into the crisp pools of the canyon. We pad down the last sandy slopes to pile in the back of the pickup truck, drenched to the bone and frozen, with a layer of red sand clinging to our soggy dresses. We bump down the rough wash singing the harmonies of an old Mormon fireside favourite:

> *I love those dear hearts and gentle people*
> *Who live in our hometown,*
> *Because those dear hearts and gentle people*
> *Will never ever let you down.*

KEEP SWEET

The Prophet's upcoming visit is usually announced at our house by a fury of deep cleaning. We take down all the curtains and wash windows and the mothers scrub and wax the floors. We rake the lawns and sweep the porches and wash all the bedding in the house because all of our bedrooms will be used for company. Our mothers and the kids will camp together and for a week all activity in the house revolves around planning and preparing grand meals for a hundred people and seeing to the comfort and entertainment of our company.

Katie, Niki, Nesta and Vicki are dressed and combed in their matching new school dresses and have matching hair bows clipped to the tops of their braids. About half a telephone pole distance ahead of me going down the Long Road toward the church, they are linking arms and skipping and chanting together:

> *Keep sweet no matter what,*
> *This is the way to be lifted up,*
> *Keep sweet with every breath,*
> *For this is a matter of life or death,*
> *No matter what, keep sweet!*
> *For heaven's sake, keep sweet!*

A few months ago, the Prophet, Uncle Rulon, gave us direction on what it meant to "keep sweet no matter what." This is a reframing of a previous teaching to "get and keep the sweet spirit of God" and has since become a mantra that we hold dear. "It sums it all up," Grandma Mem says in Sunday school. "If you keep sweet, the rest should work out fine." The simplicity of it was appealing. After all, didn't Jesus say the gospel was so simple that even a child could understand it?

We good-heartedly remind one another to keep sweet when we are playing sports, or even teasing when one of the boys smashes a finger or something. We don't swear anyway but saying "Keep sweet" is a way we keep our focus on what is important as we go through our workday. One of the mothers made a garden on the hill with the words spelled out in white rocks.

"We can all help each other. We are all trying to do the same work and go down the same path. What if a little thing you do each day can make it easier for your brother to stay on that path of righteousness?" Uncle Merrill tells us kids at school, where we have "Keep Sweet" on a big bulletin board in the hallway.

As we sit in the church hall, my nine-year-old sister Niki leans forward on the hard metal chair and hooks her feet over the bar that supports the legs. Conferences are long. All the church elders who travel up from Utah for these occasions love to hear their own voices. They read long passages of scripture and talk on until I can't remember exactly what it is they are talking about.

Father says that when he was young, the old brethren seemed as if they were trying to outdo one another. He heard enough pulpit-banging sermons of hellfire and damnation to scare Lucifer himself right up to heaven.

Uncle Charlie is the only one who bangs on the pulpit these days. I never fall asleep when he is talking. Once I was sitting in the front row and he was giving the dead cat sermon. "Have you ever kicked a dead cat?" he would say. "You kids sit up and pay attention."

I don't remember how the whole thing went but if you didn't kick the cat, then you sure should have.

I lean forward, chin on palm, elbows on knees. I look sideways down the row of chairs to my right. Two people are nodding off; my aunt is swaying slightly with her mouth open. The sun is shining through the low windows. My mind wanders off to a cold creek and squishing my toes in the slippery blue clay in the banks. I entertain myself with thoughts of riding my horse bareback through the smiling faces of daisies speckling the field like stars in a clear night sky.

I reach for Niki's hand. She has her head crooked to the side, gazing up at the ceiling. I curl my fingers firmly around her fingers with our thumbs on top. Her eyes light up through her thick glasses. I turn slightly so we can keep our game low and out of sight. We both count inside our heads, one, two, three, four, then commence to trap the other's thumb and hold it for a silent count to three. My larger thumb has the advantage but the game makes us smile. My aunt sitting behind us taps me on the shoulder and I blush, ashamed that I am being reminded to sit quietly and pay attention. I am much too old for silly games in church. I tap my sister's knee and point forward to remind her to listen. I sit up with conviction that I will listen to the words of the brethren during the conference meeting so I will feel energized and uplifted for the days to come.

One of the brethren reads familiar scripture warning about the End of Times. "In the last days, God will send fire from heaven to wipe the wicked off the face of the earth. Only those who are prepared will be saved. God said he will lift up the pure of heart while the earth will be cleansed by fire and all those who are not prepared will be destroyed off the face of the earth. Two will be working in the fields, one will be taken and the other left. Two will be grinding in the mill, one will be taken and the other left. No man knows the day nor the hour. Will you be prepared? Will you have oil in your lamp because you heeded the warning in these days of preparation or will you be turned away?"

The words from the Prophet are at the end of the second meeting. This is the part of the conference that everyone looks forward to. If there are any new revelations or any new directions from God, they will be given to the people then.

This Sunday is my day to stay home through the second meeting and help the mother on dinner with tending the babies. I like to go to church but I really do like the responsibility of being in charge of the toddlers who stay home from church.

There is a buzz as people arrive home. As God is preparing his people for the last days and the lifting up, he is revealing special teachings that will "fine-tune" his people for the work that is ahead of them. I lean in earnestly to gather each morsel of guidance from the Prophet of how I can better prepare my life. "A suggestion from the Prophet is as good as a commandment," we are taught. He is the living key to our eternal salvation.

God's chosen people on the earth are not to wear red.

I look down at my dress and run my hand across the soft, deep-red velvet bodice. My new dress. Mother made matching dresses for me and Susie. The sleeves and skirt are a white, flowing fabric dotted with tiny red hearts. My cheeks flush that I have unknowingly been offending God.

Some people say God directed us not to wear red because it is the colour and symbol of a devil worshipper. Others say it is because red is a pure colour and will be the colour of Jesus's cloak in the Second Coming so wearing red is sacrilegious, like taking the Lord's name in vain. Some families quickly rid their wardrobes of anything that has even bits of red in the fabric.

The next time we are getting school photos, I argue with my mother, who wants me to wear my new red dress. It looks so cute on me, she says.

My ever-practical mother sees no sense in getting rid of our lovely new dresses, which she has spent days sewing.

I hide my red dress and tell her I can't find it.

I've been baptized and received the blessings of the laying on of hands. I am a member of the Church of Jesus Christ of Latter Day Saints. I'm willing to embrace the teachings of the Prophet and God's will in my life. I won't wear red.

THE MOTHERS

Winter comes. Our houses are packed over the holidays with crews of people helping to finish our new house. After the New Year's Eve ball at the church, everyone is invited over to the new house for cheesecake and a housewarming and prayer to dedicate the house, which fills this beautiful big room with laughter and stories.

One of the brethren who is visiting offers to read a favourite piece of scripture to honour the mothers who run our household. "The greatest mission of woman is to give life, earth-life, through honourable marriage, to the waiting spirits, our Father's spirit children who anxiously desire to come to dwell here in this mortal state. All the honour and glory that can come to men and women is but a dim thing whose lustre shall fade in comparison to the high honour, the eternal glory, the ever-enduring happiness that shall come to the woman who fulfills the first great duty and mission that devolves upon her to become the mother of the sons and daughters of God."

Before this new house was built, our family was packed like sardines in the other two houses. Father married Mother Di, Mother Leanne and Mother Edith in the past year, making a total of thirteen mothers. Only some of the old church brethren have ever had this many wives. Joseph Smith had sixteen wives. Our family is growing really fast, and some of us kids didn't have a bedroom for more than a year.

With the new house done, we can stretch out a bit. The whole upstairs of the building is a large kitchen with a walk-in fridge, two main bathrooms and a huge dining room and living room. There is carpet in one half with couches and a piano against the wall. At the cabinet shop, when they built the cabinets for the kitchen, they also built eight big, solid, heavy tables. Along one wall are six matching high chairs that don't ever seem to be enough.

The kitchen has four stainless steel sinks, two six-burner propane stoves and four ovens. There is a warmer over the island so we can keep food warm when it is made. The mothers wanted an industrial dishwasher but my father said, "We don't need a dishwasher. We have plenty of them."

"Ha ha, very funny," the mothers said.

"I'm talking about the girls," Father quickly recovered.

✖

January hangs in the air, painted with the vibrancy and anticipation of a new year. Exceptionally heavy snowfall already sets 1996 apart from other years. Always, for us, God's chosen people, each year closer to the new millennium marks another year closer to the day of reckoning.

"Send the light, the blessed gospel light; let it shine forevermore. Send the light, and may its radiant beams light the world forevermore." My father's voice carries the familiar tune through the new intercom system to the waking ears of my entire family.

We are still getting used to this new phone and intercom system installed in all four of the houses to help manage the impossible task of finding someone who is wanted on the phone. After Father's song, he says the younger children's names, talking directly to the toddlers to get up and come for prayers.

"Dayna, wake up Mother Ruth and bring her up to breakfast. Owen, wake up your brothers. Ellie, bring Mother Sharon down for prayers. Joe, make the Top House fire. Don, make the Bottom House fire," he says. Then he takes a walk through the houses, knocking on doors and making sure the fires are getting made to warm things up.

"Let us not grow weary in the work of love; send the light, send the light." Now the song is stuck in my head. The early pink light of morning glows through my second-storey gabled window as I nuzzle the warmth of the covers for just one more minute. The door bangs closed below me. I throw back the pink floral and lace bedspread, sit up straight in bed. I can hear Father's heavy ring of keys jingling against his leg as he walks up the stairs to knock on my door. I clear my voice so I won't sound as if I just woke up.

"Hey, sweets," he says, knocking on my door. "Will you hurry up to the kitchen to help Mother Marsh with breakfast? Mother Janelle isn't feeling well." I fly out of bed, eager to help out, especially when Father asks me specifically.

Four of my younger sisters and I share two adjoining upstairs bedrooms and one bathroom. School mornings are always rushed as we run around in our long nightgowns deciding what we will wear and banging on the bathroom door if someone has locked us out or seems to be taking too long with her personal business. Then we bustle around the mirror and bathroom counter with a tail comb or a bobby pin sticking out of our mouths and a cloud of hair spray around our heads.

My father's wives often talk about how it is much easier to live in a household shared with many women than if it were just two. In a big full house of many wives, they affirm to one another, there's less drama and jealousy than what they imagine there is in smaller families with only a few wives. Anger or resentment is not typically directed at one person, which makes it easier, they say, making it sound simple: "If there was a sister-wife you didn't get along with, you can mostly just avoid her."

Dishes bang and the big pot of chicken and vegetable soup simmers on the kitchen stove. Dinner is being prepared and Mother Marsha takes a tray of freshly baked biscuits from the oven. The house is bright and inviting when we come in after school kicking snow from our boots. As I'm thirteen, my part is often to organize the younger girls with their chores. My evening job is to set the long tables and help get dinner ready to serve when Father gets home. My brothers are doing their evening chores taking care of the animals, feeding the chickens and milking the cows. Mother gets off her twelve-hour shift at the hospital at seven.

I pull a three-gallon bucket of milk out of the new walk-in fridge, pry back the big lid and skim off the heavy cream to set aside for breakfast the next morning. I line up the big jugs on the floor and pour the milk to the frothy tops of each. I can't resist and pour myself a tall glass, adding a little extra cream from the jug I have set aside. A little trickles down my chin as I gulp the rich cold creaminess of it. It is important to drink lots of milk, Grandma tells me. A young woman's body is developing and growing quickly in her teens. I need to eat lots of healthy food to have a strong body. A young woman who doesn't care for herself can't take care of her family.

I stop to read the evening schedule beside the kitchen telephone to see what my dinner chore is, just as one of my mothers' voices comes over the intercom. "Mary, dial 522 please. Mary, dial 522." I dial the numbers.

"Will you bring the zipper and ribbing for our matching dresses we are making in sewing class today?" my cousin Vilate calls. We get to sew for the last two blocks of the day and then my friends will come to my house to finish our projects in our big sewing room. We have four industrial sewing machines and a big overlock that sews like a runaway steam engine.

I'm excited for the school day since we get sewing all afternoon. I glance over the sections on the chart. *Bathe babies tonight.* I smile, thinking of my giggly, chubby little sisters splashing in the bathtub while I put piles of bubbles on their heads and play "This little piggy went to market" on their toes. My favourite "dish job," which doesn't seem like a job at all.

✺

As the numbers in our family have grown, the mothers have worked at different ideas of how to manage family meals and ensure the children are taught good table manners so we can maintain some semblance of order. They hold "mother" meetings every so often to discuss concerns and schedules, to make sure all the work gets done and everyone has a role. Father says, "Work it out," so he doesn't get involved in their meetings and house management details.

My sisters and I, the big girls, are on the meal schedules. We have a week when we help one of the mothers make breakfast every morning and then we don't have to make breakfast for eight more weeks. We make either school lunches or dinner one night of the week. The mothers recently came up with something they call the "manners schedule."

At dinnertime, some of the mothers and the big kids sit at a table with six or eight younger children. Together we eat the evening meal, making sure we all have what we need and the children use good table manners. Then each child helps with a cleanup job under the guidance of the big kids and mothers to ensure all the children get a chance to learn good habits of helping.

It seems to be going well. Mother Leanne does storytime with the younger children each night and teaches them songs. Some of the mothers like to sew more than the others so they trade "tending days" for sewing. My mother is a nurse, working full-time and taking online courses; Mother Christina is in college to get her nursing degree; Mother Mary Ann is a certified teacher; Mother Midge works at the office full-time; and Mother Leanne is also a nurse. All of them are multi-talented. Some of them work at the school a couple of days a week while some work at the office, the laundromat or the mattress factory, so organizing all of their schedules to take care of child care, meals and managing our household of almost forty children and constant guests is no small accomplishment.

✺

The bell blasts, dismissing us for the day. We pack up and sweep the sewing room in no particular hurry.

"Oops." AJ looks sheepish. There is a clunk and the familiar sound of a needle breaking in the machine. She works to get the fabric free where it has gummed up into the mechanism of the bottom bobbin. The teacher has left us to clean up, so we have no incentive to try to fix the thing. By next Wednesday, hopefully, someone else will have fixed it.

"Just finish it at my house," I tell her. She is finishing a simple dress for her little sister. All it needs is the zipper, cuffs and the facing on the neck. We pack up our projects. My friends and I walk home, enjoying the brisk wind of the cool day.

Part of the fun of sewing at my house, they tell me, is teasing Mother Marlina. She is a really good seamstress and is usually in the sewing room making something. Only a few years older than us, she is nineteen and recently moved here from Colorado City, Arizona. We think a lot of the American girls are prissy and self-righteous and when we are around them we exaggerate our country farm girl upbringing to tease a little.

She talks constantly about how she knew she was going to marry my father and move to Canada. We turn up Tim McGraw and Faith Hill a little too loud and sing along, and she rolls her eyes good-naturedly.

She says, "My father sure wouldn't have allowed me to listen to this kind of music in his house. I couldn't have imagined saying things like that before I was married." Despite her pious demeanour, she's good-natured about our teasing and is always willing to help us with a challenging piece to sew, like putting in hidden zippers, a continuous lap on a dress cuff or stitching on a binding. Sometimes we pawn it off on her and she will just do it for us, although she prefers to teach us rather than do it, so we can improve our own skills as well, she says.

"Dinner is ready," four-year-old Brad says over the intercom with Mother Di coaching him in the background. "Wash your hands and come for dinner."

Every once in a while a telephone in one of the bedrooms gets bumped dialing into the intercom system. Before someone intercepts with the code, it's a bit of family entertainment listening in on conversations or, more commonly, a child playing with the phone.

My friends AJ and Vilate pack up their sewing boxes and walk up the hill to their own houses. Their families are small and normal compared with mine. AJ has two mothers who are organized and supportive of each other all the time. Vilate is her mother's oldest. Her mother is funny, laughs a lot and is fun to be around, and she's always home. "This intercom would get really annoying," AJ comments. "It reminds me of when I was in the hospital." I know my family isn't very normal compared with those of my friends and our family has changed so fast. What's normal to us is always making room for more and a steady stream of company each night at the dinner table, but always a big warm house full of mothers, babies, hugs, good food and dishes to wash.

My friends walk up the hill through the snow in the dark. I follow my nose to the kitchen.

The turkey vegetable soup made with broth from boiling the turkey bones is served with fresh, hot, buttery, melt-in-your-mouth baking powder biscuits. While I'm eating, my seven-year-old brother Amos is telling me an animated story about his escapades to catch our Shetland pony, Shorty, with a piece of baling twine and a bucket with some rocks in it because he didn't have any grain. His freckled nose and red hair animate as he waves his arms around. I don't bother telling him it is bad table manners.

I gather the six little girls for their baths: Adree, Sara, Ellie, Dayna, Doris and Darla. With six girls between a year and a half and three years old, it takes an efficient system to get them all clean and dry at the same time. I put the littlest one, Darla, in last and take her out first and it works like a charm.

The six smiling, squeaky-clean little sisters walk up the stairs together and run to the big chair to give Father a kiss in the living room. He's been gone on a lot of trips lately with church and business but tonight he is home, so the family gathers in the big dining room in the new house and kneels in a circle on the thin industrial carpet. As usual, we have company—visitors from Utah who are here to help Father with a project—so they join the family for prayer. Father reads us a short scripture, so we will have something inspiring to roll around in our heads as we fall asleep, he says.

Tonight Father pulls out his guitar, taking a little extra time so we get more comfortable around the room. He plays and we all sing along: "All things bright and beautiful, all creatures great and small, all things wise and wonderful, the Lord God made them all."

To get a smile out of our company, Father plays his "Pearly Shells" and "Tiny Bubbles" medley and gets a satisfying chuckle from them. The prayer is full of earnest gratitude. The cellars are full, our freezers can't fit another thing in them and our bellies and houses are full, and we are moving into a new year renewing our determination to more carefully apply the directives of the priesthood and prepare our hearts and purify our lives to pattern ourselves after the Prophet, who is the mouthpiece of God.

Feeling a little sleepy and cozy on the new blue couches in the big living room, I look around at this room full of people who make up my family. Baby Charlie is asleep on the floor with his bum in the air like a stinkbug, so cozy and safe in the circle of family.

Father sings the family ballad he wrote at age nineteen when his first son was born. He called it "Jacob's Song":

There's just one man,
Who holds the keys,
To our salvation,
To heal and record,
On the earth for the Lord.

HIGH SCHOOL

I wake a little late, another birthday morning, turning me fourteen—almost too old to make a big deal out of my birthday. Morning sounds fill the house and driveway below. My bedroom window is right above the front door of the Bottom House. I dress quickly and go to the Middle House for breakfast, where the family is busily eating and readying for the day. Mother Marsha is combing Darla's hair on a booster chair and half a dozen sticky babies are eating pancakes in the high chairs. A dozen more preschool-aged children sit along the benches and kneel on chairs at the various tables. I smile and hug and thank everyone for the many birthday greetings. Mostly I'm thinking about school.

Susie has run down the hill from the little house where she shares a room with Grams and where Mother and Brittany have the other room. Mother is on day shift today so Susie brings me my birthday card, which I know will have money in it. I can spend it on goodies to share with my friends, if I want, for a birthday party or keep it for myself. Mother will give me my birthday present later.

Sue checks the names and grabs two brown bag lunches off the cupboard. "Hurry," she says to seven-year-old Chelsea, who is struggling to put her shoes on by the door. "I have your lunch. I'll walk you to school on my way to the high school."

I'm in grade nine now and going to the high school. Susie and I have a green Yamaha TW200, which we share with Father. The deal is, he says, it's his and we get to ride and take care of it, and he will ride it whenever he wants. It's a good deal for us, since he seldom does.

I've already promised Nesta, who is nine now, that I would drop her off at the elementary school on my way if she would help me clear the four long tables, which had been set for a breakfast of poached eggs in milk, applesauce and toast. She is waiting at the door as I shove my lunch bag in my backpack with my homework books.

She waits as I kick-start the motorbike, then she starts climbing on behind me. "Wait until I'm ready or I'll tip over," I scold her. The bike is on the big side for me but I've already grown since I first started riding it. I'm quite comfortable with a passenger now.

We are about to head out when our brother Don comes running out of the house. He has a piece of toast in one hand and his lunch in the other. His hair looks as if he just crawled out of bed and he isn't wearing a jacket. He is usually late for school but today he managed to get up after, I'm sure, the fifth person tried to get him out of bed.

"Let me jump on the back," he hollers.

I don't feel confident enough as a driver to have two passengers. "Keep your foot down until I start going," I instruct. Once I get going it isn't too bad.

The school made a rule that we can't ride our motorbikes on school grounds during school hours, so I have to park my bike down in the trees below the church house, which is also where we have our high school.

The big yellow bus is in its usual spot to the side of the pad when I walk in. Grandma Mem is always early. She loves school. She has never taken a year off from school since she was four years old and started kindergarten.

My hands are frozen into two claws. I blow on them and rub them together while I fumble with the combination lock on my locker.

Uncle Merrill, our principal, does assembly with us each morning. We sing and say prayer and read from the *Student Star*, a church-published biweekly newspaper from Salt Lake City filled with inspirational pieces or the latest word from the church.

Most of the forty or so kids are already sitting in the front lines of chairs in the big hall. As I walk in, the first bell blasts directly above me. I jump and drop my Book of Mormon to the floor with a loud bang. All eyes turn to me as I scoop up my book, stand and straighten my skirt with one hand as I walk up to take my seat. Most of the boys sit by the piano against the wall. We girls sit in the middle, taking up two lines. A couple of the boys sit closer to us, or even with us if they have a sister in the group. The boys naturally stay quite separate from the girls as we move about the school for our classes throughout the day. It doesn't need explaining or enforcement. It just is.

Uncle Merrill leans against the podium, a black clipboard in his hand. As he starts down the list of names, cousin AJ hands me a shiny gift bag with pink tissue paper sticking out the top. I give her a look of surprise, smile and peek inside. It's heavy and smells of lavender.

Andy is called on to say prayer. He walks up to the second step of the stage, turns and thanks God for his grace in a few hurried lines we can barely hear. We listen with arms folded and heads bowed and amen our agreement with his words. We grab the brown hymn books and turn to page 208, "God of Our Fathers, Known of Old," to practise the harmonies while Grandma Mem plays the piano and plucks out the tenors for the boys.

As we sing, my mind wanders to when this building used to be the dairy barn until our fathers sold the quota and the cows when the stock market crashed in the eighties. When I was quite little, after the hay from the top of the barn had been emptied to feed the cows, we would strap on our brown leather roller skates and scoot around the smooth wooden floors. The vaulted ceilings of the church hall still have the angular shape of a dairy barn.

I would have been five going to check on the cows in the big dairy barn with my uncles. I remember jumping over the gutters, helping my uncles scoop the sloppy manure and watching as the heavy chain pulled the dung all out the back doors. I remember peering inside the stainless steel vats, watching the hot steam rising off the shiny steel and petting the warm noses of the pretty black and white calves that got weaned early from their mothers.

After the assembly song, we take turns reading from the designated piece of scripture. Then Uncle Merrill takes a sobering minute to remind us to be prayerful throughout the day and be earnest and diligent in being clean and honest in our personal lives so God will see fit to restore the health of our ailing Prophet. He reminds us that the Prophet's stroke was sent as a test to the people and his recovery would depend on our willingness to overcome our weaknesses and keep sweet no matter what.

I silently resolve to make this fourteenth year of my life more prayerful and keep the sweet spirit of God on me at all times, no matter what. What better time than my birthday to take full responsibility for my eternal salvation in the hereafter so I can be reunited with my family members for eternity in the next life? I add a line for the speedy recovery of our Prophet, dear Uncle Rulon, that his health would return and he would be able to come to Canada to guide and direct our lives to the will of God.

There is a stampede for the lockers to grab books and then thunder up the stairs to the classrooms. We have Grandma Mem for English first class. She can recite dozens of poems from memory and has us memorize one a week. "If minds are active," she says, "they are healthy." Alzheimer's, she says, is a disease of the stagnant mind. Weakness, for her, equates with ungodliness.

Grandma Mem has read *The Complete Works of William Shakespeare* and has an extensive and eloquent vocabulary. Slang annoys her, as does the improper ungrammatical speech of popular culture, especially among teens. Swearing, she reminds us often, is a weak mind trying to express itself forcefully. When we overuse words such as "cool" or "this sucks," she lets out an exasperated, exaggerated holler and puts both her hands into her already frazzled hair, which is pinned into a frantic bun, saying through her expressive face that being around our ignorance is equal to the trials of Job in the Bible. She sends the offender to the back wall that is covered by her personal collection of books and has him or her retrieve a thesaurus to look up five words that could be used to communicate our point.

She believes in reading real literature, books with substance. She can't stand the thought of anyone wasting their time reading the drivel of romance novels like Harlequins. You are what you eat, for sure, she says, but more importantly, you are what you put into your head.

ⅈ

The bell rings for a class change. We go to our lockers to get our textbooks for our next class. I will be back in her classroom. I get myself a drink from the fountain in the hall. The hall is crowded with my cousins getting to their lockers. Vance opens the big exit doors to let in some of the fresh spring air so we can catch a glimpse of the sun that peaks through the grey May sky. Dandelions open up to smile at the sun, looking, on their green backdrop, like the fabric in a fresh new Sunday dress.

I dial the combination to my lock and am not really surprised, but pleased, to see a couple of chocolate bars sitting inside on top of my books. Michelle smiles at me.

"From Terrill," she says as she heads down to her science class.

Terrill is a grade-ten boy who has a crush on me. I know he got one of my friends who knows my combination to put the candy bars in my locker. We don't do the dating thing in our religion. Boys and girls are to treat each other with respect. To get one's heart set on a person does not leave it open to God's direction. We all know we want God's will first and foremost in our lives. These secret school crushes are flattering but put me in an awkward position. Flirting or encouraging boys' attention would be scandalous on my part and little more than playing with fire. Already one boy has called me stuck on myself and stuck up because I ignored him when I heard he had a crush on me. I don't think I am stuck up; I just want to be a good girl and don't know how to act around a boy who "likes" me.

Seeing the candy bars, Lana raises her eyebrows at me. To lighten the situation, I make a show of being surprised by finding the candy and generously break the bars and give them out to my friends. I quickly head to class and give Grandma Mem the last piece.

Next class I have math with Grandma Mem. Father has always said she is the best teacher in the world. Grams says her oldest daughter became a teacher when she was six years old and started teaching Uncle Mac to read. She never dreamed of taking maternity leave for any of her fifteen children. She is determined that even a pack of scruffy farm children will have as good an education as anyone. My father's oldest sister and my mother's stepmother, she is respected by both of my parents.

She tells her math students, "I sleep beside my phone and you can call me any hour of the day or night with your questions. There is no excuse to not get your homework done." You could wake her out of a dead sleep at one in the morning. She would ask which page you were on and the number of the question and she could walk you through the question without even having a book in front of her.

The lunch bell rings and we head to our lockers for our bag lunches. All of the high school girls gather back in Grandma Mem's classroom to eat. She's been reading us *The Robe* during lunch as she can eat and read and knit a lacy afghan at the same time. Grandma Mem keeps a brush and comb and hair spray in her desk drawer; while she reads, Daisy starts coming her hair, teasing up her thin grey strands into a smooth graceful bun.

Most of us have a comb in either our backpacks or lockers. Soon there is a braiding train going down the line of desks. We all have long hair that has never seen scissors. Our long hair is an important symbol of our faith. Hair is a woman's crown and glory, the scripture teaches. At the time of the resurrection, we women will use our long hair to wash the feet of our exalted husbands, as Mary Magdalene did for Jesus in the Bible. Engrossed in the reading, we practise every kind of fancy French-braided crowns and poofs and twists. Mir practises doing a ribbon braid weave. With our long hair, braiding is an essential skill as well as an important statement about our womanhood. My father tells us in church, "You can tell more about a woman than she will ever know by the way she combs her hair." Father says hair should be functional and neat, not excessive displays of vanity.

Grandma Mem also teaches the high school band classes. She can figure out any instrument she picks up and she's got our scruffy bunch of farm kids playing our brass instruments pretty well.

She is stern and gruff at times, but she still makes it fun to hang out with her.

Being idle is a sin in Grandma Mem's book. She encourages us to always have some needlework we could be doing while she reads. She never missed a day of school to sickness in her fifty-some-odd years of teaching and believes personal care and health are not just a lifestyle but a moral responsibility.

Often, our lunch-hour discussions turn into lectures on our responsibility as young women to learn and care for our health as we become mothers, which we feel assured we fully intend to be. She speaks to us openly about health challenges associated with lack of nutrition, exercise and drinking enough water. Chewing raw vegetables, she says, not only is important for vitamins but also gives a person stronger bones and straighter teeth. "In China," she tells us, "when they started refining the rice, the rich people started getting sick from eating soft white food. The poor people, who were eating all the fibre the rich would throw away, were well."

"Varicose veins," she explains one day while drawing a diagram on the board, "are caused from the pressures on your legs of wearing too-tight socks that pinch off your circulation. Also, don't sit too long at a time or you will get hemorrhoids. Health is an attitude."

She says to us girls, "Don't have any more children than you want to take care of." While this is practical advice, it is also a statement loaded with obligation. Grandma Mem has given birth to a small army of her own, and it is no small order that a mother in Zion has no business shirking her responsibility to motherhood. A woman denying the blessings of God is denying her purpose as a wife and mother.

She often reads or tells us stories about our pioneer grandmothers and the hardships they faced crossing the plains to bring their families out west so they could serve God without the persecution of enemies of the Saints. She tells us of women in the church whose faith was so strong they could heal their sick babies, or mothers who had to bury their small children along the wagon trail and never wavered in their praise or their faith in God. Women, she reasons, are still created the same. It is our minds that have grown weak. If we can rise to the strength of character and faith of our pioneer grandmothers, we too will be able to accomplish what they have done.

We young women are called to be mothers and raise pure sons and daughters who will dedicate their lives to this work, as in the Book of

Helaman in the Book of Mormon, in which the mothers had raised their young sons with such faith that they could walk into any battle and be undefeated because their faith was so pure and strong.

A mother in Zion must never curse. She should learn a musical instrument, sew the family clothing, grow large and bountiful gardens, preserve food and learn to cook well from basic ingredients. We will not know what the priesthood will call us to do, and so we must be prepared. We won't be able to call on our mothers for a bread recipe or to cut our sons' hair. Grandma Mem says, "Never go to bed with a messy house. What if the Saviour were to visit your home during the night? Would he find a clean priesthood home? Or would there be a television and dirty magazines lying around?"

In the early days of the Mormon Church, the priesthood directed that every household should have a piano because "a song from the righteous is like a prayer unto God." Dragging one of those things across the plains in a wagon must have been no small labour of devotion, and since our houses all have one, the least we could do, Grandma Mem says emphatically, is learn how to play one.

"God will have a tried people." Grandma Mem echoes the message that is spoken so often from the pulpit on Sunday. An important aspect of being a Mormon is having the faith and strength of character to get through the trials and tribulations God feels are needed to test his people. Through us, the strong women of the faith, we will raise a nation that will build a New Jerusalem for the Second Coming of Christ.

Beside my mothers, grannies and aunties, I learn to cook, garden, sew, bake bread, prepare potatoes a hundred different ways, play piano and sing. I will find my place among these women and work shoulder to shoulder, united in our preparation for the Great Destruction when God will send fire from heaven and wipe wickedness off the face of the earth.

As committed wives under the priesthood of a faithful husband, we will rise in the morning of the last days when Jesus returns to the earth. As devoted as the mothers of the army of Helaman in the Book of Mormon, with my husband, I will raise strong and faithful sons and daughters to labour tirelessly in the work of God.

❧

School is finally out. The day has warmed up and all I want is to jump on my motorbike and spin up the road, feeling the wind whistling past my ears and my long braid and skirt flapping in the wind. My friends and I are going to go up on Cranebill Hill, make a fire and cook some food over it. We'll take some goodies, along with the chocolate cake with chocolate frosting I made last night.

Around five o'clock, Penny and I borrow her brother Luke's stick-shift pickup truck, load up some firewood and goodies and drive around to grab all our friends. Five girls are packed in the single cab of the truck and the rest climb in the back. We pop in a Tim McGraw country cassette tape and belt out our rich sopranos and harmonies. Country music is mostly church approved by our families. We feel silly when we get together and make inside jokes and quote our favourite books and old shows. AJ is the comedian of our friends; she sings emphatically and makes funny faces, keeping us laughing uncontrollably.

We have a twelve-pack of iced tea the girls pass around while I get the fire going. Our great-grandmother on Grams's father's mother's side was half Cherokee, we say, and we talk often about our proud Indigenous heritage. I always say that my skills at making a fire are owing to my Cherokee ancestry. Later we will all end up piled in Grandma Lois's living room talking over one of our mixed tapes of mostly church approved music while we each work on crocheting our afghans or other needle work.

We are a cheerful group of good friends fully enjoying the simple pleasures of life. Having the gospel in our lives is our greatest blessing and will be a fabric that keeps us connected as we go through our lives. In a few more years, many of us will be getting married. We will be young mothers together as our mothers were, and when we are called to go help build Zion, the New Jerusalem, I know these dear friends and cousins will be among the Saints.

SUMMER AT THE POST MILL

Summer arrives and with it my shifts at the post mill begin. Hyrum and our older cousin Spencer are the crew bosses for our crew. I'm back to steel-toed workboots, yellow hard hat and Decidamp earplugs expanding my ear canals. There are six of us girls and a pile of boys who trade shifts back and forth. As summer heats up, I enjoy being out at the crack of dawn and watching the pinks of the sunrise change as the sun sweeps across the swamp north of the mill. I don't mind the work but I miss long summer days in the garden, swimming in the pond and tending Britty. The boys make jokes all day and lift the heaviest things for me. I feel like a lady even though we have dust caked inside our nostrils. If I am stacking and getting behind, someone will jump off the loader and help me catch up, or if a particularly large and heavy post comes down the stacking ramp, someone will help me with it.

I am keen to learn to run every machine at the post mill. I take only short turns at first so I don't slow production. Over the summer I become quite efficient running the post peeler. My favourite task is running a chainsaw, bucking the ends off mis-sized posts. Running the big IT28 loader well enough to keep up to all the production on the landing is a challenge I never quite master. But feeling that sense of power in running a giant machine, I can tell, is an addictive thrill. Now I know why boys like to drive.

⋈

Working in the post mill is hard on dresses. I wear my four oldest dresses to work. They are full of holes from snagging on branches and equipment. A skirt with any kind of volume in it is not practical, and light fabrics look awful. The other girls and I start making "bag dresses" for work. We find a large bolt of dark, heavy fabric at Fabricland for a dollar a yard. Two and a half yards is ample to make a drop-waisted dress with a gathered length of skirt. Nearly every one of my female teenage cousins has one of these very practical garments. I am a little more vain. I sew my dress with a more fitted bodice and pleated skirt, and a sweetheart neckline, but it sports the same giant parrots in dark orange, greens and browns as the rest of them.

The next Sunday when I'm home, I'm hanging out in the kitchen with Mother Leanne, who is stirring something on the stove. "Who would have decorated their house in this crazy fabric?" I wonder to her, laughing, admitting it really isn't up to my fashion standards.

Always very proper and professional as a nurse, Mother Leanne often has a remark about our "fashions." She smiles and says, "Most people would be wondering who would *wear* that ugly fabric." We laugh together. Part of the beauty of our "fashion," we post mill girls tell one another, is that it is practical and functional and very inexpensive. Two dollars and fifty cents for a whole new outfit. Who could beat that?

In our world, we girls are cool. We don't have any Hollywood or designer fashions to keep up with because we don't watch television. We buy some of our clothing, for sure, but the way we layer our clothing and put things together is our own special flair. The denim jean jackets and vests are stylish. My sisters and I sew matching plain pastel dresses to wear with our vests.

We wear stretch denim leggings under our dresses. These are more comfortable and more functional for our lifestyle of riding horses and motorbikes than the long nylon stockings that wrinkle, snag and pinch our toes.

It all makes for lots of coordinating to get the look just right. It is only on trips to town, when some stranger makes an offhand remark about polygamy, that I really even remember that people think of me as weird. We teenagers usually travel in a herd and we have good wholesome fun going to the Dairy Queen for Sunday afternoon treats or making an extra stop at the Hi-Way Cabins to smile at the cute boy who works there and buy a screamer while running errands for our mothers.

✎

We're working in Sundre, Alberta. This is one of the Sundays when we don't come home for church. We got permission to drive to the West Edmonton Mall with some of the boys. There are four or five boys and six girls. The boys keep saying, "This is so weird. Why do people keep staring at us?"

"What are you talking about?" the girls and I ask. "People always stare." I realize it is true. The boys look just like any old Alberta cowboy rednecks in their button shirts and ball caps. It's only the girls who carry the torch of being different with our long braids and homemade fashion.

"We don't care. We like being different," is what we have always said, but sometimes I do care. The boys get off so easy. The beginnings of questions prick at the back of my mind. Why do I have to look so different from the rest of the world when my brothers and male cousins don't? I think about the "parrot dresses" we make for our work on the crew, the adjustments we have to make for riding horses or other chores, and the challenge it was to hide our long underwear under our Highland dancing costumes. The boys aren't required to think about their clothing quite as much as we are. I think about what I've read about feminism and whether I think women should be equal to men or if that is even possible with how different our bodies and our lives are.

I shrug off my doubts. I know everything the church teaches us is for a reason, and to prepare us for the time of the Great Destruction that is coming so soon. We each have a role to play in God's work.

Ten Weddings

My oldest brother, Jake, is the coolest guy I know. He's tall and handsome, a great hockey player and our father's right-hand man, but that means he is rarely home because he works long hours on the logging crew.

Now he and most of my male cousins his age are on a church "mission," giving all their time, work and money to the church. Their men's singing group, called the Mountain Men, has recorded an album of church hymns and inspirationals, which I find mixed in among the dusty collection of church-approved cassette tapes in the glove compartment of Jake's truck. These consist of mostly people in the church singing popular songs and some sermon tapes, and a few old country singers like Roger Whittaker and Johnny Horton. Uncle Rich has recorded a few cassettes of him playing his guitar and singing old country songs that were popular when he was young.

Most of the Mountain men are twenty or twenty-one by now and not married. At the end of August, Uncle Rulon is coming to visit for a church conference weekend. The Prophet is coming to Canada and this means there might be some marriages in our community. The Prophet is the one man on this earth in these latter days who has a direct connection to the will of God. He can receive prophecies and give revelations for the people. It is our greatest blessing to have the Prophet visit our community. He holds the sacred key to perform the celestial marriage covenant that seals people together for time and all eternity. Without this sacred ordinance, people cannot get to the highest degree of the celestial kingdom.

This weekend some of the young men and women will be given this blessing to know their place and assignment in God's priesthood work, as it is only the Prophet who assigns marriage placements. Those who've entered into the sacred marriage covenant will be called upon to raise faithful sons and daughters to prepare for the Second Coming of Jesus Christ and the building up of Zion, the New Jerusalem on earth.

It has been a long summer of fence posts for me, long hot days or long dirty nights, and as I've never been at the crew houses with Jake, I miss my big brother. We gossip about him getting married this weekend and we all know he likes Mother Midge's younger sister Treena.

"Please take us to the Dairy Queen to get sundaes," my cousin Daisy and I beg him.

"Okay, if you both rub my feet for thirty minutes, I'll take you to get ice cream."

He lies on the couch and props his head up on a pillow and before we have his socks pulled off, he is nodding off to sleep. Drowsily, he stirs to tell us to rub harder. I knead the soft skin in the arch of his foot with my thumbs. His feet are clean and pink. I look down at my own clean toes. Normally at summer's end, my feet would be as tanned and callused as saddle leather, but not this year. Three months sweating in steel-toed boots and what I have are wrinkled pink feet.

"Can I comb your hair?" My five-year-old sister Hanna is standing over our snoozing brother with a yellow plastic cup of water with a grey comb sticking out of it. He grunts and she takes it as a yes. She sops water onto his hair, then combs it smooth. In a couple of minutes she is joined by Chelsea and Joni, who are a couple of years older. Chelsea has a handful of elastics and barrettes. Concentrating, they part his hair and work to fasten it into tight ponytails, which stand up in little spikes on his head. He snorts occasionally, annoyed by the drips of water running down his face.

The eternal thirty minutes is over. I pat his cheeks. "Wake up, Jake. Dairy Queen time."

He mumbles and sits up. Our little sisters giggle into their hands. He reaches up to touch his hair.

"Look in the mirror." They hold up a hand-held mirror and are elated by his expression.

"I got to get Mother Zelpha to cut my hair tonight," he mumbles, pulling the ponytail holders and little bows out of his hair. He quickly smooths his hair with his pocket comb and puts on his ball cap.

We pile into his truck and tell him we have to go pick up a couple more of the girls. I'm only a little surprised when he turns on the truck and a Tim McGraw tape starts playing. I reach over to turn it up, asking with a smile, "Is this church approved now?"

A few stops around the block and the truck is packed with six girls—only one over the number of seat belts, we reassure him, as no one is willing to sit the trip out. "Jake and Treena sitting in a tree, K-I-S-S-I-N-G. First comes love, then comes marriage, then comes Jake pushing a baby carriage."

We laugh and tease him about getting married. We know Treena likes him back, and I think it is so romantic that they could get married to each other. He pays for our ice cream and we laugh and talk, taking up two tables in the back of the DQ. I sit close to him, soaking up this special time together.

✖

Conference weekend is in late August, so Friday and Saturday are work project days and we also need to get ready for a big barbecue at the pond Saturday afternoon. There is a lot of company up here visiting from Colorado City and Salt Lake. The weekend will be a big event.

They start Friday. All the men meet in our big kitchen for breakfast. Father and the men will make a work plan for Friday and Saturday of who will work where, which tools and materials are needed where and when, and then off they go. This weekend the work project is building a house in a weekend and taking it from a concrete foundation to ready to paint in just a couple of days. On the corner at the top of the hill will be a little duplex house just right for two small families.

Father spends the day going back and forth between the hardware store and the work sites, making sure the crews have everything they need. Any extra hands that can be spared can be put to use in the kitchen at the Middle House, cooking to feed the big crews three meals a day. Then, of course, there's the barbecue on Saturday afternoon over at Uncle Brandon's place on the sloping lawns beside the pond.

After breakfast cleanup, I ride the motorbike by the work project. In a few hours, the walls are up and the trusses are getting lifted on with a crane and anchored down. There is a crew ready to start with the stucco on the outside, and electricians running wiring and plumbers working on the inside. It's like watching the efficiency of an anthill. Everyone knows their role and their place.

We take muffins around to the crew for a mid-morning snack. The day is heating up but attitudes are cheery. People are excited to be part of such a project and speak in awe at what can be done when people work together. It's like an old-fashioned barn raising. The house will have windows and doors hung and most of the wiring and plumbing done by the end of the day.

Friday night is a community social, a program with singing, telling Bible stories, acting parts and, always, treats.

Saturday morning will be hanging drywall and mudding. That's when the waiting begins—while the paint dries.

Mother tells me to head over to Uncle Brandon's house by the pond to see if there is anything I can help with for the barbecue that afternoon. My cousin Goldie is washing and cutting potatoes and precooking french fries in the big fryer on their side deck. We scrub ten five-gallon buckets of oversized brown potatoes under the garden hose. We put them one at a time into the wall-mounted french fry cutter and pull the heavy arm down, which forces the long white strips out the bottom and into a bucket. Some of the potatoes are so big they have to be cut in half to fit into the contraption. We have the oil heating and fill the big metal baskets with fresh juicy strands, then settle them to bathe in the bubbling hot tub of oil. We are just precooking them so they will cook more quickly, because the line to get french fries is always so long. It takes forever to cook enough for everyone to get some.

"Who do you think will get married?" Goldie asks, giggling, while we work.

"There are a few I know for sure. Father told Jake, Brig and Jared they would all get married this weekend." They are all twenty years old.

"Yes, but which of the girls will get married?" We both laugh nervously thinking about which of our older cousins could be eligible for marriage. "It would be so romantic and nerve-racking to be waiting for that call from the Prophet," Goldie says. "One time this girl was at the Prophet's house for her sister's wedding. After the ceremony, the Prophet told her to stand up and a man who was brothers with her sister's husband to stand up. He married them right then and there in what they were wearing. Can you imagine? But when the Lord inspires the Prophet to what is God's will, then everyone can just feel how right it is. They were the best couple and were so perfect together. However inspiration comes through the Prophet is a blessing in the lives of those who are ready to receive it."

I nod. "Yes, you have to be ready to do whatever God says is right."

Before the crowds start to show up for the barbecue, I ride my motorbike over to Aunt Leona's. The sewing room is always where I find her, often with Mir. Fara is standing in the middle of the floor in a smooth white dress. Aunt Leona fusses around her daughter, straight pins poking out of her mouth, pulling and pinning here and there to get it to fit just right.

I can't believe it. Fara getting married? She is only sixteen. "Just because she is sewing her dress doesn't mean she is getting married," Aunt Leona reassures me.

It is all so exciting. I need to go find my friends to see what little details they know. This is the sort of thing where people get told just as much as they need to know and that is all. Is Jake actually getting married? Jake and Treena have liked each other for a long time, but that still doesn't mean they are going to get married. They could both marry someone else and then their youthful crush would be just one of those stories. But I sure hope they get married. Treena is just beautiful. She would be perfect for Jake.

At the barbecue people make an attempt to subdue the gossip about the weddings that will take place at seven o'clock at Uncle Rulon's office. How many will there will be? Who is marrying whom?

I guess my father has been telling the new brides and grooms all day, and they begin showing up at the house dressed and combed in their finest. My heart flutters with relief when I see Jake and Treena holding hands and smiling as if their faces might bust. The surprise of the day is Hyrum. He's almost nineteen and was our boss for the summer, but no one thought he would get married. He's holding the hand of Cecelia, who is one of the Chatwin sisters. Since Father married Mother Marsha and Mother Zelpha, the Chatwins have started coming to stay for a few weeks each summer, doing projects for Father and camping and having a blast. I'm thrilled Hyrum will marry one of the sisters. Now our families are even more connected! With his new wife-to-be, Hyrum walks up the stairs to say hello to Grams in the kitchen.

"Well, I'll be," Grams blurts out. She starts crying as she hugs them both.

Over the evening, ten couples get married. All the Mountain Men get married on the same day. Fara gets married and so does Nancy! They both marry Cecilia's brothers. This means we are part of the Chatwin family forever now. What a joyous day. Families are joined. Girls become women and move from their families' homes to create lives and families of their own.

I am happy for my brothers, especially for Jake. It is so romantic that he got to marry his childhood sweetheart. But now all the big girls are married. Marriage feels different now that it's happening to my friends. It will be so different without all of them around, organizing projects and doing fun things with the girls. Fara is only three years older than me. Now that these girls are gone to start their families, we are the big girls. They seem happy and excited about starting this next part of their journey. I'm thankful "the Canadian girls" who married "the Yankee guys" will have each other. Their new husbands are industrious, good priesthood men. They are building houses they almost have complete and have stayed committed in their service to the priesthood, preparing for when God and the Prophet would be inspired for them to move on with their lives.

It looks exciting but marriage is the farthest thing from my mind. I don't plan to marry any time soon. And I feel certain that whenever God calls on me to move on with my life, I'll feel differently. I still have plenty of other things I want to do before I start having babies. I know from Mother's stories of her work as a midwife that birthing isn't always easy. Of course, I know there is no greater calling for a woman than to raise the children of Zion—but I'm okay with waiting for that great calling just a while longer.

CLEANING UP AFTER BOYS

Staying at the Ryan Ranch with Grandma for the summer is the best. This means a swim in the Moyie River after each long, hot, dusty day making fence posts. However, Grandma still expects the girls to help with the meals and the cleaning, even after we have put in a long day working with the boys. That isn't a problem but she never even asks the boys to help.

Already I've learned that the traditional division of work doesn't seem fair. Watching Grandma Mem, it seems like it is just my lot in life to suck it up. I also know there will be lots of days in my future when the boys will still be getting up at four in the morning to go make fence posts and I will get to snuggle back in the covers with my babies for a couple more hours of sleep after I've gotten up to make breakfast for my husband. Still, there are days when I want to yell at the boys, "It's not fair!"

We all get home excited to release our feet from the sweaty prisons of our workboots. We are a bunch of farm kids who like to have bare feet in the summer, so having feet sweating in hot workboots and never tanning in the sun is its own special kind of hell. Next to Decidamps, they are the worst part of the job.

The boys head straight to the river and pile in in their work clothes to soak off the day's layer of sweat and grime. Grandma has a big pan of potatoes for us girls to peel and vegetables to chop before we can join them. I think again about some of the reading I've done on feminism. As I watch the boys in the river from the kitchen window, I start to get an idea how it all started.

There are twelve of us to eat the evening meal of buttery mashed potatoes, ground beef gravy, corn, steamed cauliflower and broccoli and bread fresh from the oven with homemade strawberry jam. Nothing is better than Grandma's cooking. There is room for ten at the table; Grandma usually takes her plate to her room or eats after the crew and she actually expects one of us girls to move, to make room, if one of the guys comes in later.

The boys put their dishes in the sink and we wash them and put them away. After the meal, we lounge on the couches. Grandma comes in with a basket of fresh clean sheets. "Mary, come upstairs and help me make the boys' beds." The boys, who sleep in those beds, keep right on sitting on the couches next to me.

"Boys should make their own beds," I mumble and glare at them in exaggerated frustration while they grin.

Grandma is a no-nonsense kind of lady who is hard of hearing. She doesn't hear my mumbled complaint. It would take a lot of energy to actually explain my questions and reason with her about her obvious bias. It would probably end with "Oh, it'll just never hurt ya. Just go do it." I get up to help her.

For her, this kind of labour division isn't even a matter of fairness. For her, there is a clear and obvious difference between how boys and girls work: what's easy for one is just more challenging for the other. When everyone does his or her part, it all works out and everyone is taken care of. It is just the way things are. Girls wake up half an hour earlier than boys do to make breakfast and pack our lunches for the day. Why complain and argue? The world has no use for a lazy woman.

❧

One week my cousin Penny comes up from Creston to help Grams and me. We call Grandma Alaire's daughter Mandy to get a ride to stay a few days with us too. Grandma sends us girls out to the trailer to gather up the boys' laundry, put clean sheets on the bed and scrub the bathroom. We snoop around a bit as we are changing the bedding. One boy we know has a secret crush on Penny.

I sprawl on his bed, flipping my hair over my shoulder. "Which one of the boys do you suppose slept on this bed?" I make the words smooth together like Dorcas in *Seven Brides for Seven Brothers*. Penny shoves me with an embarrassed giggle. From my vantage point on the bed, I can see a small wallet-sized photo of her smiling from the inside shelf of his nightstand. "Whoo!" I tease her. "He falls asleep gazing at your face."

"Yes," she replies defiantly. "Well, a certain you-know-who paid my sister to get a picture of you from me." It gave me a weird feeling knowing that a boy I didn't know very well had a picture of me and thought I was cute. He is on the night shift and his bed is in the back room.

Penny starts running down the hall. "I'm going to see if he has a picture."

"Don't be rude," I holler, running after her.

"Ha," she says, holding up a Book of Mormon with my school picture from last year poking out the top as a bookmark.

"Well, I'm glad he's reading the Book of Mormon while he's looking at my picture," I blurt sarcastically, my face flushed.

I'm not sure why but I feel a little giddy while the two of us make up the beds in the room. "Hey, let's short-sheet their beds."

We don't want to look like we are flirting with the boys who "like" us, so we tuck up the sheets of several of the boys' beds. It is a common prank to do when someone gets married. You take the top sheet and tuck it under the top of the mattress, fold it halfway and lay it so it looks normal. When the person goes to climb into bed, they will be able to stick their legs in only halfway and will have to remake the bed if they want to sleep under the sheets. We find some marbles in one of the guys' drawers and put a few of them under the bottom sheets so it will be annoying to get them out.

"Let's put saran wrap on the toilet seat too," Penny adds. I think that one is funny but pretty mean, and it is worse for girls.

"Boys stand up to pee so all it would do is get pee all over the place and we will have to come clean it again."

Penny agrees with my logic. I feel a little guilty. The boys will get home at four in the morning after a long night's work and when they climb into bed they will have to get right back out again.

My remorse doesn't last long. The boys come in for their breakfast around ten in the morning and make only a few satisfactory comments about it, and we get lots of giggles.

✿

When I lie in bed at the end of the day, all my muscles tired from my shift at the post mill and from working in the kitchen, I sometimes think about my life. What will I do? I know I won't always work at the post mill; eventually I'll get married and I'll be too busy raising babies to work with a crew anymore. It's likely, though, that as my babies get a bit older, I will be able to do some other kind of work. Mother, after all, is a nurse, and Mother Christina and Mother Leanne are nurses too. Mother Midge works at the office. Mother Mary Ann is a teacher. I think I could be a teacher. No matter what I do, though, I will never stop having to cook and clean up after boys. Maybe, I think to myself, before my exhausted body finally forces my mind to stop churning, I will learn more about feminism.

SWIMMING IN DRESSES

"Laura Ingalls!" A boy shouts out the window of a green jacked-up pick-up with dark tint and a chrome straight pipe. Black smoke belches and fills the street around us as the truck roars up the main street.

My cheeks flush, though we pretend we didn't hear them. Mandy and I focus intently on being in an engaged conversation with each other, with lots of smiles and laughing.

Although I'm a *Little House on the Prairie* fan and adore Laura Ingalls, I know the town boys are not shouting her name at me on the street as a compliment. She wore two braids with her hair parted in the middle and her dresses were peasant-style smocks. My smooth French braid, which reaches past my waist, with a stylish wave that gracefully frames my face, is fresh and fun. My dress, with its A-line drop bodice and box-pleated skirt, looks more formal than peasant. I don't cover my face with makeup because I don't have anything to hide. Boys can be so dumb.

In my world, I'm smart and popular. Encounters like these remind me how people in Creston see women from our community: simple and old-fashioned.

Being a kind of visible minority and living life in the glare of the media is just part of life for fundamentalist Mormon women. The boys just look like cowboys. We say it doesn't bother us that people stare all the time and ask curious questions about our clothes. I am proud of who I am and love my family and religion but the truth is I kind of resent that the boys never really get stared at.

Except when we all go swimming. Then, we all get stared at equally since we all swim fully clothed. The boys, who always seem to have advantages at other times, get the short end of the stick when it comes to swimming fully clothed. They swim in denim jeans and long-sleeved, cotton button shirts because that's what they own. Girls at least have the option to choose some lighter fabric for swimming, and our dresses generally float in the water. Some dresses are terrible for swimming but others float along in lacy rippling patterns and even have useful applications, making bubbles that hold you up as you float. Swimming in dresses isn't much of a problem.

⚜

I turned fifteen in May and it's a sizzling hot day in July now. We are home from the post mill with an extra Friday off this weekend and are eager to spend it with friends. Mandy and I walk up past the 7-Eleven to meet her brother Ty at the Dairy Queen. The sun is bright and since we are done our bit of shopping, our plan is to get some ice cream and head to the river. The boys sit at a table in the back corner. All three wear button-up shirts with different plaid patterns but it is their form-fitted ball caps—pulled down tight on their heads, faded and worn with the beaks curled deeply into a little tunnel above their eyes—that are the signature look our boys go for. Our fathers used to wear the old trucker-style hats with the flat beaks and the mesh backs that stood four inches from the tops of their heads. *So* not cool.

Ty offers to buy our ice cream. We decline but he insists. I tell him I'll get a small hot fudge sundae. He knows I'm ordering that because they are only a dollar fifty and returns and hands me a Turtle Blizzard. I smile and shake my head. "You didn't need to. I owe you one."

I know full well he will never let me buy for him. While we talk and laugh and finish our ice cream, I think about the boy in the truck who called me Laura Ingalls. Our boys are way better than town boys, I conclude. I'm so happy to be with my own kind. Mandy and I climb in the back seat of the extended-cab pickup Ty drives, the one with the headache rack and a fuel tank in the back. Next stop, Goat River.

This time of year the water is reasonably warm, but it is the pristine sparkle of the water and the impressive moss-covered cliff walls of the canyon that make this place special. We pull the truck into the hairpin off the main road. We walk the bottom road to the Chimes, which is a rocky shelf with a deep section where we can jump and dive right into a fast current. The real swimming hole is up at the Trolley.

The river cuts through jutting rock walls and opens up where round river rocks have been deposited on the east side of the river, which gets the most hours of sunshine. The swift current of the river runs into the cliff face above the rock beach where the water has carved a seemingly bottomless pool. The crook of a low bench that juts out makes the perfect diving and lounging platform, which we call the Main.

Our parents have directed that it's fine for us to swim at the river as long as there isn't a bunch of "goobers" swimming down there mostly na-ked in skimpy bathing suits. We can see only a man fly-fishing from the rocky beach, a boy playing in the water with a bucket and a dog running around on the rocks along the narrow banks of the river in the curving canyon. We walk along the steep rocky bank, then swim across sections of the river twice. Part of the fun of this place is the adventure to get to it.

It gets pretty busy around cherry harvest time when all the Quebec-ers come to town to pick fruit. There is one little sandy beach down the river where they hang out in the afternoons, playing their drums, singing or just napping in the sun. They have long, shaggy dreadlocks that remind me of a horse's tail full of dog burr hanging in ratty clumps. They speak French really fast and sometimes swim with no clothes. They strip down to nothing and jump in the water. If that happens, we quickly avert our eyes. We are reminded to guard what goes into our minds. Images of nu-dity can play in the mind and provoke immoral thoughts.

By the time we get to the Main, Mandy is shivering. Even on the hottest days, when we would call the river "as warm as bathwater," it is still chilly. The sun will be off the swimming hole soon, blocked by the canyon walls.

We have a rope swing tied onto the Tree. I feel a bit like showing off so without hesitation I dive from the Main to retrieve the end of the rope, which bobs in the current. I hold the rope with my teeth and do some bouldering up the ten feet of rock face to the rock platform.

"Oh, pretty brave," Terrell says, bracing himself to give me a hand up the last few feet.

"Well, I would like to see you do it in a dress," I say as I coil the rope into my right hand to keep the rope and my skirt from catching. I pull the rope taut so my back is against the cliff face.

To jump off the rope swing, one must be high enough to not hit the water and low enough to run off the long section of the steeply slanted rock face. I've done it dozens of times but still have to build my courage. I run and jump, sailing out and around, circling over the swimming hole and timing my drop to the right spot so the fast current will push me back down, but not holding on too long to smack the rock face beyond.

A good scrambler can get from the lower jumping point we call Slanty up to the next ledge we call the Border and then up to the mid-point called Port Hill. This ledge, with a big red heart spray-painted on the side of it, is an impressive forty-five feet high, depending on the water level. A few weeks ago, Amy and I stayed for almost an hour one evening, trying to get up the courage to do the jump. I tuck my skirts between my legs and hold them with my knees so they won't fly up, and I hold my hands in so they don't slap on the water. It's just taking that first step that is hard. Once I'm in the air, feeling the rush and the butterflies is addictive. I feel so alive!

The Tree is the highest point jutting over the deepest pool between the canyon walls. A determined pine tree has rooted on the ledge and reaches for the sky. This cliff is over sixty-five feet high and of course it is the ultimate challenge for the daredevil boys. I'll never dare do it and I hold my breath each time someone is preparing for the jump from the Tree.

I've swum with the Oler boys many times before, and to say they are fish is the only way to describe how they swim. It's as if they can sprout gills and stay under for twice the normal time. They think it's fun to push people off the main rock; then, when they are coming up for air, they dive in and push them down again. This is a game called "push-off," which I'm sure is a lot more fun when you are the bigger and stronger players. After the sixth or eighth time gulping water and getting water in my nose and ears while I'm pushed under yet again before I can get a breath, by a boy twice my size, I drag my soggy self onto the rocks next to Mandy, telling them I'm out of the game. I'm a drowned rat with my hair plastered to my face and water streaming from my layers of drenched clothing. The hot rocks warm me through my wet layers and the sun caresses my face and brings life back into my numb hands and feet.

I lean back on my arms and look up the impressive moss-covered faces of the cliffs guarding this beautiful and sacred place. It feels like a cathedral, like a place to go to pray and be close to God. A few minutes ago I thought I was about to go meet my maker, but if I had to, this would be the place to do it.

BRIGHT EYES

One evening when I am fifteen years old and have been working at the post mill for my third summer, I'm folding my laundry on the floral over-stuffed couch upstairs in the community birthing clinic where my mother, the community midwife, lives and is always on hand and on call. I'm making stacks of my neatly folded white undergarments, whistling the theme song from *Anne of Green Gables*, which I'm learning on piano. The tune transports me to a world of tall blowing grasses and warm ocean breezes on Prince Edward Island. My Gilbert Blythe holds my hand and we skip with a picnic basket through wildflowers. Anne and Gilbert's love withstood any challenges life could throw at them. A few weeks ago, we begged Father to give us permission to watch *Anne of Green Gables* at Grandma Lois's house for Michelle's birthday. We know from experience the answer depends on how carefully we frame this question. We all showed up to his office together with our best puppy dog eyes.

The Prophet has advised us not to watch television and to prepare for the time of the Great Destruction. The church warns relentlessly of the dangers of relaxing our vigilance and allowing the devil's tools into the home. A dedicated priesthood home must bolster its guard to allow only that which is sacred and holy to enter. Homes should be clean and peaceful so that the spirit of God will always be present there.

"But," Father responded sensibly to our plea, "the destruction isn't going to happen today. Go watch your movie."

I muse about the love story of Anne and Gilbert. I know my own love story will be very different. I'm still only fifteen years old. Susie will marry before I do. My father's oldest daughter, Susie is bright-eyed with a glowing smile and genuine cheer that easily lights up a room. She is authentically selfless, modest, humble, strong and hard-working. She has a gentle heart and laughs easily at any situation, which always breaks the tension or lightens the mood. Sue gets the attention of probably every man in the church who considers himself even somewhat eligible as a suitor to the bishop's precious, beautiful daughter. Fortunately for all my father's friends, this could potentially include them, as polygamy certainly is an option.

My sister and I work for our father, which is the same as working for the church. We never take a paycheque for our work but always know we will get what we need and a bit of spending money. After Sue finished grade ten she kept working, driving the crew to do fence posts. "Sue's my right-hand man," Father says. "I don't know what I would do without her."

Some think she will marry the Prophet. Many young women have married him in recent years and it is considered a very high honour to a family to have a daughter deemed worthy of marrying our elderly Prophet. Sue reflected my own feelings when she told Father, "Whoever I marry, I want to have my own children." We have never discussed it, and we all respect our older cousins who did marry the Prophet, but theirs is a journey neither of us feels called to.

Our heroes were the pioneers of the Old West. Like Cinderella, our princesses had calluses on their hands. But I've never wanted to be the twenty-fifth wife of anyone, even if it means moving into a palace. Whatever they gain in luxury and financial security, they sacrifice in children and life experience. Certainly, I am going to be a mother, and I see myself having a more active role in family and community life than sharing a dull, quiet, spiritual life with dozens of other women. They will get to live their calling to be mothers of Zion after the Second Coming of Christ, which will be soon upon us. When this time comes, the people are taught, the Prophet's body will be renewed. His wives will then bear his children and live perfect lives in the highest degree of the celestial kingdom in the golden city of Zion. I respect that theirs is an important spiritual path in the work of God but I've never felt that path is for me. I don't imagine myself in a house packed full of wives and no children. I feel certain God has different work for me and I guess that is how Sue feels about it too.

✺

Sue sits silently on the arm of the couch for a moment and watches me. I stop and give her a funny, questioning smile.

"I'm going to marry Ben Johnson," she blurts out quickly.

"Who is Ben Johnson?" I don't know this name. She shows me a school photograph of a gangly-looking kid who looks about fourteen.

"Handsome," I remark, a little sarcastically.

"This is outdated but it is the only picture Mother Edith could find for me," my sister explains, a bit flushed.

"Well, that's a relief. I hope he has grown up a lot."

"Don't be rude." I feel a knot in my stomach, which I'm sure is an extension of the one in hers.

"In two weeks," she tells me. "I'm moving to Utah."

We stare at each other. These days we've mostly kept our private thoughts to ourselves. She has been working so much these last few months. I can't imagine a world with her being that far away. I'm happy she will have some good friends to share life with. Five of the girls got married in the last few years and are living in Colorado City. She will have lots of babies to hold and friends to invite over for birthdays.

"I'm not worried," she adds. "In a couple of years, you will be moving down too." I continue to fold the clothes. She is probably right. All the good church boys I know are my cousins, so I'll be marrying a Yankee too. But that feels a long way away.

ஐ

For the next couple of weeks we pack Sue's stuff. What does she need to take on the airplane? Mother and I won't need all the room in our suitcases, so she can fill them as well.

This is the first trip I've ever taken with just my mother, father and sister. We drive to the airport and fly to Salt Lake City. Someone picks us up at the airport and rushes us directly to the Prophet's house. My sister quickly dresses and combs her hair.

"Hurry," some people said. "We are already late."

"Well, what are they going to do?" my mother snaps defensively. "Have the wedding without her?"

I change into the nice dress I brought and we walk together into a large room packed full of people. People are sitting on lines of chairs, quietly waiting for the bride. Next to the tall thin man with steel-grey eyes is an empty seat in the front row, so I'm guessing this is my sister's new husband, the kid from the picture. He definitely looks well grown up and he isn't at all bad looking. Sue walks across the room in front of all these silent onlookers and sits in the empty chair. Mother and I sit to the side. Ben is Jake's age. They say he is a hard-working man and has just finished building his own house. She will move into her own, nicely finished, brand new little home.

"It sure beats living with the in-laws," my mother concludes.

I fixate on the fact that the first thing my sister is ever going to say to her husband is "I do." I don't even think she has had a good look at him since she sits beside him, looking straight ahead as the Prophet speaks. "Wives, cleave unto your priesthood husbands, honour your sacred marriage covenants, and God will bless you in your lives."

They stand together before the Prophet, right hands together in the patriarchal grip. The Prophet recites the familiar words of the marriage covenant and they repeat where necessary.

The light crepe satin of Susie's western-style wedding dress pleats gently against her curves. She and Mother Janelle designed and sewed her dress over the last few months and she looks radiant with the silver accents on the bodice and collar reflecting the light and matching the toes on her white cowboy boots. She is curvaceous, strong and beautiful. Her face and hands are a deep tan from many hours working in the sun. Her cheeks flush; her hazel green eyes seem far away. I wonder what she is thinking as her new husband puts a simple gold band on her finger. They lean forward stiffly and touch their lips together.

After the ceremony is complete, the next wedding starts. My father marries Ben's sister Jenny, and just like that she will be taking Sue's spot flying home with us.

The wedding is followed by a fabulous dinner in a large banquet hall at one of the elders' houses. Then, with nothing left to do, we load the luggage into Sue's new husband's big diesel-engine Dodge pickup. They are off on a honeymoon, driving down the California coast through the redwoods. Sue is a quiet person and Ben seems pretty quiet too. I really wonder how they are going to do. They look terrified, like awkward teenagers at their first church dance.

"Well, you should know each other after that." I try to sound jovial. Tears come out of my eyes when we hug. I'm happy that she's going to start her new life and it feels wrong to be crying at a wedding, but it feels like we are leaving her alone with a strange man.

On the flight home I get to know my new mother, Jenny, a little bit. She is a nice, quiet lady just a little over twenty years old. She is fashionable and loves sports. Talking to her makes me feel a bit better about leaving my sister with her brother.

ᴥ

The next time Sue comes home is for a funeral. Our cousin Savannah was riding with her brother and some of his children from work. The roads were icy and the car coming toward them lost control and hit them head-on. The others were injured but our cousin suffered a bad head injury and died a few days later in the hospital.

She and Sue were the closest friends growing up. We all Highland danced together, swam in the pond and rode horses.

In her later teens, Savannah became wilder and worldly. She cut her hair and wore tight jeans.

She did decide to marry in the church and became a third wife. She decided the marriage wasn't right for her, so she left her husband and had a boyfriend outside the religion, which meant she had very little to do with the community and family. She was working and getting by, then found out she was pregnant.

Shortly before Christmas, she decided she wanted to raise her child around family and friends within the values of the religion and community. The relationship with her baby's father broke down and she moved in with her brother. She had been home only a few weeks when the accident tragically ended her life and that of her unborn child.

Her death leaves us all reeling with questions about her status with God. How are we to feel about her? How does God feel about her? She was an adulterous woman, which is one of the greatest sins in the sight of God. Had she done enough to be forgiven of her sins? Will we see her again in the hereafter? Jesus forgave Mary Magdalene.

"She was wearing her long underwear when she was died," others affirm. I feel a bit of reassurance that at least she had the protection of the sacred garments when she faced her judgment day.

"God said, 'Leave judgment unto me,'" Father reminds us. "I'm thankful the only job God has given me to do is to love, and that is what I plan to do."

"Perhaps it is for the best," one of the old aunts states gravely. "We have never had a child in our family born out of wedlock."

Susie and I stand together and I feel her body stiffen at these words. I know we are both thinking about the Savannah from our childhood, so full of creativity and life. Sue and Savannah both loved horses and driving trucks and neither was afraid of a hard day's work.

Perhaps it's for the best that God said to leave judgment to him, are the words that run through my mind.

SWEET SIXTEEN

"Sweet sixteen and never been kissed!" The words are written in red cake goop on the Dairy Queen ice cream cake the girls bought for me after our Saturday shift at the post mill. We all giggle, knowing it quite literally is the truth. I've never even come close to kissing a boy. I've thought about it for sure, though, and have a wild crush on the cutest, most handsome boy in the whole church. Short of shaking his hand in the long lines in church and a few shy smiles, I've barely spoken to him. He knows who I am, of course. He is two years older than me and I'm almost certain I will marry him, so on lazy sunny afternoons at the river, I allow myself to imagine his strong arms around me and his soft lips lightly kissing my hair and neck—after we are married, of course.

I pull myself out of these indulgent fantasies and remind myself that God saves the best for those who keep their hearts open and directable and their minds pure. My mission as a woman of Zion is to prepare to serve God with all my heart, no matter where I am directed to go. I know God will not give me any assignment or any challenge that is too great for me to bear. I know I will have a love-filled marriage and a happy home, no matter what my marriage assignment entails.

Michelle just got married. She dated her husband for a whole month. They went on hikes and kissed in his truck. After he would drop her off, we would bug her to tell us all about it. She was on cloud nine for a month and was so excited when they finally got married.

Two of Uncle Mac's daughters who had been my close friends grow-ing up both recently married Uncle Warren Jeffs. He's gotten many wives recently, at least as many as Father. Lots of the young women seem to be wanting to marry men of high church standing. I've heard some are encouraged or even directed by their fathers that this will be the way to ensure they get into the highest degree of the celestial kingdom.

I've wondered and prayed about being a plural wife. I've prayed about it with an open heart. I have thought about who I would want to marry and how my life would be as part of a bigger established family. I'm sure we all have. But I feel certain that if it is to be my assignment from God for my life, I would feel it.

Women love to tell their wedding story. They tell and retell how they found out who they were going to marry and the adorable, awkward way they met their new husband and the surrounding events, including sweet inspiring words of guidance from the Prophet. These stories are told with reverence and are cherished as one of life's memories. Most of the young women I know well who have become polygamist wives have told me they just always knew they would be plural wives, so it makes sense to me that this is something women get as an inspiration from God. Most of my friends, though, are first wives married to young, good priesthood men. It makes sense to me that the church needs plenty of strong young men and women to raise strong sons and daughters who are resilient in their faith to go through the trials and tribulations of the last days and the Second Coming of Christ. I will be one of these. I fancy myself working beside my husband to build the new city, not one of many wives moving into an established household to be a jewel in a well-jewelled crown.

⠩

We've had a girls' crew doing fence posts on Saturdays for a couple of months now until school gets out for the summer, and then Father says he needs us to get back out to the crews.

Saturday happens to be my sixteenth birthday so I spend it at the post mill with all the girls. Glo, our crew boss's wife, makes us tacos and we fill the evening with silly pantomime games that involve singing, dancing and lots of giggles, eating ice cream in our long nightgowns and flowing cotton robes. The house is full of girliness. Spencer, who is our crew boss and cousin, one of Uncle Mac's oldest sons, lives at the Ryan house with his two wives and small children. He rolls his eyes in humour.

It feels as if I have been waiting forever to be old enough to get my driver's licence. Now that I finally am, the province has changed the licensing program so it takes a whole year to become an independent driver. I'm going to get my learner's permit right after school on Monday. I remember wondering in school with my classmates if we would even have time to get our driver's licences before the world was going to end. But now that the time is here, it's looking hopeful for me.

Sue and Michelle were our crew drivers but now they are both married. I'm the oldest one of the lot now and if I can get my licence quickly, I'll be able to drive the girls to work. Father has concocted a plan to have the girls' crew trade with the boys' in Sundre, Alberta. I will change my learner's licence over to Alberta and will be able to get a full driver's licence in a matter of weeks.

When school is done for the year—for me, it will be the end of high school completely since the school only goes to grade ten now—we pack our work clothes and head to Alberta. The Sundre house is similar to the Cranbrook house. The main house isn't large but it is on a big property with a few acres that are as flat as a pancake. There is a grassy field where the boys have set up a volleyball net and play football after work. There is a garage, a shop and a barn. The garage has been converted into two bedrooms and a bathroom. Several travel trailers are parked behind the house and serve as bunkhouses. The barn is a low, wide building. The interior has been finished with plywood walls and ceiling. There is a window in each wall. It is a comfortable bunk room where the girls will sleep. The house is a few miles out of town, but only a short dike separates it from the Sunpine lumber mill.

We will be on night shift for the next month. Each morning, with the sound of a post peeler's high-pitched notes humming in our ears, we will scramble over the dike and fall asleep in our barn bunkhouse.

My grandparents and great-grandparents were Alberta people before Grandpa Ray moved to BC. As I watch the sun fall behind the flatness, only to appear again a few hours later to peek over the northeastern edge, or when I see the dance of the northern lights and marvel at the strokes and colours God uses to paint the endless canvas of the Alberta sky, I realize I have the prairies in my blood. The wind blows my skirts and hair, chafes my face and tells me the stories of my ancestors. "I've been here a long time," the wind reminds me. I imagine my ancestors looking at this same expansive sky. The sun can be shining one minute and then billowing clouds appear from nowhere and fill the foreverness of the endless expanse.

I think again of my great-grandfather; after his years at sea and settling a farm in Idaho, he answered a call in Canada to come claim the "last best west." I imagine he must have felt right at home under this blue sky that must feel similar to a life at sea.

This family. My family. God blesses me, too. I let the wind caress my face and I am happy.

Banana Peel

While I'm walking home from church, my father stops beside me and rolls down the window of his pickup. "Jump in, sweets."

We drive slowly down the roads of Lister, the sun bright on the thick green fields almost ready for the first cut of the year.

"So, I hear you are swinging your butt when you walk, trying to attract attention. That's what Uncle Mac said. He thinks you should clean up your act so you don't get in trouble."

Uncle Mac has always been one of my favourite uncles and is such fun and a dramatic entertainer, but a scolding from our father's oldest brother and his scathing disapproval and lectures on proper moral behaviour can make you feel very small indeed.

"So, according to Uncle Mac's report, I am dressing provocatively and being suggestive with the way I walk," I repeat back. I'm sixteen years old and basically a grown woman but still under my father's priesthood direction. My face turns red. I feel ashamed somehow but I'm not sure what I've done wrong. I can't believe he said that. "Why is he looking at my butt?" I blurt defensively.

"Calm down. I'm sure he has your best interests in mind." Father laughs at my awkward embarrassment. He isn't taking our little talk too seriously but I am offended.

"I do think some of your dresses are too tight," Father continues. "That one is too tight."

I'm wearing one of my favourite Sunday dresses. It is dandelion yellow and makes me feel like sunshine when I wear it. It is formal but made with stretchy suiting material with a tiny white print on it. The skirt is straight with a small split in the back. It is tapered and fits well.

"It's not tight. It's fitted," I argue.

"If it wasn't tight, it wouldn't need a split in the back so you can walk," he says. "You look like you're wearing a banana peel."

"How is it my responsibility to worry about the boys having impure thoughts? It isn't my fault I got Blackmore curves," I argue.

Father laughs again. "Just dress modestly," he tells me.

I get out of his truck annoyed and angry. I know I'm supposed to just obey my father. I wonder as I walk, do boys really have these runaway brains that they can't control? I wonder what the books on feminism say about this kind of stuff. Father wants me to get rid of some of my favourite dresses. I wonder if it is in me to defy him. I consider wearing them anyway as a deliberate statement of my defiance. I let the "I will show you" in me have just a few minutes of time. Then I consider going overboard the other way and doing what I've seen many of my cousins do: they seem to have somehow transcended and become the epitome of the perfect sweet woman with even their voices changing and their faces taking on expressions of long-suffering goodness.

I really like the dresses so I decide on a compromise. I give one of them away—it was really too small—and I wear the others when I know I won't be seeing Father. I doubt he actually even notices what I'm wearing most days.

The yellow dress looks good on me.

INSPIRATION

The pending time of destruction hangs over our people. Father marries a young woman only a few years older than me. Wedded bliss is off to a rocky start for them when she tells him on their wedding night that she hadn't wanted to marry him but had done it because she didn't want to disappoint her father. She makes it clear that she is not interested in the life of the family or being his wife.

They work out that she will go with our crew of girls working the day shift, packing plywood at the treating plant. There are only the six of us staying in the big rambling Cranbrook house, which feels a bit strange after the bustling crew life of the summer. We eat our dinner and pack our lunch for the following day, then lounge around in front of the fireplace on the overstuffed couches in our flowing nightgowns. I'm sixteen and the only driver of the group. Amy, Vilate and AJ are fifteen. For all intents and purposes of community life, we are adults. We work away from home all week. We shop for and cook our own food. We check in with our parents occasionally and on weekends we go home to help our mothers catch up with baking and laundry or assist in community projects or social activities. We've all finished our formal studies through grade ten, since that is the furthest Bountiful School offers. Any further education we do will be through correspondence. But in these days—the last days—the focus of our people is not on academic education but on our spiritual education. We must prepare our hearts and our minds and our homes for the Second Coming of Christ and the building up of Zion.

We've just met this strange girl who is now going to spend all of her time with us. She opens up to tell what to us is the most tragic story of how she found herself sealed for time and all eternity to a man she felt she could not love. Even her flat, matter-of-fact retelling of the experience is upsetting to me. We all listen, horrified.

She had been in love with another man, she says. For months she had felt inspired that she was to join his family as his second wife. But her father was so set on her marrying Winston Blackmore that she had gone through with the marriage so as not to disappoint him. She tells us flatly that, as she was standing up in front of the Prophet holding my father's hand in the patriarchal grip of the marriage covenant, listening to him repeat the vows of the most sacred of all covenants that Mormons can enter in this mortal life, she had been praying that a bolt of lightning would strike her before she could say "I do."

Her horrifying tale contradicts everything we believe and think we know about church weddings, which are the most sacred and the highest honour we could hope to have blessed into our lives.

We sit flabbergasted. A look of disgust spreads across Amy's animated face. She blurts out what the rest of us are thinking: "Why did you do it?" It sounds like an accusation even though this poor girl has just shared her innermost struggle with us, but her words express the judgment and disgust we are feeling. We pity her and at the same time loathe her for being weak. For whatever wrong she felt would have come with saying no to her father's will or to the Prophet's will, breaking the marriage covenant is ten thousand times worse. A priesthood release usually requires immorality by one party or another. For her to ask for a priesthood blessing to be released from a good priesthood man would be almost unheard of. Much worse still is a marriage being void because of the great and unpardonable sin of adultery. But if a marriage is ended by adultery, there is almost no chance the priesthood would ever again bless a union of that person. That person will have essentially given up her birthright.

"You should have said no and told someone how you felt." We shake our heads with conviction. I feel better somehow now that we have identified her error. I somehow feel that her fate is owing to her not being honest with her heart. It is a young woman's responsibility to keep her heart open and unattached. But it is also important that you are honest when you say yes and that you feel you can uphold the marriage covenant. Forever is a long time to be married to someone you don't love.

My mind runs over and over her story as I curl up in the cool, fresh sheets on my single bed in the corner hall bedroom. She made a covenant before God and the best option for her now is to make the most of it. At least my father is a kind man. She could have done worse.

"She is my wife and I will do right by her," my father says to his family as a partial explanation for her offish behaviour.

The young woman sticks it out for a couple of years. She almost begins to show interest in family life. She and Father have a son together. Then, as quickly as she had come, she leaves, taking her son with her.

Only after she is gone do I hear him speak of his experience on their wedding night. Hearing these words from your bride makes you think long and hard, he says. And then, talking about his son, he adds, "I know that little boy is going to come find his dad some day but right now I know he needs to be with his mother."

✎

"It is important that you tell the Prophet if you feel your marriage assignment is not right for you," my father counsels us young ladies. "Keep your hearts open for the direction of God in your life, but God gives you inspiration for a reason. Learn to listen to where he is guiding you. The first question the Prophet asks a young woman is 'Do you have someone in mind?'"

I wonder, when it is time for me to get married, who it will be. I sometimes still daydream about the Yankee boy and wonder what it would be like for him to kiss me. I guess I do have someone in mind. But I try to stay open to the direction of the church. I understand that the end of days is coming and I want to do my best for my family and my church.

✎

I am awakened by my seven-year-old sister Chelsea crying outside my bedroom door. She seems half asleep and is sitting with her legs pulled up inside her flannel nightgown, her back to my door. Her hands are cold.

"Come climb under the covers with me and tell me what's wrong," I say soothingly. She snuggles into the warm blankets beside me and wiggles her feet under my leg.

"The destructions," she whimpers. "I don't want to get left. I dreamed the door was locked and I couldn't get into the house. Everyone was getting lifted up and I was left." Her little body shudders next to mine and I pull her close to comfort her.

"That is never going to happen," I reassure her as best I can. "Jesus said, 'Let the little children come to me.' You are a sweet little girl and Jesus will always look after the little children, no matter what happens. Whenever you are afraid, just say a little prayer and ask God to watch over you. You don't need to worry about the destructions if you keep a good spirit and ask God to have your guardian angels watching over you. When I get scared, I like to sing a little song about Jesus to remind me that he is close and watching over me." I sing softly, her body relaxes and her breathing grows even.

"Listen to the Saviour's plea, let the children come to me, let the little children come, come to me, come to me."

Awaiting Placement Marriage

It's 1999. Life feels like a teakettle building up steam. Soon the time of destructions will arrive. It feels a bit unreal that it is coming so fast. Soon, too, it will be time for me to get married. That feels unreal too. I'm sixteen and when I think about the boys my age who were in my class, I wonder if Mother thought Father was silly and immature when she was sixteen. I laugh when I remember that I wanted to marry my cousin Andy when we were in grade one.

I grew up listening to Father tell the story about how badly he had wanted to marry our mother when they were teenagers. "Jane was the most beautiful girl in the world," he'd say. Father talked about them being schoolmates together. They were the only two children in their grade all through school. They did their homework together. She was neat, well behaved, sweet and beautiful. He was sassy to his teachers, rushed through his work and rarely did his homework. "Around about the age that boys start to notice girls, I noticed Janie wasn't just a regular girl. She was lovely and I wanted desperately to be good enough that she could be my wife."

On a conference weekend when the Prophet came to visit in May, they married on a Sunday. They were young, both eighteen. Their world needed for them to be grown up and so they were.

I wonder how grown up the world will need me to be. I will be getting my marriage placement soon. I keep thinking about other marriages. I think about my parents and I think about my Aunt Debbie too. I've always thought my parents' love story is cute and that my father is romantic when he's telling it, usually when he's playing his guitar to a group of company. Mother has never really liked it when Father talks about it, though. She doesn't think it's very thoughtful of the other mothers.

My mother's and Aunt Debbie's experiences of placement marriage were as different as they could be. It's been eleven years now since the fire that took my aunt away in a station wagon. Mother has a photo Aunt Debbie sent of Jolene smiling in her fresh-cut bob, dressed in her sharp cadet's uniform, looking so much like our beloved Grandma Joanne. I don't know if I miss them anymore but it's good to see the shiny eyes of my old friend.

So many times I've thought about Aunt Debbie and what her life was like. It's hard for me to believe her when she says that my father is a bad man and that everyone in the church is abused. At separate times when I've had a chance to be alone with each of my parents, I ask my mother and my father about Aunt Debbie's marriages. When she was fifteen, she married Grandpa Ray, who had already been diagnosed with leukemia. Father told me he was only thirteen years old and tried to talk her out of it. He said Grandpa tried too. Grandpa had said, "I'm a sick man. Why would we do that?" Father said she cried a bucket of tears and was persistent, telling her father that God had shown her she was supposed to marry Ray Blackmore for the rest of time and be his eternal wife. On the Prophet's next trip to Canada, they were sealed for time and all eternity: my young aunt married my dying grandfather. They had a little daughter who they say was a great joy to Grandpa Ray in his last days. After Grandpa passed away, Aunt Debbie was placed to marry Uncle Charlie Quinton, another older patriarch in the church with grown children. That time it was Mother who tried to talk her out of it. But for whatever reason, Aunt Debbie had also been insistent that she marry this stern patriarch. She stuck through a few years she said were mentally abusive. She had two boys before she got a church release from him and then was married as the third wife to Marvin Palmer, who is the father of her last five children.

Inspiration works in many ways.

In the fall I spend a month driving Andy, Branny and Matty to do plywood every day since none of them have driver's licences. Father buys a brown 1980 Lincoln Versailles at an auction. It's in mint condition and floats along like a dream. It's my car for a while and I drive the boys on the plywood crew to Cranbrook and back every day for work. Father doesn't want us to stay at the Cranbrook house since I would be the only girl there. "Just come home and sleep in your beds," he says with practicality. "I trust you but we don't need to give anyone any room to question your virtue." It sounds sensible but feels like a major inconvenience since it adds more than an hour onto the beginning and end of each day, which really cuts into my sleep time. It's no problem for the boys, though, since when I drive around to pick them up in the morning, they each climb in with a pillow and sleep the whole way to work.

I enjoy the freedom of driving and having the power of the steering wheel and the feeling of a full tank of gas. This morning we picked up a couple of extra guys so Andy is sitting in the front middle seat. His feet are both on the passenger side, crowding Matty, and he's got his pillow propped against my shoulder. He's sleeping like a baby. I've always been good friends with these boys. I used to wish Andy were a girl so we could be best friends. But we've always been told that girls mature much more quickly than boys, and it certainly seemed to be true. These boys seem so carefree and boyish, still fully engaged in their own entertainment. They live for hockey and hunting and it seems to be all they care about. They won't be thinking about getting married for another three or four years possibly. They can stay anywhere and do anything they want with barely any questions asked. As long as they wear jeans and a button-up shirt, no one thinks twice about how they look. As long as they don't drink alcohol or watch movies, no one cares what they do.

If it weren't for my father's wish to curb wagging tongues, we could all be sleeping in beds only ten minutes from the work site, getting more sleep and hanging out after work. The boys do complain a bit about this extra bother because if they didn't have a girl on the crew, they would have more freedom. "Well, it's too darn bad y'all can't drive, isn't it?" I say sarcastically. "This must be hard for you."

❧

Soon it is time for my marriage placement. Mother and I go to find Mother Janelle. She also helped Susie design and sew her wedding dress. Mother gives her some money and we sit together; I tell her how I want it to look and she draws it on paper. The shimmery, flowy fabric I've chosen from Fabricland is called Cloud Nine and will hang beautifully in the A-line pattern I want. I choose a light, gauzy crepe for the accent that shines without being gaudy.

Mother Midge gives me the wide brocade lace for the bottom of the skirt and the lace collar with intricate patterns down the front almost to my waist. The back is fastened by eighteen pearl buttons set closely in a line. Mother Marsha gives me her vintage white leather lace-up boots with a small, square, three-inch heel.

"Mary, come try on your wedding dress," Mother Janelle says over the speaker system. I can hear the tease in her voice. My wedding dress and upcoming wedding are certainly the big news in our house.

She pulls pins and clips threads as she helps me into the delicate fabric and fastens the long string of pearl buttons up the back. It's a perfect fit with no room for overeating from now until the unknown date of my matrimony.

"Let me try a few practice hairdos," she says, "so you can decide just how you want me to comb it for your wedding." In addition to sewing complicated dresses and fabrics, she's particularly talented with elaborate updos and braids. She weaves a thin white ribbon into two side French braids and divides the back into three long, intricate braids to loop up into a clip.

We look in the mirror. I look like I've been dusted with a layer of fresh snow. My cheeks and lips look pinker, my blue eyes bright.

"All ready to be a blushing bride." Mother Janelle stands back to admire her handiwork. She and I sit together on Mother Susan's bed. They tell me stories about their weddings and we talk about the weddings of their friends. The stories are romantically mysterious as we retell the diverse ways God places a young woman with her time and all eternity.

It is not up to us to question the ways God does his work, whether it is to inspire the heart of a good priesthood woman to the direction of her life or to heed the Prophet. When the Prophet joins two lives, that marriage is blessed with all the blessings and happiness that are available to anyone on earth and in the highest degree of the celestial kingdom. When the couple puts their faith and focus on their sacred union, their lives and their posterity will prosper. I have been taught this. I believe this.

Now that it's me, I don't even really know how I feel about it. It feels a bit like a dream.

THE END IS NEAR

"If I left right now, I could be there by tomorrow morning." Mother's voice is filled with determination.

Sue is to deliver her baby the first of January. The church has issued strict direction that no one should travel at this time. The dawning of the new millennium most certainly will be the hour of the lifting up. We need to be in our dedicated homes under the direction of our priesthood heads.

Mother and I are sitting at the kitchen table at the clinic where Mother, Grandma and Mother Leanne live. Mother has been talking on the phone several times a day with Susie. Mother has no intention of leaving her daughter to deliver without her. She and Father argue extensively about this.

"What is it really going to hurt? If the end comes, I'll be safe there," Mother says. She explains to Father that she will stay with Susie until we get the okay from the church that it is safe for her to travel home.

My father insists. My mother stays.

Sue gives birth to a son on the second of January in the year 2000. A week passes and the planet appears to be intact. I watch Mother become like a caged grizzly. She needs to see her daughter and new grandson.

She gets special permission from the church, which gives this direction to my father to pass on to her: "If she circles around Salt Lake City, it will be safe for her to travel." In the last few years, the Prophet has received revelation that Salt Lake City has become one of the most corrupt and wicked cities on the earth since its bid to host the 2002 Winter Olympics. "Driving through Salt Lake has become like a madhouse of construction and detours. That chaos has to be the work of the devil," my uncle, who is a long-haul truck driver, says at Sunday dinner, only part sarcastically.

In the last two years, the Saints living in the Great Salt Lake Valley have been instructed to sell their homes and businesses and move south to Colorado City in preparation for the turn of the century and the great lifting up. Together, the Saints can be more united in their faith and their service to God and the church. Those in Colorado City and those of us here in Bountiful are all grooming our lives to "be led as if by a thread," and we feel ecstatic to be the ones chosen to carry out the long-awaited prophecies lived out in these last days. The Harvest Festival was bigger and brighter than ever this past fall. It was a time of celebration for the abundance and the honour of having God's one and only Prophet on the earth guiding us, God's chosen people, ten thousand strong. Now fall has ended and the new millennium is here, along with my sister's new son. My wedding dress hangs in my closet. I feel as if everything is about to happen or is already happening. God is testing his people. The time is near upon us.

2

MARRIAGE

2000–2011

MARRIAGE

The year 2000 continues. "The times are short" is the message each week from the pulpit: "Prepare your lives and your hearts for whatever wrath the Lord will bring to the earth. The millennium is upon us."

My family gets ready; our food storage rooms are full to overflowing. We guard our thoughts and actions. The warning from the pulpit is that we will be cut off from the Prophet for a time. For how much time, no one knows. To those of us just coming up to marriageable age, this is terrifying. The Prophet is the only one who can perform the sacred marriage covenant. We might be old maids the next time we have a chance to see the Prophet so we can marry and move on with our lives.

Despite working diligently to keep my heart open to whatever the Lord directs for me, I am sure I am falling in love. I'm still daydreaming about the same boy who caught my attention when I was fifteen. He is from the US, and visits often with his family as one of my older cousins married his father as his second wife. I think he must be the cutest, sweetest, nicest, smartest and probably the most devout boy in the whole church. Every time I see him or shake his hand at church, I get butterflies in my stomach. I pray to God, asking if I am to marry him. I work hard at keeping my heart open and my thoughts pure, preparing myself for God's direction in my life, but I know where I hope that direction lies. When my father asks me if I have anyone in mind, I tell him about this boy who is almost daily in my thoughts and prayers.

Although I think I know who I would like to marry, I don't really want to get married yet. I'm almost seventeen and I am princess of my world. I have my driver's licence, a vehicle, lots of friends, work and the confidence of my father. However, the prospect of doing dishes at my father's house until I am an old maid doesn't sit well with me either. My grandmother married when she was my age, and in the context of these urgent times, getting married seems the best way to support the Lord's work in these last days.

❧

The second time my father asks if I have anyone in mind for marriage, I tell him again of this young man I feel hopelessly infatuated with. His response is matter-of-fact, almost distracted: "Well, that isn't what the Lord has in mind for you."

I'm confused and deflated. Romantic tales of young love have taken so much space in my teenage mind. My father has told and retold the stories of how smitten he was with my mother, how he had prayed to God and knew she must be his wife. My brother Jake and beautiful Treena had liked each other for four years on the sly. They asked for each other and were given a church blessing and are now the most in-love young couple with a dreamy love story. Similar stories of love and inspired marriages are told and retold in the church. I'm sure I've kept my heart pure and my prayers earnest to fully receive inspiration from God as to the affections of my heart.

Vilate is the one friend I've confided my romantic girlish dreams to. She reminds me gently of church wisdom: "God saves his greatest blessings for those who wait for his direction." I affirm with determination that I can do whatever God wants me to do. I esteem church leadership and wholeheartedly trust my father's priesthood to be the direction in my life. I know God has great blessings in store for me and my only challenge is to have my heart ready to receive those blessings.

Winter ends but the world goes on. While we await the time of destructions, the excitement of marriages in the community causes a stir. Two of my cousins are leaving to the US to get married. Father tells me I am to travel with them and get married in Salt Lake, where the Prophet will perform the ceremony. Mother is in Victoria doing her midwifery training and won't have time to make the trip as it will be a quick trip down and back. Father assures her it will be fine. He will go with me.

Mother tells him firmly that if he takes me to Salt Lake to get married, she will charter a jet and will fly there the next day at a cost of about ten thousand dollars. My father rolls his eyes. She is being so unreasonable.

"My daughter is not getting married without me," she asserts.

I don't go.

Instead, the next day my sisters Mandy, Katie and I go to Victoria to spend a few weeks with Mother. She is working with a midwife in Victoria to get her required birthing experience for her training. She lets me take her car with a tank full of gas. We buy a map. I drive while my sisters navigate and together we find hidden parts of the city filled with flowers, trails along the ocean and little shops.

It's April. I will get married when the Prophet comes up at the end of the month, Father tells Mother. We girls, Grams, Mother and Brittany all pack into Mother's Yukon. I drive the whole way home. I still haven't got direct confirmation from my father as to who this new husband will be but I will be meeting him for the first time once we arrive home. My heart flutters more with each mountain we summit, closing the gap between my childhood and my life as a married woman. Mother kisses me and drops me off at the corner to walk up the hill to the Middle House. Who will be this knight in shining armour?

On the big deck in front of my father's house is the dreamy young man I haven't yet been able to force out of my thoughts. My heart leaps in hopeful surprise. Maybe I will marry him after all? Father knows my inspiration has set my heart on this man. From the porch he smiles at me walking up the hill. I'm instantly conscious of the movements of my body. I tuck my messy hair behind my ear. "How was the drive up? Did it get any shorter?" I'm being cheeky and he laughs, disarming me. He jumped in at the last minute with some of the guys coming up from Utah, he explains.

Tomorrow is my wedding day. I will marry a good someone. I wish desperately my girlhood crush weren't here.

♣

The next day I marry his best friend, Sam, and he marries one of my best friends and cousins.

As the young newlywed couples, we share a honeymoon trip to Utah. The proud grooms are excited to show their young brides their hometown. The Roundy uncles are round and jolly and Grandpa Sam and Grandma Shirley welcome me warmly into their family. We ride dirt bikes, play baseball, go on picnics and go camping and spend two weeks meeting the in-laws amid endless awkward hugs and handshakes and introductions. The Holms grandmas host a double reception for us.

The "honeymoon" is awkward at best. I'm sharing a bed with a man I barely know and I get my period. While my husband is taking me for a rip down the Crick on his friend's four-wheeler, my foot slips off the buddy peg and I end up with wheel track bruises all the way up my thigh. He's beyond embarrassed so I spend the rest of the week trying to not let anyone notice I'm limping. We learn how to kiss, though, which is quite nice for both of us. I'm becoming quite fond of my husband's quiet, slow humour and personality.

Mercifully, finally, the honeymoon is over. We come home. I move with my husband to Alberta, where he is working with one of the company logging crews. I don't look back.

TWO PINK LINES

My marriage assignment is God's will in my life. It is part of a greater work he is playing out on the earth at this time. Our lives are dedicated to his service. We know he will deliver on his promise. We will rise together in the morning of the resurrection as we commit our lives, our hearts and our purity to each other. I will do my part.

I look forward to years of service to "the work" in our long and productive marriage. To having lots of fat babies together, to raising faithful sons and daughters who go on to dedicate their lives to the priesthood. My husband is nineteen and as a first wife I fully embrace that he at some point will take other wives. His mother did not come to Canada for our wedding. Upon seeing us when we stepped out of the car in her driveway in Colorado City, she told her son, "I'll for sure make it to your next one." To this we all just laughed good-naturedly.

Together Sam and I will live the fullness of the gospel and the law of celestial marriage as our fathers and forefathers have done. We have both kept ourselves clean and pure for a priesthood marriage and are committed to creating this life together, come what may.

We spend the summer under the windy, mysterious Alberta sky. In the afternoons before it is time for me to start on the evening meal for the crew, I go for long walks in the tall blowing prairie grass out to the ravine looking over the Red Deer River. My heart swirls like the changing expanse of the endless sky and I listen to the gentle advice of the wind. Is this love, this ache inside me to be near him and this longing for his touch? I wonder at the completeness I feel when we are together, and the overwhelming loneliness when we are apart.

I fall in love with my husband, and in one short summer, I am a woman.

My husband is kind. He is patient and funny. He makes me laugh. I respect his willingness to work long hours when needed, which often requires him to work on weekends after a long workweek. Compared with my mother when she first married, I have a life of luxury and leisure. I cook and clean for only my new husband and a few other guys in the crew house. I do my best to cook good meals for him and the crew and pack delicious healthy lunches. I keep the house neat and busy myself with baking or sewing to fill the hours until he returns from work, when we play tennis or go for a short hike in the evening. I want him to feel proud that he got a good wife. I will be a good mother as well.

We make the six-hour drive from Alberta to Bountiful every two weeks for church and to see family, through the Morley First Nations reserve and Banff National Park. If we are not in too big a hurry, I persuade him to take a short hike with me or just sit next to a beautiful stream, holding each other.

❧

One day in October, after we've been married for six months, we visit Bountiful for another weekend of church and family time. It's my husband's birthday and I feel especially proud of him and of our new marriage. We're in our bedroom in the mobile trailer where we stay when we visit Bountiful. Sam lies on the bed, still dressed in his suit after the evening priesthood meeting. He is flipping through a book of scripture his mother gave us as a wedding gift: *Faith Like the Ancients*, true stories of pioneer heroes and the hair-raising challenges they overcame through their unwavering faith in God. His socks are on and his hair neatly combed over. He looks sharp. My heart swells as I hand him a small foil bag, the silver pattern reflecting the light. He reaches inside and pulls out the little plastic stick. He raises his eyebrows in surprise. "I'm late," I tell him. "Should we try it?"

We stare at the little window, elated as the two pink lines form into a cross.

❧

The baby is growing, changing my body, my identity, my life.

My husband beams with pride, holding my hand as we walk together. He talks to my round belly while we lie in bed together and tries to guess which part is moving against the contours of my body.

❧

The birthing clinic is the active centre of community life these last months. In our extended community, sixty women have delivered or are due within the next year. When I go into labour, both recovery rooms are full. Mother fixes her bed for me for after delivery. I labour all day and all night with a birthing team who spell one another off. Grandma Mem walks beside me up and down the hall and shows me how to do side steps up the stairs, holding the railing. Mother's gentle, cool hands wipe my face and then in the wee hours of the morning, when I am quite certain I can't do one more minute, her firm, confident voice helps find my determination. The delivery room is warm with low light. Calm women's voices and expert hands move about the room, reaching for this, supporting me for that, a voice in my ear to breathe or move and then to push. With my mother's hands guiding him, my husband catches our daughter and cuts the cord.

I am a mother.

✤

My husband's father is the chief of police in Colorado City, Arizona, and head of security for the Prophet. My father is the bishop and presiding elder. Our fathers have been close friends for years. Together they pace up and down the hall outside the birthing room, coaching my husband now and then and sending me words of encouragement on sticky notes through the nurses.

The baby is still wet with goo as the two zealous grandpas beam at their shared granddaughter.

"She is the best of both of us," they say, looking at their combined genetic material in this one tiny little girl. We are officially bonded eternally as family.

Our little Starla is the fourth of my parents' four grandchildren born this year. My sisters-in-law bring the babies: Stella is four months older with her chubby cheeks and blond curls; Jenna, two months older with her soft dark hair and shiny dark eyes; and our skinny little Jeron just made it out two days ahead of this adorable little person who chose me to be her mother. I don't think I've ever seen anything more perfect. All of us young mothers gleam at the good fortune of our babies. I couldn't have imagined anything like the surge of love and emotion that floods my heart as I hold these little ones, already feeling the bonds they share with one another.

With our little daughter, my husband and I become a family all our own. We learn how to be parents in the same awkward way we learned how to be lovers and partners: with patience.

GOD GIVES LIFE
(AND TAKES IT AWAY)

"The Lord's judgment is spreading across this nation. The earth will be cleansed by fire."

I clutch the telephone, bewildered at what I am hearing. Judgment Day is upon us. "It's all over the news," my mother's voice tells me. "I watched with my own eyes. An airplane flew right into one of the twin towers in New York City."

She is watching it on TV at the hospital where she works on maternity. I glance nervously over at my round-faced, three-month-old daughter sleeping peacefully in her bouncer chair beside the sewing machine, where I have been patiently stitching her a tiny romper with the remnants of the fabric from the new dress I just finished sewing for myself. My goal is to finish them for the family pictures we are having taken this weekend when we go home to Creston for church. Family photos matter little if this is the hour of the Great Destruction.

After spending my pregnancy wondering if the world would end before my daughter was born, I pushed that fear aside and let myself become absorbed in the all-encompassing task of caring for a new baby. Today I'm alone with my daughter in the Green House, one of the many crew houses the company owns in the Sundre area near the Sunpine mill, where only a few years back I worked with the boys. I have no car. Is it better to go outside or stay in the house? Restless and uneasy, I can't make myself sit down to finish sewing the project that was of such importance to me just moments ago.

I wrap my baby in a blanket and strap her in the stroller. I walk the few miles down the busy highway to the main house, where another crew of cousins live. Ada is the main crew momma here taking care of meals. They have a television and have rigged an antenna so the guys can watch the hockey games and the Grey Cup football playoffs.

The house is filled with smells of baking bread. A batch of cookie dough is mixed up on the table. Everyone is crowded around the small black box. Guys from the shop are still in their blue overalls and have grease-covered hands with rags hanging out their back pockets. Uncle Karl, who drives a logging truck, has stopped by for lunch and a bucket of hydraulic fluid for one of the guys whose machine broke down on the mountain. We press together, clamouring our questions about what this can mean. The news announcer says they suspect it was a terrorist attack.

Uncle Karl shakes his head, speaking to no one in particular. "No man knows the day nor the hour. Well, my friends, as for me, I won't be caught out of the line of duty." He puts on his dusty trucker cap with the flat brim and heads out the door.

Before I get up to see if I can help my cousin's wife in the kitchen, I whisper a silent prayer to our gracious God for those people who lost their lives. I pray for the safety and protection of my little daughter. God gives life and God takes it away.

✺

The attack on the World Trade Center is awful but, for now, the world goes on. My husband and I celebrate our second year of marriage, our healthy daughter and the move into our very own first home. "The only thing more wonderful than having a baby," I tell my husband, "would be having two babies." Shortly after weaning my daughter from breastfeeding, we become pregnant again. The Lord is good.

✺

The Lord is good and he speaks to us through the words of our Prophet. As we await Judgment Day, his words have often given us comfort. It is with increasing anxiety that we hear of his poor health: "Our dear Prophet's illness is a test of the people," we hear each Sunday. The Prophet, Uncle Rulon, had a stroke a few years back, which limits his mobility and reportedly has affected his memory and his speech. Most Sundays, as we gather in the big converted meeting hall, we hear a few words from the church leadership in Utah via telephone. Uncle Warren Jeffs is by his father's side day and night. He speaks for his father or helps the Prophet to say a few inspiring words directly to the people. We talk often about how hearing the voice of the Prophet fills us with a sweet spirit that gets us through the week.

More frequently these days the church calls a fast day. The people are called to fast and pray to ask God if it be his will to help get the Prophet through a particularly difficult time. Because I am pregnant, I cannot safely join my family in fasting but I dutifully pray.

Uncle Warren Jeffs reminds us each week in his firm but gentle voice that if we have enough faith, God will renew the Prophet's body. He will be made whole and young again and lead his people until the Second

Coming of Christ only if the people demonstrate great displays of faithfulness and prove our worthiness to be the ones to usher in the New Jerusalem.

New revelations are coming from the pulpit weekly. Some of them are small practical changes for people to make in their lives, such as making clothing plainer, more modest. Uncle Warren reveals that these last days call for more direct measures, as only the purest of heart will be allowed to enter the kingdom of heaven. We should all be vigilant to ensure we don't have a wolf in sheep's clothing among us. Tensions rise. A culture of vigilantes rallies. There is constant pressure on people to report others who are not following church teachings to the letter. Wives report husbands, who then must go in for priesthood corrections. They are to repent from afar and send their means to support the priesthood work and prove their worthiness that they may then be asked to rejoin their families in Zion. There's a growing sense of urgency in everyone in our home community and in our sister community in Utah.

⚹

"Something is going to happen. We need to be prepared," Sam says. My husband is kneeling beside our bed after a long telephone conversation with his father. I mark the section I am reading in *Purity in the New and Everlasting Covenant of Marriage*, which was assigned a few weeks ago for couples to read. I kneel beside him for our evening prayer. On Sunday evenings my husband talks on the phone for hours to his father in Utah. I know it is not my business to ask about their conversations. The bits he offers tie into the messages from the pulpit. "The times are short; Judgment Day is nigh upon us. The Lord is doing his housekeeping, making sure the hearts and minds of his people are pure and clean, so we will be worthy when he sends his only begotten son to save the children of man."

Several men have received priesthood corrections and lost their families. Like King David in the Bible, an adulterous man will lose all that he has. It will be given to someone else. These are grave and serious times, yet we are a blessed and chosen people to be doing the Lord's work in the last days.

Clinging to my priesthood husband and the safety net of my family and community, I believe I am prepared for the challenges that are coming.

JUDGMENT DAY

Nothing could have prepared me.

June 3, 2002, the day before my daughter's first birthday, starts out like a normal Sunday. I put on a crisp Sunday dress and smooth my nylon socks so they don't wrinkle at my waistline. I slip into the bathroom to pouf, sculpt and braid my long hair while Starla enthusiastically pulls everything out of the bottom kitchen drawer and rattles it across the kitchen. With some hair goo, I entice a curl on the top of her head and stick a small bow to her head with extra gel. We walk from our trailer down the hill to Grandpa's house where the family is washing up after breakfast and setting up chairs in the Middle House, all dressed and combed in their Sunday finest. Starla stands but hasn't taken her first steps yet. Stella, sturdy on her feet, comes running to smother her little cousin in kisses, knocking her over. Jake's two wives, Treena and Lydia, walk in the house a few minutes late carrying the cutest little duo, Jenna and Jeron. With my father's children and grandchildren, gathering for Sunday school is a wiggly mass of low attention spans. We optimistically gather in the big room on Sunday mornings. Mother Leanne works with a group of children to practise a song. We sing and pray and listen to pieces of inspiration together before going to church. My brothers and their wives all work away at the logging camps and post mills each week as my husband does, so Sunday is our day to reconnect, hold babies, share stories and, of course, eat.

Sunday dinner is the family meal our life revolves around. My father's wives, the daughters-in-law, the married daughters and the big girls have groups so each group takes a turn to make Sunday dinner once a month. It's an ambitious and satisfying task to plan and prepare this feast for over 150 people every Sunday. If I miss Sunday at "Grandpa's," as I now usually refer to my childhood home, I do feel I'm missing out.

This morning Father left early and no one really knows where he went. He's not back in time for Sunday school so Jake leads us in singing songs with the family. Father arrives shortly before church. He is serious and matter-of-fact. He tells us he received a call early in the morning. Warren Jeffs, speaking for his father, Uncle Rulon, revealed to Father that the Prophet had received inspiration that Father no longer holds the priesthood. I feel my stomach move up to my throat. How could this be? This means Father no longer has standing in the church, nor is he sealed to his family. When a man loses his priesthood standing, all that he has will be given to someone else. This is something that was rare in the past and only done in extreme circumstances of adultery. In the last two years, however, our aging Prophet has been receiving this revelation regularly. The community has been watching as devoted fathers and respected men in the community are stripped of their families and invited to serve the church as "single angels." The constricting grip of fear and foreboding has been tightening over the church, but never did anyone imagine this could happen to a man so highly revered as Winston Blackmore.

Father is a beloved and highly respected spiritual leader of a congregation of more than ten thousand people in Creston, North Idaho, Salt Lake City and southern Utah. Father is well known for his open-door policy and his free church bed and breakfast, as well as for his compassion and for encouraging people to repent; he'd say, "Where there is life, there is hope. As long as you are alive, you have an opportunity to correct your life before God."

When Father shows up briefly in the middle of our Sunday school session, he tells Jake he needs to go for a drive and will not be attending church today. Mother's brother Jim has been assigned to be presiding elder. He will lead the service today and share the news of my father's fate with the congregation.

The Prophet has been saying, "God will have a tried people." It is echoed from the pulpit at church that there will be many tests in these last days. Now I wonder if this is a test to see if Winston Blackmore is humble enough to take a correction. News of his priesthood correction spreads through the church like wildfire, shaking the congregation to its core.

Since the Prophet has stated that Father no longer carries the priesthood, the church will require him to give up his leadership and ministry and be rebaptized into the church as a lay member. The church directs that he can get his priesthood reinstated and his family can be resealed to him. Most of his wives and older children feel that is what he should do. Some of his family say that giving up his church office will mean Father will have more time with his family. Life will go on and soon this will be barely more than a bad dream.

But my father says he can't get rebaptized if he didn't commit any sins, and his family was sealed to him by God and blessed by the Prophets. He says he and his wives have honoured those covenants and no one needs to redo them. He says he knows he has not lost his personal connection with God and someone telling him he has doesn't make it true. "Jesus Christ is my Saviour," he says, "not Warren Jeffs."

Most of the family choose not to go to church this morning. We pack salads, cold cuts and twenty watermelons, load up our family and go down to the farm to have a family picnic with the cows. We hold each other and cry in fear and confusion. I don't know what this means. None of us do.

BACK TO THE FOLD

My husband is connected to the inner workings of the church through his father, so now his warnings that "something is going to happen" make sense but anger me. He already knew about Father's excommunication and has had time to mentally prepare for this. On Saturday night, while I was still blissfully ignorant, my father-in-law had left Colorado City with a truck and a trailer and a few young men to gather my husband and his family to take us back into the fold of the faithful and away from the turmoil of the crumbling church leadership in Canada.

Only two weeks before, I was bursting with sharing the joyful secret of my pregnancy with Mother and Sam. Now I feel as if the world is coming crashing down. How am I to bring another life into this world in these uncertain times? I watch the young men on a church mission load all of my worldly possessions into a trailer. The baby crib goes in first, then the bed and the beautiful solid wood dressers Sam and I bought for our first anniversary. They dismantle the little home we have lovingly created. I don't even try to help. I sit on the stairs and weep. In one day, my father went from being one of the most esteemed men in the church to being publicly chastised and rebuked with no explanation. I feel I'm losing the whole world.

It takes them only an hour to load our life into a trailer, ready to head to Utah.

"I'm not going," I say, finally standing up to face my husband. How can I leave my family like this? I've had only a few hours to process this life-changing decision. Our whole world has been shattered. I need to grieve with my family, to listen to their questions. I am strong and I can help them. My siblings need their big sister. I can't just leave.

Without any hesitation, my husband tells me to do what I need to do, but he is going. My father-in-law comes to talk to me. We quote scripture at each other, perched on the little porch of the blue and white trailer that has been our home under the pine trees. We are both well versed in church doctrine so it's a pointless rally using one scripture to contradict the argument of the other.

He references passages and examples from the Bible and Book of Mormon, when whole cities were destroyed because the people did not follow the Prophet. Nothing he says can convince me.

I am adamant. "My father has done nothing wrong," I say to my father-in-law. "You are one of his best friends. You know him better than anyone."

My father-in-law, who is usually lighthearted and jovial, responds sombrely that he loves my father but there is a lot I don't know about him. He says it is not our role to question; it is our role to obey the Prophet, as the Prophet cannot commit an error. He says we must be humble enough to be led as if by a thread and that he's praying my father will find the humility he needs to accept his correction and come into the service of the Prophet.

We've always been taught that every person is important in the eyes of God and that each soul is worthy of being saved. Did Jesus not speak of the shepherd who leaves the flock to go looking for the one who has fallen away and is lost in the wilderness to bring him back to the fold? I feel certain that our leaders must care deeply about us and will take care to lovingly explain away this confusion. I've always felt with conviction that each of us is important to Uncle Rulon. He would not just let the flock go untended. He loves my father.

"If my father is wrong, why would God allow so many people to be led astray by the failings of one man?" I challenge my father-in-law. I sincerely feel there must be some breakdown in communication, some jealousy or misunderstanding.

My despair shifts to determination. Good men run this church and I will go talk to them. I tell my father-in-law that I will go. I tell him I want to go to Utah and talk to Uncle Fred and Uncle Rulon themselves. These two beloved patriarchs have led our people for decades; they love us like their own families. My father-in-law says he can arrange the meetings for me.

It's early afternoon and I walk around to hug my goodbyes to my confused and weepy family.

I climb in the back seat of the white Ford Excursion, next to my daughter's car seat, and bury my face in a pillow. I am nineteen years old and I'm pregnant with my second child.

We really need to sort this out. My family needs me to get to the bottom of this.

There's no way I'm going to stand by and let rumours and lies decide our fate.

✎

We drive through the afternoon and night and arrive by dawn the next day. It's Monday and my little daughter's first birthday. I'd imagined this day would be filled with cake, and cousins together with our three little girls—Starla, Stella and Jenna—in our beautiful BC home. Instead I'm in Colorado City, Arizona, a town that's in shock from the news of the day before. Few people are going to work. As our Prophet has grown more ill, his son Warren Jeffs has become increasingly involved in the management of the church and the details of his father's personal life.

Those close to my father know there is no love lost between him and Warren Jeffs and the supremacy of the Jeffs family name that evolved over the last few years. Father insists that we are all equal in the sight of God and the Lord doesn't care what a person's last name is. Many people in the church are already saying that my father was to be the next leader of the church and Warren Jeffs manipulated his aging father to remove my father from leadership so he cannot be a threat to his ever-tightening control on the church.

Just a few hours after we arrive from our eighteen-hour drive, Sam and his father hold good to their word. They take me to see Uncle Fred, bishop and presiding elder and essentially mayor for Colorado City and Hildale, Utah. He is one of the founding fathers of the town and community. His has led this community for nearly half a century to build a thriving centre for God's people. Under his leadership the town has become a progressive and expanding metropolis with good schools and members trained as doctors, dentists, teachers and other professions. The community celebrates several times a year with elaborate festivals and a flair for the arts. He built a zoo and parks and put pride in the beautification of the town. He is a visionary, a beloved father figure and leader and one of the most well-respected men in the fundamentalist Mormon Church, and a good friend of my father and my mother, who were frequent guests in his home.

If there is anyone who will give me a straight story about what is going on in the church, it will be Uncle Fred.

We arrive at Uncle Fred's early Monday morning just before the weekly work meeting. Dozens of men who work for church and municipal businesses meet early at his house for prayer and breakfast and to await their assignments or seek his counsel.

The roses are in full bloom climbing the arch and along the path to his familiar front door. All conversation stops when Sam, my father-in-law and I walk into the big sitting room. Uncle Fred sits in a large easy chair. Men stand around him and sit in rows of chairs lining the room. Each man holds his ball cap respectfully as hats are not worn in priesthood homes. Most of these faces are familiar and have been guests in my father's home over the years. All of them know my father well and, I'm sure, share some of the weight of the pain in my heart.

So many questions run through my head and heart. For all my determination to leave with a list of answers, all I do is sit next to him, bury my face into his shoulder and cry.

"I love your father." His words are slow and deliberate. "He is a good priesthood man." Uncle Fred puts his hand on my shoulder and the room sits in silence.

I suppose I got the answer I came for, but not clarity. Why did he say that? We were told Father no longer held the priesthood. Uncle Fred's words simply add to my confusion. I want him to fix it and to make everything go back to the way it was.

✤

Over the next few weeks, Sam calls several times to try to secure an appointment for me to see our Prophet, Uncle Rulon Jeffs. In response to my husband's requests, Uncle Warren Jeffs, his father's right-hand man, only instructs my husband to tell me to get my heart in the right place. If I pray earnestly I will receive my answer, he counsels. An unfamiliar feeling of anger rises in me. To question church leadership is something I've barely even let tug at the corners of my mind. I am struggling with a decision that could mean the cost of my eternal salvation and I am not worth five minutes of the Prophet's time? I'm flabbergasted. Always I've imagined my soul being guided by caring, nurturing and inspired leaders.

"This is a test for all of us," my father-in-law says to comfort me. "It is not up to us to question the way the Lord does his work. Our job is to follow as if led by a thread."

My father-in-law moves out of his bedroom to give his space to Sam and me and little Starla. It is a large room, with a private bathroom and a whirlpool tub, ample for our needs. As soon as we arrive, my husband buys a new Dodge Ram pickup truck and starts working out of town so he is gone during the week. Financially, it's a tough season for us with a baby and one on the way. My three mother-in-laws are gracious and generous about sharing their kitchen and meals with us. I find true friendship in many of the children. This part is easy for me—to gather them up and fill my time with hikes and activities. I get to know the children well.

Susie's house is my real sanctuary. Although I miss Canada and the rest of my family terribly, it is a joy to be in the same town as my sister again. Since my husband is gone, I get up early, strap my baby in the stroller and walk across town to my sister's house for breakfast. I often stay into the evening, especially if her husband is also away.

Susie has an old green Oldsmobile sedan. The heater is stuck on despite the sweltering temperatures of a southern Utah summer. We load up our babies and bomb around town to the fabric store, the grocery store or the thrift centre. She has a good garden scratched out in the red dirt that grows tomatoes and roses really well. Being country kids, we are always looking for a chance to take our shoes off, play in the mud and get our hands in the dirt. Our feet and clothes become stained a dull orange from the red southern Utah dirt.

Doing God's work is the whole purpose of our existence. We are all in this together.

Despite Our Fasting and Prayers

On a warm weekend in September, three months after Father is excommunicated, Sam and I make a quick trip to Canada to see my midwife, who also happens to be my mother. We've decided we will have the baby at our birthing clinic in Canada, where I have medical coverage. I can see a midwife in Utah for some of my care if needed. We leave early to return to Utah with our daughter early Sunday morning so Sam can get to work. The US border denies me access until I can get the paperwork started for my immigration.

As we turn back from the border, Sam gets a call on his cellphone—the call none of us were supposed to receive. Despite our fasting and prayers, despite the songs of unity and hope sung by the thousands, on a sunny September day, Rulon T. Jeffs, the Prophet of God, has died.

I wonder about all of those prophecies that he would live on into the millennium until the Second Coming of Christ. Is this just another test for the people? The Prophet died. I never got to ask him my questions. Now he can't fix this. The church is slipping into chaos. Nothing makes sense anymore.

Those who attend church that day relate their experiences of when Warren Jeffs walked in to tell the people that the Prophet had passed on. One of Uncle Rulon's wives, who is also a nurse, had been by his side constantly in the last weeks of his life. She relates her testimony that she felt the Prophet's spirit leave his body, then she relates what she describes as the mantle of the Prophet resting on his son Warren Jeffs, and how she knew his work would live on through him. She says she knows he will continue the Lord's work leading and preparing his people for the Second Coming of Christ and the building up of the New Jerusalem.

Many describe this day with deep conviction and fall seamlessly into this idea with reverence. They say the prophecy has been fulfilled and that the Prophet has been renewed and will live on through his son. They say he will continue to lead the people as if from another room, where his son can seek his counsel. No one, including me, wants to question the will of God, but for so many of the people this doesn't add up. This is just never the way succession of church leadership has ever been passed forward. Questions and confusion spread over the congregation like an ache.

⥁

It was prophesied in the last days that sons would turn against fathers, fathers against sons, brothers against brothers. I look around me now; somehow the devil has crept into our hearts. Community, family and working together were always the things we said set us apart.

On a Sunday session Warren Jeffs tells the people that they must declare their loyalty publicly, once and for all. "If you are not for God and his work, you are against it." Many take a journey to Utah to seek the counsel and guidance of the priesthood. They return changed. They no longer speak to any family members who are not following Warren Jeffs. In Canada, the split runs down the middle, with about equal numbers of people following Warren Jeffs as not. In Colorado City, many more follow his ever more strict and secretive teachings.

My mother is more torn than most of us. As caregiver of the community, she is close to everyone, especially the women. Her father's side of the family and her two daughters are following Warren Jeffs. Her brother has been assigned as the new bishop. My father's family and her children and grandchildren are mostly pulling away from Warren Jeffs's teaching. Mother worries that if she doesn't follow Warren Jeffs, she will lose her daughters and siblings forever, while if she stays in the church, she likely would still be able to reach out to those who have left it.

We play tug-of-war with her in the middle.

Finally, she rents a house and moves into Creston, unwilling to take sides among her family. "I won't choose between the people I love," she says.

Unbeknownst to us, Mother also files for divorce from Father.

The church teaches that without a priesthood release from the marriage covenant, any other relationship is considered adultery before God. I want to know why she needs to add getting divorced on top of what is already going on. I question her. She has always seemed so independent, living her life the way she needs to. I don't see how she can't continue that, even if she lives in town. I worry about her choice to divorce my father in these precarious times.

I feel confused. I know how committed my mother is to our family unit and I love her, but I was raised to have pity for the divorced and seeing my own mother this way is hard. God promised King David that for those who are faithful, theirs would be a glorious eternal life surrounded by family and a multitude of descendants as numerous as the grains of sand on the seashore. Why would Mother give this up? In these last days, being sealed to a good priesthood man is of utmost importance. A woman's connection to her husband, we are taught, is her opportunity to be exalted to the highest degree of the celestial kingdom of heaven. Single men and women can never become gods and goddesses in their own right who will eventually be lord over their own worlds but can only serve as single angels for eternity.

This worry brings up a deep, unsettling childhood fear of losing my mother, a loss that could extend beyond this life into the next. I remember the saddest story ever told from my childhood Sunday school lessons. We had an old cassette recording of my great-grandfather Gallup reading "To the Buffetings of Satan" at a church conference. We listened to it sometimes in the car.

In the story, a young missionary is invited into a dilapidated home of obvious poverty. A haggard woman sits smoking at a meagre table with a half-consumed bottle of alcohol on it. She is surrounded by several dirty children. In a great mournful tale, she recounts to the young man her testimony of the truth of the gospel of Jesus Christ of Latter Day Saints and tells him she had sinned the terrible unforgivable sin of adultery and was no longer worthy of God's blessings. She had resigned herself to a life of suffering and the punishment that would come of it. She had sealed her eternal damnation.

She had once been married in the church, had been sealed in the temple, but had allowed herself to be seduced by a charming man who had promised her a life of glamour and luxury. They would live in California by the sea and eat in fancy restaurants. She was too beautiful a woman to waste her life as a servant to her husband, he had told her. She had fallen for it. She had followed him, believed in his grand tales. After taking her virtue and using her in unthinkable ways, he had abandoned her with three small children, telling her he had never wanted to be a father. This was not a life for him.

The story struck a warning in my developing morality—that a man could possess such evil and be so trivial about family and commitment. This story taught me that there were men of the world who did not want children or to fulfill their role and calling to be fathers. Even more, I learned that a woman can throw away her blessing of God's directive to be sealed to a good priesthood man and to raise faithful sons and daughters in a priesthood home. I understood from this and other teachings that my birthright as a virtuous mother of Zion was one of my greatest possessions. A long, lonely life of suffering can be the only result of allowing the temptations of Satan to speak louder than God's words. I fear for my mother.

❧

Mother's decision has big ripples. The mothers say they feel abandoned by her. "She didn't just divorce Winston," several of them told me. "She also divorced us." In Mother's careful, calculated way, she says only what people need to hear and just keeps showing up to care for the ones she loves. Mother puts Brittany into public school, which concerns us as well. The ominous familiar warning echoes in my mind: the sins of the children will be on the parents if they can stand before God and say, "My parents never taught me."

My ten-year-old sister insists on wearing only her dresses to school, but gradually she and Mother both go to church less and wear pants more. Slow and steady, Mother weathers the storm, loves her kids, takes care of women and creates a life where she can connect to family both in and out of the religion.

❧

Father asks Jake, Hyrum, Pete, Joe and me to meet him down at Mother's house in town to talk to her. Father sounds bewildered that Mother wasn't gloriously happy in her work of service for the family and community. I know Mother felt a lot of satisfaction in her work but she always took on so much of the pain of others. I also know how deeply this division in the church is hurting her.

Father offers to build her a dance studio. He is frustrated and offended that she can't see the value and conviction it took for him to take a stand against Warren Jeffs and stand up for the teachings of Jesus Christ, which are teachings of peace. "Come help me make it better," he urges.

I find Mother lying on her bed in a puddle of tears. Watching the breakdown of the bonds of her family and community that had been so loving and cohesive is tearing her apart. "All of this suffering to follow the directions of senseless proud men makes me so angry. It just makes it worse that they are doing it in the name of God," she cries helplessly into her pillow. Mother is careful about what she says to us of her anger toward Dad, but we have watched them both carefully in their very public lives. Mother has often felt that Dad makes fickle decisions and could do so much more as a minister and a community leader to help people in our community. While he feels he has supported her in so much of her journey, I've seen him ask the impossible of her, whether in the name of the church or just bad judgment. My brothers and I are adults now and there is something unspoken we now understand about my parents. They both have reasons to feel the way they do. And, we fear, neither of them knows how to make things better.

A ROUND BELLY AND A TROUBLED HEART

As my belly grows the world around me seems to collapse. I wonder how I can justify bringing another child into such a crazy, mixed-up world. When I am in Utah spending time with my sister and my husband's family, who are dedicated followers of Warren Jeffs, I start to wonder if the teachings of Warren Jeffs are correct and my father has fallen away from God and is leading his family to hell. Then I return home and spend time with my brothers and their families. They are all as they were when I left them: thoughtful, generous, hard-working, good people.

I witness with dismay the way the split between my father, with the more moderate Mormons, and the Warren Jeffs followers is changing the community I grew up in and still love. Bountiful School has long been the centre of community life and pride for us with a student body of over 250 children. Many feel that if they just don't debate church leadership at school, they can continue as normal. These children are all close friends and cousins who have been friends since birth. We can't imagine it being any other way. However, the principal and at least half of the staff declare their loyalty to the leadership of Warren Jeffs. To the parents' alarm, they begin teaching his new prophecies and revelations to the students. As more families denounce Warren Jeffs and stop attending church, the children are caught in challenging positions, with some telling others that their parents are apostates, which is the worst thing you can call a Mormon.

It all goes down like a bad divorce, where one partner feels entitled to everything and wants the other to have nothing, and the other takes the side of the martyr and doesn't try to fight for a fair separation of the accumulated assets. Father is firm that he will not fight over it. "We will go find somewhere else to have school," he says. The Split creates deep wounds among a group of people whose lives have been so intertwined. Only a short year before, we would have gone through hell or high water for each other.

As the skirts on the girls of the Warrenites become longer and their hairstyles get higher and smoother, other families begin cutting their hair and wearing jeans or shorter skirts. In these challenging times, some days it feels as though God has forsaken us. The constant pestering of the media only adds to the noise and the chaos.

❧

During this time, many family members from Canada who are following Warren Jeffs make the trek to Utah to see the Prophet and receive his counsel as well as to visit family and friends. Several times my daughter and I catch a ride back home to make my deadline on my border-crossing date.

On a Saturday morning, Rett, my father-in-law's third wife, knocks on my bedroom door. "Someone is here to see you."

I braid my knee-length hair, dress my little Starla and lift her over my now enormous baby bump, carrying her down the long hallway of my father-in-law's house. In the foyer, Aunt Marilyn, my father's sister, who has taken very little interest in my life so far, and her husband stand waiting to see me. They fuss over my daughter and Aunt Marilyn keeps touching my belly and asking about my pregnancy. My uncle keeps talking about my older brothers. He says he is hoping they will have the strength to stand up for the priesthood despite what my father and his family are doing. A knotted flare of anger tears at my gut. How dare they?

Even though I was named for her, Aunt Marilyn has never gone out of her way to see me or know me. Now they've come to take the little church orphan under their wing and console me for the fact that my father, my brothers, my mother, for certain, and all the rest of my family will burn in a fiery hell for their disobedience and unwillingness to acknowledge Warren Jeffs as the one and only spokesperson for God.

I nod along, biting my tongue. If I say anything, I will just burst into tears. I don't feel nurtured by either of them. I wish they would just stop talking and leave me to my lonely questions. I wrap my arms around my daughter and feel my baby move inside my round belly. Their evangelical missionary work falls on a troubled heart.

❧

A few nights later some ladies ask if I would like to join them to go to a party. We tell the babysitter that we are driving into the neighbouring town of Hurricane for ice cream but actually we go to a friend's house to watch *A Walk to Remember*, which has just been released.

I'm surprised by their invitation. The church has strict rules that television in any form is forbidden. One of the church crimes my father was accused of and admitted to was telling a group of church brethren that

God would not smite them for watching the old John Wayne movie *Mc-Lintock!* The same middle-aged men who had watched the movie bore witness to church authorities of my father's counsel, which directly defied church rhetoric, and these middle-aged men included my father-in-law. Now this very sin was happening in his own family. I join them for the movie but regret my decision when I end up sitting in the corner listening to a roomful of self-righteous women gossip and criticize my family. I hate them in that moment. They all lied to their babysitters and are committing the sin my father was kicked out of the church for.

When we return, I crawl into bed with my daughter. I feel absolutely miserable and alone.

Coming Home

It's December, the chilly desert wind has whipped all the leaves off the trees and the rain feels like shards of ice. In a few months I will be a mother of two. My mother-in-law pays for me to take a child development class from Aunt Jeanie. I don't take my parenting lightly but I didn't realize how critical each stage is. I read: Don't let your children look upon their own naked bodies. This will instill vanity and pride in nakedness. Don't give in to your children's whining. They will learn to be deceitful. Children learn immorality in the first few years of their life and this behaviour follows them throughout their lives.

I barely sleep after my first class. Starla throws a fit when I try feeding her oatmeal and suddenly I am second-guessing every strategy I've ever used to calm my daughter. I am horrified that my child might learn to be a thief and a liar by the time she is three years old. She could be learning immoral thinking and behaviour even as a toddler? Now I can't tell if I am letting her cry for mere trifles or I am letting her self-soothe.

"It takes some practice," Mother Val encourages me. "I was still learning with my fifteenth baby."

⁊⊕

Late in December, my body enlarged with my eighth month of pregnancy, my mother calls me in Utah. My cousin's one-year-old baby has drowned in the bathtub. I went all through school with my cousin and can't imagine her anguish. I hold my little daughter and sob. I am planning to go home for my delivery, so I will find a ride a few weeks early to go to the baby's funeral. A few phone calls later, I locate my cousin who has come to visit family with his wife and their children and will have room for Starla and me to ride home with them if we pack light.

After I squish in beside the toddler car seat in the back seat of their minivan, we wait several hours, as my cousins are thrilled that they will have an appointment to see Uncle Warren before heading on the long trip home. Our toddlers are getting restless and the trip hasn't even started yet, but the wait will be worth it, they say, for even a minute with the Prophet.

I offer to sit in the car while they go in, as I don't have an appointment to see Uncle Warren. "That would be such a waste," my cousin's wife declares. She will ask for me if I can at least shake his hand.

I sit by the door in the little waiting room, letting my daughter walk around before she has to be strapped in her seat for the next twenty hours. Several of the wives I know well come out to give me a hug and admire my baby. Uncle Warren's brother Seth is managing his appointments and tells him Winston Blackmore's daughter is here to see him.

Warren Jeffs comes into the entrance. His fixed, penetrating eyes bore into me. I instantly remember my teaching: "The Prophet always knows your heart." I make brief eye contact but can't make myself keep looking at him. I pick up my daughter, who begins to fuss. I shake his hand. He holds my hand for what feels like forever and keeps his intense gaze on me. As a distraction, I turn to let my daughter shake his hand. To fill the awkward silence, I say, "Starla, say 'We love you, Uncle Warren.'" He seems satisfied and finally goes to his office.

My ears are burning with shame that I hid behind my one-year-old daughter and told a lie because I didn't have the courage to look him in the eyes and ask him the real questions I have.

As we get ready to go, I feel I need to scrape the lie from my tongue lest God smite me down for blasphemy. God promised the people that never again would the keys of the priesthood, which Joseph Smith had fought so hard to restore, be taken from the earth.

I don't know who the true Prophet of God is but I don't love Warren Jeffs.

⚬

Once in Canada, it is heartbreaking seeing my cousin and the small, lifeless body of her perfect, sleeping angel baby, but the funeral makes it worse. This is the first funeral I have ever been to that my father does not officiate, and if I hadn't seen the little dead baby myself, I wouldn't have even known it was a funeral. The focus of every speaker and song is Warren Jeffs and the hellfire and damnation that will fall on the enemies of the priesthood. I am sick at heart seeing my cousin, who just needs to cry over her baby.

Less than a month later, there is another little hole being dug in the community cemetery and another tiny white casket with a baby inside. Peter and Millie have lost their tiny perfect baby daughter, little Vicki Jane, after only three days on the earth. We all file in line into the church house, shocked that we are here again so soon. This time my father does the service for his granddaughter. The service is a celebration of life with poems, songs and stories. We hold each other, laugh and cry, together sharing the joy and sorrow of knowing her and saying goodbye to this little life.

The contrast is like night and day. "By their works ye shall know them," Christ said. We see these works. For most of my family who are still uncertain if Warren Jeffs is the spokesperson for God, this is their moment of clarity. Warren Jeffs speaks only of destruction, destroying families and destroying the community we all love.

ᛞ

On a cold February night at midnight, my perfect son rushes into this world—in the Creston hospital this time. My mother is not feeling stable enough to do a home birth after losing one grandchild only weeks before. The doctor arrives, catches the baby and is on her way. Holding my little Kayden, I know only joy. His first night on earth, he and I are the only occupants of the empty wing of the maternity ward. I swaddle him close. In a few months I'll have my twentieth birthday. There is still a lot I don't know, but looking into his already blue eyes, I promise my remarkable little son I'll give him a good life.

ᛞ

With our son a month old, our little family of four travels back to Utah. We settle into family life in our new little apartment. Sam works around town for a bit and we enjoy some time together. I confide in my husband that I do not believe Warren Jeffs is the Prophet of God on the earth. I feel strongly that I cannot endorse his teachings, nor do I want my children to grow up in a world that teaches fear and hate. I tell him I don't want to leave our marriage, and I wonder how we can raise a family together with our conflicting beliefs. I feel like the walls of Warren Jeffs's teachings are steadily being erected around me more each week.

That old wholesome feeling of being in a town of like-minded people who are comrades in the work of God is gone. Colorado City feels like a city of spies with an ominous dark cloud of foreboding hanging over it. How will I go on living here? How will I raise children here?

Sam's answer is simple. "Just don't tell anyone."

My mother-in-law coaxes us each week to go to church. For several weeks, I have used the excuse that my baby is so small I want to keep him home, but April conference is just around the corner and my excuse sounds weak to be missing the church event of the year.

Starla stays home with her teenage aunt, who is tending the children for the morning. I swaddle baby Kayden in the little crisp white tuxedo I sewed him for the naming blessing he received last Sunday. The uncles and great-uncles gathered over at Grandfather's to give this small boy a name and a father's blessing. Eleven strong men in his family circled around my boy to put their hands under his round little body. His poker-straight black hair contrasted with his white skin, and his giant blue eyes stared brightly at this circle of men who supported and gently bounced him in unison.

The long services of conference Sundays are familiar to fundamentalist Mormon churchgoers. In Canada, my father says, a bunch of farm kids can't sit that long so church meetings are under an hour and include more songs than sermons. For April conference the brethren are well prepared. These Sundays there is an earnest anticipation to attend meetings as followers look forward to new revelations and teachings, which are coming from the pulpit weekly. It is a season of great excitement and vigilance as God is carefully sculpting his people's every action to ensure preparation for God's work in these last days. These "last days," I think, are dragging out into last months, last years, and it is troubling.

Sam and I sit in a side wing so I can leave if the baby starts to fuss. An hour or so into the service, Warren Jeffs begins a thirty-minute prayer, asking God to send fire from heaven to destroy the enemies of the priesthood. His voice carries through the room. His followers revere his voice as the sacred voice of God himself. As his eerie voice rises in fervour, my guts churn at the graphic imagery of this fiery destruction he is conjuring as if casting a spell. He calls to all who can hear his voice to unite their faith that God will send fire from heaven to destroy the enemies of the priesthood off the face of the earth. With repetition and changes in cadence he rouses a great spectacle with his thin arms stretched above the audience, reaching as if to heaven. The enemies of the priesthood, he circles back through the incantation, are all those who do not unite in uplifting the one person on earth who speaks directly to God. "God said," he affirms, "'If you are not for me, you are against me.'"

My mouth tastes bitter with bile welling in the back of my throat. This meeting hall has always been a peaceful and inspiring place to hear inspiration and connect with the Saints. Today it is packed with thousands upon thousands of family and friends who, less than a year ago, would have sworn their lives and treasure to protect my father. Today they gather uniting their faith and prayers calling on God for his destruction. Without question they are entrusting the power of their faith and turning their trust blindly over to Warren Jeffs. Susie is here; my cousins are here, Fara, Sharon, Amy, Daisy, Marigold. My father has treated them all like his own daughters.

My head begins to swirl with blackness. I've been standing for quite some time now holding my two-month-old son. A heavy weight is forcing down on my chest. It feels like I'm gasping for breath. I put my swaddled son into his father's strong arms. Heavy blackness is constricting and presses around me. Desperately, I run through a side exit door and collapse on the sidewalk, sucking at the thin desert air. Doubled over, I hold my head in my hands until I can breathe again.

My concerned husband follows a few minutes later. With tears in my eyes, I tell him, "Sam, the devil was trying to kill me in there. It felt like Joseph Smith describes in the Sacred Grove when Satan is trying to get him to stop praying and a blackness comes over him so thick he nearly dies. There is evil in that room." I am well aware that the words I say to him are church treason. To even think, let alone speak, against Warren Jeffs could bring doubt and hardship on a family. Believers are to guard their dedicated homes with diligence that no one or thing should enter the home that has not been consecrated to God. My mother-in-law would be horrified that a non-believer has been living under her roof, desecrating her home with doubtful thoughts of her beloved Prophet, Warren Jeffs.

Sam is patient with my spiritual struggles. He is a natural-born peacemaker. He waits just long enough, then offers his alternative perspective to consider. "Well, maybe you have a bad spirit on you, so you are not pure enough to go into that holy gathering and pray with the saints of God."

My body feels heavy and weak. The adrenalin and fear run their course and fatigue settles in.

"I just know I'm not supposed to be here." I struggle through tears. "I don't need to ever go into that building again. I want to go home."

❧

These goodbyes break my heart. Leaving the church is the forever kind of goodbye for a believer. The only thing to cling to is that loved ones will see the light and will be rebaptized and re-enter into the fold.

Sue comes over to help me pack up the trailer from our little apartment in my father-in-law's basement. As I'm saying goodbye to Susie, we both hold on extra long. My optimism insists it will be only a short time before she too will need to get out of this imploding cloud of darkness.

But Sue's husband is as different from mine as possible: Ben is a very strict and devout man of the church.

When we hug our last long tearful squeeze, I thank her for keeping me alive this long year, for loving my babies and for being my refuge from this caving-in, suffocating world. I think I understand what she means then, but I don't. She says softly through her tears, "You can't leave me. You are the only one who knows how I feel."

I could not imagine the cruel separation the future has in store for us. If I could have known, I would have never let go of her. Instead, I do.

❧

I leave Colorado City with my babies and head back to Canada. Sam stays behind to work. I wonder about our future. Many women have left their husbands who do not follow Warren Jeffs. When I told Father I was moving home, he told me to honour my marriage covenant. I love my husband and we are proud of the little family we have created, but this time leaving feels different. I don't know what the future holds.

I move in with my mother, not really sure what to do next. Always a sensible woman, Mom brings me home the GED preparation book and I book a test date for August.

I look at the two perfect people I have brought into the world: nothing is more important to me than building a world worthy of them. I want them to spend their afternoons chasing minnows in the creek and riding bicycles and ponies with their cousins. I want for us to grow delicious food together in a big family garden, swim in fresh clean rivers and lakes, camp and hike, dance and take piano lessons. I want them to pray and sing "Jesus Loves the Little Children" and "Love Your Neighbour" in Sunday school, and I never want them to hear about destructions and hellfire and people burning off the face of the earth.

Back home, it feels as if I'm seeing the Creston Valley for the first time, the towering beauty of the Skimmerhorn mountains where shale slides climb steeply from the rocky, treed foothills. They support the rugged cliff faces, which thrust to the sky in impressive columns. From the Devil's Chair protrude two adjacent pillars to create a throne for the gods.

Water seeps into the weathered lines to cleave away rocks from the ever-changing face of this sentinel that has always felt like a guardian watching over my family home. Determined roots and lichens cling to this supporting structure, home to the sure-of-foot bighorn sheep and small critters that seek refuge here.

Each day I notice the light as it passes across this graceful silhouette, the pink of the morning rising to kiss its gentle curves. Each morning, the light casts this beauty centre stage and worships its texture and grace.

As the slanting light turns to amber each evening, this monument is covered in a blush that plays on the smooth surfaces and reveals another kind of beauty. The seasons change the costume; clouds reveal the moods. I watch the dance and the changing expressions across this tantalizing face.

I am home.

❧

Barely a month later, unexpectedly, my husband shows up at Mother's house. He has decided he too no longer feels Warren Jeffs carries the inspiration of God. "And," he says, "I called Jake and he gave me a job."

I dress my babies each Sunday and coax my husband to sit with me at my father's Sunday school meetings. This morning I watch as my Starla runs screeching to hug her little cousins. The three of them in curls and ruffles look as fresh as smiling daisies after a summer rain. My father directs church gatherings and community socials. Our toddlers get up to sing "Jesus Once Was a Little Child" with the children's primary group at church. I'm thankful for the terrible twos, ponies and cousins.

Beneath the vitality of community life there is an ache that is almost visible. The Split has left deep wounds that will be slow to heal. But I feel lucky to be here with my family and community. I feel hopeful that we can work together with the other survivors of the Great Destruction to piece our community back together for our children to grow up in. We will support each other and grow together to serve God, build community and raise our children.

Sam and I buy a small house together in Cranbrook, closer to his work. When our kids are older we will move home so they can stay connected to family and enjoy community life.

I feel so lucky to have this second chance at life. I am certain that Jesus Christ, the Prince of Peace who stood for love and hope, does not want my children to live in the fear and darkness of the world Warren Jeffs is creating. Though not on a burning cloud, I feel that God has indeed lifted me up from the Great Destruction.

FEMINIST AND POLYGAMIST

In August 2004, I participate in a community meeting to discuss and make a plan to build up our school to support the educational needs of our children. When our school split, each half of the community ended up with half enough teachers and barely enough to limp forward with elementary school up to grade six. The rest of the kids did the Homelinks program with different parents helping them focus to get through their studies.

I've just got my class two driver's licence to drive our school bus, so I could borrow it to take loads of kids to the lake and to the skating rink. Dad tells me he wants me to help out at the school for the year and drive his kids back and forth each day. I ponder with my husband for a few days. Kayden is a year and a half and if helping to rebuild our school is going to be my calling, I want to get on it so my children can enjoy going to that school with their cousins. I tell Dad I feel we don't need more helpers; we need more trained teachers. I tell him my decision to start college in the fall. He is thrilled.

Mother Ruth, Mother Elise and Treena are all attending college to get their bachelors of education. In September, I join them in their second year and Millie starts taking classes for her grade-twelve upgrade. We are an elaborate collage of child-care exchange and carpooling as we figure out our class schedules, homework and family time. Our kids have the sweet life of cousins and our three little girls Starla, Stella and Jenna spend almost every day together for a few years. The students and faculty of College of the Rockies in Cranbrook become quite familiar with our oddities around campus with our long skirts and braided hair. We soon develop a group of eclectic friends. Mother Ruth has a quick wit and humour that takes people off guard and challenges their stereotypes. She laughs easily at herself and others and people are drawn to her. As soon as anyone meets Ruth and her sister-wife Elise, they usually say, "Well, there goes the assumption the media makes that these women are only in college because the men have sent them. I don't think anyone could send Ruth anywhere she didn't want to go."

※

So begins my foray into the world of education and becoming a career woman. Sam and I have been married for four years now. I take extra effort to ensure I never falter as a Mormon wife and mother and that my family life won't be the cost of my education. I eagerly embark on this journey.

I'm religious and conservative by nature or at least by my upbringing. I'm observant and in new situations I try to learn the rules to make the best decisions as they come up. During my first semester of college, I live in excited but nervous anticipation that somehow I'll be found out as an imposter. I sit in the front of the classroom and ask my teachers careful questions when I don't understand material. I take advantage of extra access to my instructors and tutors and ask peers to proofread. I do all the readings and extra readings and come highly prepared for exams. I learn quickly that most peer study groups are just for hanging out and gossip. I carefully isolate myself to a back corner of the library to avoid interruptions from chatty friends. I decline invitations to coffee and drink socials. School ends and parenting begins when I pick my children up at 6:00 p.m. Whenever possible, weekends are for my family. When I get a perfect mark in my first semester, I learn where I can relax a bit settling into college life.

Without strict rules from the church to govern our every decision, we all must figure out the edges for ourselves. I still feel a strong commitment and loyalty to my Mormon heritage and the teachings of Jesus Christ and want this wholesome family life for my own children to grow up in. Dad says that the teachings of Christ are so simple that a child can understand them, so it seems that religion has complicated a whole lot of it. I'm on a journey to clarify my own values with Mormon teachings, and just as with Warren Jeffs's teachings, there are quite a few that don't make much sense to me. I've decided to ask myself, Is this custom or value about religion? Is this what God has said we should do? Or is it about tradition, just the way we've always done it? Those, I've decided, are fair game for change. Wearing long, loosely fitted dresses just because my grandmothers did isn't a good enough argument for me. Did God tell me to wear a dress? I ask.

My upbringing included plenty of warnings about the evils of alcohol. My grandfather Ray Blackmore was as staunch a Mormon as ever lived. He said never in his life had alcohol touched his lips. On the other hand, Sam said his father and grandfather enjoyed beer on family camping trips and such. He said it was never a big deal to him, but I hated it when he drank as it went against the moral principles I was raised with. He reasoned good-naturedly that Jesus drank wine, and maybe the Mormon rules against coffee and alcohol didn't make much sense in terms of one's ability to be a good person. Determined not to be a prude, I finally decide to try some of his beer and see what drinking alcohol is all about. So at twenty-three I drink my first beer.

It isn't until my second year of college that I begin developing my own college social life. I join the ladies' hockey team, the Kootenay Wildcats. We travel out of town a couple of times to hockey tournaments and I have my first experiences winning gold in a team sport, bar hopping, drinking beers and the glorious good fun of dancing the night away to live music with a dozen hockey gals.

🕉

From 2004 to 2007 the media insists that the government isn't doing enough to rid Canada of its "dirty little secret," polygamy. The Bountiful Women's Society, a group led by community matriarchs including my vocal aunts and mothers, works hard to interface with the media and public to dispel accusations that women in the group are held against their will or are forced to marry and don't have a voice.

Our Bountiful Women's Society group is invited by the advocacy organization Beyond Borders to its international conference in Winnipeg in February 2005. A discussion about Bountiful and polygamy are on the agenda. A group of fifteen of us women make the journey to Winnipeg to speak on behalf of the women in our community. Aunt Sue describes herself as a self-proclaimed happily married independent fundamentalist Mormon—a polygamist who doesn't belong to a particular faction but follows the teachings of Joseph Smith. She gives a presentation about her home and married life, her children and her values. Overall, we are well received at the conference, making meaningful personal connections with various women from the organization over the two days. They are surprised and impressed to meet us and learn that there are groups of polygamists who do not follow the doomsday regimen of Warren Jeffs.

Later the next fall, the Bountiful Women's Society hosts a polygamy summit. They invite the press, service professionals and the interested public to come meet women of Bountiful and hear them share stories of their lives and values. These women open their homes and hearts, sharing about growing up in large families, co-parenting with sister-wives and the joys and challenges of living this seemingly strange style of collaborative patriarchal family structure from the women's perspective. The message is stated clearly to the crowded room of cameras and scribbling reporters that these women see their lifestyle as a legitimate choice to raise their families.

Living so openly is the kind of hard work that at first bonds people as they rally together. But then it becomes exhausting, personally and spiritually. The many hours of preparing, organizing, speaking, interviewing, welcoming people into homes, feeding, feeding and feeding, talking and talking, repeating over and over: "We are here, we are Canadians, we are alive and we are not going away. We choose to be here. This is our family. We love our family and we don't need to be saved: we just deserve to be here."

For all the effort it takes, we feel it mostly falls unheeded.

Most media groups cover the summit in similar ways, belittling the value, efforts and innovation of the women to advocate for their families and lifestyle. The headlines and articles that get written over and over take the same spin: "Under the directive of the male leadership, the women of Bountiful community speak out."

✺

Banding together to open our story to the outside world is a strengthening force of sorts for a season. It is now our normal to have a television crew show up every six months to get a sensational clip of this or that to be twisted for some voyeuristic news article. "Who made the front page this time?" we ask in sarcastic excitement each time Bountiful makes the headlines. The pictures are usually of a pregnant and frazzled mother wrestling a toddler while trying to load her groceries or on her way to a doctor's appointment. My cousin's wife looks particularly young and doesn't wear makeup. She's in her third pregnancy in her mid-twenties. She's already made the front page several times as a "teen mom."

"Oh goodness, I hate this," she says, folding the paper laid out in front of us. "It's so embarrassing. I look like a child."

In our community as well as in Colorado City, the Warren Jeffs group move to further distinguish themselves from those who have not followed him. In a matter of a week, tall privacy fences have been pounded up along property lines. Carefully made signs hang above each door that say "Zion" in painted lettering. The dress styles and fabrics have become plainer and more conservative. The women's hair is more quaffed, into fantastic puffed architecture rising off their foreheads with perfect braids and feathered scoops.

For a season it seems that all conversations at church gatherings are tearful retellings of how a sister or mother walked right past in the grocery store or looked the other way when a family member tried to talk to her. We all learn first-hand what a cruel weapon shunning is. I can see why many church societies historically have used it as a weapon to inspire conformity and discourage dissonance.

We follow rumours that the Warren Jeffs group are building massive compounds across the western states. Their cohesion and productivity are impressive. For the rest of us, our sense of community is unravelling in bickering and blame as people struggle with creating a new paradigm for raising children, consuming alcohol and working together. Watching them makes us long for the old days. Mother and I continue to call Susie a few times a week. She answers the phone and we talk about her gardens and her children and she tells us over and over how blessed she is to be following the Prophet.

Then one day when Mother calls, an unfamiliar woman's voice answers the phone. She says she has just moved into the house and she doesn't know a Susie. Mother immediately calls Susie's mother-in-law, who confirms in a sweet voice, "Oh, I think Susie moved. No, I don't know where they went." Families have been moving in the dead of night without leaving a note or a trace as to where they went. They've been called on a secret mission and are doing God's work so others are just happy for them that they have received their calling to go to Zion and never ask questions. We see a real aerial photo of the Yearning for Zion Ranch in Texas and worry about the ever more constricting secrecy that has swallowed our friends and family in these last short years.

In our community, many families try to reconnect with family values from before the preparations for the millennium. We return to calling our father "Dad" and he reminds us that the sacred undergarments were intended to be part of the marriage covenant and were not required for children to wear. But as the daughters cut their hair, pierce their ears and give up skirts to squeeze into low-rise jeans, parents struggle to create boundaries and guidelines for their children. A few families decide they are done with religion altogether.

⁑

There isn't one day of my classes that I take for granted. I know how hard women in history have fought for the right to get an education and it is a right I treasure. My mother's journey for her education and career was hard earned. Studies were never easy for her and witnessing her stress and tears imprinted on me the value of getting an education. As long as I can remember, my mother was taking this course or that course. She sat at the kitchen table, massaging her temples with her fingers as if sheer determination would will her headache away and replace it with the information in her textbook. I admired her work ethic. I still do.

I remember a few times Grandma Mem commenting that the singer and actress Cher was her same age. She included remarks about Cher being an ungodly feminist and being one of the bra-burning hippies of the sixties and the radical feminists of the seventies, but I think she held some esteem for this powerful woman. I also have an idea that Grandma Mem is a feminist too, even if she would never have called herself one. She worked all her life supporting education and helping women to better themselves and their lives. I've decided my husband, brothers and father are also feminists because they support their wives getting an education. Even in the early days of the church, Brigham Young understood the value of women getting an education. "You educate a man; you educate a man. You educate a woman; you educate a generation," he is noted for saying. Grandpa Oler taught music and mechanics and shared his love for theatre in our little community school. He told us often, "God reminds us that we are saved only as fast as we gain knowledge." His sons and daughters studied many different trades and careers and he was particularly proud that so many of his daughters got a college education. Since I first heard about feminists from Grandma Mem, and now as I study the feminist movement in my sociology class, there is no doubt in my mind that I am a feminist.

"How can you be both?" Tia, a new friend in my sociology class, asks me in genuine curiosity. We are discussing movements and labels and opposing ideologies. "Like really, how can you be a Christian and believe in the big bang theory and evolution?" she challenges me playfully.

I'm only half joking when I tell her what I've determined is my new personal label. "If I must be called something," I muse, "if I must describe myself with a label, I will be a radical optimist fundamentalist feminist Mormon." I enjoy the paradox of it almost as much as I enjoy the benefit of living in seemingly opposing worlds. Going to college, new friends, learning and intellectual debate wake up unknown parts of my mind and I feel alive with curiosity. I feel supported in both worlds as my journey to become a teacher is praised and supported by my husband, father and community.

"I feel I've got a solid argument for Christianity and science," I continue through her skepticism. "The theory of evolution simply states that species change over time, and there is plenty of evidence that this is true. Humans coming from a piece of slime that happened to grow legs is as big a leap of faith as is that God created the heavens and the earth in seven days."

To me this argument is simple and rational, using the gaps in each narrative as evidence for the other. I don't feel that one proves or disproves the other. They are both simply trying to tell the same story with different pieces of the puzzle. I love my astronomy classes and the teachings of Christ. I feel the same way about being a feminist and a fundamentalist Mormon.

Lightheartedly I dismiss warnings about feminists not making good wives, or feminists not liking men, or feminists hating polygamy or the priesthood. I feel certain these statements describe an older style of feminist. I am indeed a feminist. And if Grandma Mem could follow the priesthood and be a feminist, then so can I.

Despite my enthusiasm to join the ranks of the noble cause of women fighting for women, I find it perplexing to be emerging onto the feminist scene but then be getting the message that somehow I'm not the right kind of feminist.

My sociology teacher is, I suppose, trying to challenge me to look more deeply into the opportunities provided to women through the work of feminists. Education, she points out, is a predominantly female profession and has always fallen into traditionally accepted careers for women. I can't really call myself a feminist for choosing to become a teacher. I'm not trying to crack any glass ceilings and there isn't anything radical about my dream to move home to improve education within my family and community. My plan to build a home on family property, teach school, raise my family and teach my children the values of education, growing food and community might not be a radical one.

⚬

In Creston, an anti-polygamy group, Altering Destinies Through Education, states that its mandate is to help women from polygamist families overcome barriers to education. The chair of this group befriends my mother. Mom suggests I go ask them for funds to help support my pursuit of a bachelor's degree in education, since the costs for transportation and child care are piling up.

A month later, I'm invited by these ladies to travel with them to attend a University Women's Club meeting where they have applied for funding for their program. They've asked me to do a small presentation about my journey to get an education. Miriam is also taking university classes and has agreed to join me. We all carpool to the meeting in Cranbrook on a snowy December night. The ladies give us a binder to use in our presentation with some ten-year-old newspaper clippings they want us to talk about at the meeting. We are shocked and horrified that they expect us to stand up at this meeting and repeat outdated media stereotypes to perpetuate an image of ourselves as being mindless puppets of a religious patriarchy.

In Cranbrook we are welcomed into the festively decorated home of a doctor. Mir and I talk easily over our tea and cookies. They ask us about our lives, our goals, our education and our families. Later we are informed by Altering Destinies Through Education members that their money is for women who are leaving Bountiful and polygamy, and therefore I don't qualify for any of their financial assistance.

✒

The following spring, a local government organization that accesses resources as a safety net for women in the Creston Valley reaches out to some of the professional women in the Bountiful community. They invite four of us to an information session to learn about some of the services they have to offer. Some of their funding is running out and they need to do some outreach to qualify for more. They receive additional funding if they offer programs to the vulnerable women of the Bountiful community.

They take us through their programs and we are all surprised that so many services exist, including support for child care, transportation, education and relocation. Mir and I both have young children and continually more costs. We book appointments to see if there are any of these services we can access.

The women in the office are professional and friendly and the questionnaires are long and personal. At the end of the several-hours-long interview process, the woman who sits down with me explains in very plain terms that the services at her organization are for victims of polygamy. She asks me slowly and clearly if I identify as being abused in any of the obvious or not so obvious ways she has covered in the last several hours.

I tell her I do not, but that I have two small children and am finding the financial barriers quite challenging.

I leave her office feeling frustrated. I spent two afternoons of my life so somebody could check off some boxes on a grant application form. I wonder what the women look like who do qualify for services. Do they have dirty, tattered dresses and matted ratty hair as they escape into the night?

For the first time I think about this word, *victim*, and what it means to require someone to identify herself this way. I wonder if these women have ever considered what they are asking me to trade for their help.

I use my determination and creativity to find solutions. I pay for my university, dignity intact.

❧

In college I develop a thick skin and a sassy, argumentative persona. People are surprised to find I am from a polygamist community. Most people I meet are curious and kind, but those who are not always make a bigger impression. One day I meet two men who are of the latter kind. It is a late afternoon in the college library. Staying late is a luxury I don't allow myself often as I have babies to care for at home. Fortunately my mother comes to my rescue to get my kids to bed when I need a few extra hours and have a big paper due the next day. This is one of those nights.

Two young men loudly debate the only practical solution to deal with polygamists. "Someone should just take that Winston Blackmore, cut off his balls and throw him into jail. I don't know why the government hasn't dealt with those rapists yet anyway," says one.

While I try to keep my eyes on the computer, my blood is boiling. I interject into their conversation, catching them off guard. They start backpedalling when they learn it is my father they are suggesting should be castrated and incarcerated. We have a curiosity-driven conversation. They apologize when they acknowledge that we are talking about real people, and that perhaps polygamy and rape are not the same things.

After I walk away from those two young men having spoken my mind, I feel validated but upset. I find it hard to build a life and feel safe in a world where an irresponsible media is depicting my family as abusive and grotesque. It is unsettling that complete strangers speak as violently as self-proclaimed vigilantes without asking questions or confirming their information. It was hard for my father to speak against the church and split with Warren Jeffs, and every day my family struggle with their loss and grief and what it has meant to lose contact with close loved ones. My father is a good man and my community is made of strong, good people. I still have questions about why Mom divorced Dad but I also know balancing her life in the service of women and the church has not been easy. I know that living with my faith and with my blossoming commitment to feminism is not straightforward.

When I arrive home, my children are already in their beds and Mother is reading them a bedtime story in the little nursery off the kitchen. She kisses them both quickly and I take her spot as she hugs me and heads out the door. My heart is full. I feel constantly lucky to have a husband who supports my education and my independence at college. I don't have any doubts that I am where I should be, for myself, for my family and for God's will.

FEMINIST FIRE

When Starla is six and Kayden is four, I transfer from College of the Rockies and complete my bachelor of education degree at Southern Utah University, only an hour away from the stunning red cliffs of Zion National Park. I enjoy my studies in Utah and every spare minute I spend exploring the cracks and canyons of the red mountains. After my first summer of classes, I rarely wear skirts to school and enjoy dressing the same as the other Mormon moms in my classes.

One day my art history professor comments that the production of *The Vagina Monologues* by Eve Ensler has caused quite a stir and was protested when it toured through Utah, particularly at SUU. Living in Mormon Town, Utah, is giving me an opportunity to notice my own European-Christian-centric values compared with the diversity and broader world view I experienced at my college in Canada. My teacher is careful to avoid judgment as he shares thoughts on cautioning any culture that finds itself wanting to censor art. He is a petite man of careful, beautiful language and asks thoughtful and provoking questions. His comment about the value of understanding the experience of women compels me to head straight to the library to get the book.

Each night after I tuck my babies into bed, I read by the light of a dim lamp. My heart bleeds for women, our secret fears and pain and the confusing longing and betrayal of our sexuality.

Eve Ensler's words echo in my mind: "When you rape, beat, maim, mutilate, burn, bury, and terrorize women, you destroy the essential life energy on the planet." I stare at the ceiling. My six-year-old daughter is stretched out between her brother and me. I watch as her little toes find warmth under my leg and notice her silky straight blond hair like feathers over the pillow.

Tonight my mind goes to my aunt Debbie. This last summer, when I was home during my break, she gave me a copy of her book, *Keep Sweet: Children of Polygamy*. I read it, putting it down often, until I just couldn't stand it. Aunt Debbie talks about the great Old Barn as a place of terror where dark and disturbing things happened to children. Her story has the same imagery as my childhood but is filled with yelling and beating and unspeakable horrors. On her visits, she talks a lot about sexual abuse.

She talks about violence. At times she seems obsessed with it. She asked each sister and niece if any of us had been sexually abused. She said she learned in her training that people will often block out those experiences but will still show characteristics of sexual abuse. Most of us, she said, show signs of being sexually abused.

Eve Ensler reminds us that it is important to listen to women's stories the way they choose to tell them. When I hear the voices of *The Vagina Monologues*, I feel that fire the feminists are talking about. As long as there are women who aren't safe, feminists have work to do.

❧

We haven't had contact with Susie for a couple of years now. I often think of Susie and that final hug we shared before I left. Mom presses forward and files a missing persons report across the United States and files for grandparent visitation rights for Susie's children. "I just need to know they are safe and have what they need," she says. There have been rumours of Susie being seen in various locations, but that's it.

In August we are surprised to see news reports and photos confirming that "the worldwide manhunt for fugitive polygamist leader Warren Jeffs ended when the self-proclaimed prophet was arrested. ... Jeffs, who was on the FBI's 10 Most Wanted list, ... is wanted in Utah and Arizona for alleged involvement in underage marriages, rape and sexual assault" ("Polygamist Sect Leader Captured in Traffic Stop," *Los Angeles Times*, August 30, 2006). We can't imagine what this could mean for family members following the church. There are still many people, even those out of the church, who feel the cohesion of Warren Jeffs's church is evidence of a righteous path and still many others who testify of his holiness but feel too weak or unworthy to follow his teachings.

In 2007, a relative puts Mom in contact with Jon Krakauer, a writer who recently published a book about fanatical fundamentalist Mormon sects in North America. His book *Under the Banner of Heaven* documents violent crimes committed under religious pretense by radicalized Mormon followers. Mr. Krakauer offers to help my mother find my sister. They are able to confirm through the sheriff's office in Custer, South Dakota, that Susie's husband, Ben, is indeed the spokesperson for the fundamentalist Mormon compound being built near the Black Hills. With help from the sheriff and Mr. Krakauer, Mom is able to get Ben's phone number. He agrees to a meeting to appease the conditions of her visitation rights.

Excited and eager, eight siblings and four nieces and nephews load into Dad's fifteen-passenger van with our mother and drive eighteen hours across state lines to see Sue. My mother had planned to meet Sue, Ben and the children at the park but as we get closer, Ben refuses to take our phone calls. She decides we're going to just head out to the compound. When we arrive, the gates are open and the watchtower overlooking the brushy hillside stands empty. "Let's just go in," I convince Hyrum, who is driving. We stop fifty feet inside the gate and have only a minute to wait before boys and men show up on four-wheelers. They all have longer hair and ball caps with dark sunglasses. Hyrum, Mother and I get out of the van and walk over to talk to the men. They stick to robotic responses, asking us politely to leave as they have called the sheriff to remove us from the property. I immediately recognize my husband's cousin Tom, who was married to my friend Holly from Colorado City. I start peppering him with questions about his wife and kids and asking him where my sister is. He keeps his expressions placid.

Our mother begins reasoning with these men in their silly disguises. She worked with the midwives to deliver many of their children and has known all of their families for years. "I just want to see my daughter," she says firmly. "I know Susie is here. I'll just wait right here until she comes out to see me. If you want me to leave, just ask her to hurry."

The radios they each carry beep and blurp and a voice from the tower says he can see the sheriff's truck approaching. This makes Mother begin to start frantically knocking door to door and yelling out Susie's name. It's heartbreaking watching her. Starla and Kayden climb out of the van. My six-year-old daughter is looking nervously at her older second cousin on the four-wheeler, and my four-year-old son runs up and down the dirt piles. We can hear the sheriff's truck on the dirt road. Tom says to me, "Please excuse me for this." He pulls off his hat and removes his wig, looking a little smug. Hyrum and I roll our eyes at him. We are angry and disappointed when the sheriff makes us leave their private property. Mother starts to cry. For a minute we stand and look at each other. Only four years before, we had been working side by side. We understand their conviction to serve their Prophet and God, but why can't they let the poor woman see her daughter? Why can't we just see our sister?

✒

At the end of the fall term, just before we move back to Canada and our daughters will transfer to our little school at home, Mom has organized for Peter and me to take our families on a cruise to Mexico with her and Brittany. Millie and I drive with our kids to meet them and go on our first-ever family vacation. Stella and Starla are in best-friend heaven and four-year-old Kayden weighs down his pants with more rocks and seashells than he can carry. It turns out our families make really great tourists and Sam and I determine to make family holidays a priority.

On our drive home, Mir's little sister Linda, who is five years younger than me, catches a ride home with us. She's just finished nursing college and we are both moving home. Linda and I never stop talking and laughing all the way to Canada and from then on we are close companions. I'm reminded of Grams saying that if ever a woman loved another woman, she had loved Grandma Aloha. Sam and I have a conversation one night about him taking a second wife. We both think Linda is great. I feel certain if ever there was a woman I would share my life and husband with, it is Linda.

I've run a four-year sprint doing classes in fall, winter, spring and summer semesters, and some online, to get here. Finally being settled, with my kids in school with their little cousins, feels reassuring somehow. We settle into a routine of classes and after-school lessons.

One afternoon in April, I get a text message from Sam. "Did you hear about the Texas raid?" I turn on my computer and connect it to the internet. I cannot believe the horrifying scenes in front of me: a full-scale US military invasion of the Yearning for Zion Ranch in Texas. We've heard they've been building something but I couldn't have imagined the scale of this operation somehow engineered and built in the last five years. In front of me I watch law enforcement officers armed with automatic weapons and SWAT teams with snipers descending from armoured helicopters accompanied by armoured personnel carriers, set on a backdrop of a gleaming white temple and log structures made from the lathed logs that I knew my cousins had made here in Canada. They are responding to a local domestic call that was made by a female who identified herself as "Sarah," claiming to be a sixteen-year-old victim of physical and sexual abuse at the ranch.

It looks just as I imagined the Short Creek raid did in 1953. Small children are loaded on large buses and screaming babies are taken out of their mothers' arms by strangers. Eventually a total of 462 children are taken by Child Protective Services at Fort Concho. Over a hundred adult women choose to leave the ranch to accompany the children.

I've just finished making dinner and mixing a batch of bread when

Sam gets home from work, so I drive over to find my mother. At her kitchen table we watch the videos online together, looking for Susie's face among the women, hopeful we won't see her. The last we knew, she was in South Dakota, so that is reassuring. As I watch the scared, familiar faces of pregnant young mothers in their long pastel prairie dresses, my guts turn and my heart aches. This so easily could have been me. I think of my little tender-hearted, blue-eyed boy. I can't imagine him going through something like this. Some kids would just never recover from that. I cling to my mother and cry. "Maybe I can help them," I tell her. "Do you think I should go down there? Maybe there is something I can do?"

The mothers with the nearly five hundred children in state custody write letters to the governor of Texas and one father writes a letter to President George W. Bush. Mental health workers at Fort Concho support their claims about children being subjected to demoralizing interrogation sessions and invasive physical examinations. Girls are asked to do pregnancy tests and complete body X-rays. Women staying at the Fort Concho shelter tell the press that the temporary housing is very crowded and that the children are frightened. They say it is like being in an internment camp. I watch the television with nervous anticipation. Several of the mothers from the Yearning for Zion Ranch go on *Larry King Live*, telling of their horrifying experiences and asking for help to get their children back. They show camera crews through their living accommodations at the ranch, begging to have their children come back home.

They decline to discuss the allegations of abuse. Their awkward rigidness and the controlled sweetness in their voices, as well as their matching head-to-toe, loose-fitting clothing and unusually sculpted hairstyles, do nothing to appease the concerned public that these women could keep their children safe from a church leader perpetrator. The 911 call ends up being a hoax and the woman responsible is later arrested and charged with several offences. The community feels they are victims of religious persecution. I can see why they feel this way. From what I could see, it didn't look like they were wrong either. I know these women and how they think, or at least I used to. But listening to them say they have choice—I now disagree with this pretty strongly. If you have two choices and one is family and heaven and the other is loneliness and hell for eternity, those are not choices. But it's hard to see how this justified a military SWAT operation and forceful removal of children. I would argue most of low-income America have very little choice in their lives. We are born into a culture, mindset, socio-economic status and location, and mostly we live our lives and don't move out of it much. I do agree when they say this experience is traumatizing their children and they are worried about the long-term effects of it. Prisons are filled with adults who came through the foster system. I just think that when you take away someone's right to parent their children, and children's rights to their parents, you should be good and sure you can give them something better.

DAD'S ARREST

The following September, I'm home doing my practicum, following the dress code at Mormon Hills School. I look cute and feminine in my plucky floral skirts and I enjoy the fervour of being a fresh university student eager to make a difference in the world. Weekends I spend with my husband, wearing jeans, doing house renovations and getting ready to sell our house in Cranbrook. Our children are now seven and five. They are both enjoying their first season of minor hockey. Sam stills works in forestry as a machine operator. The fall passes in a lovely flurry of family and career life. Winter arrives.

꘎

Today I arrive at school on time and wait for the delayed school bus. It's January and a foot of snow fell overnight. School has been delayed to 10:00 a.m. because the school bus can't get out of Uncle Guy's driveway in Kitchener. Dad has just finished breakfast with his kids at his house, which includes flipping pancakes and frying no fewer than six dozen eggs for the forty or so kids who get up in time to eat a hearty breakfast before school. I spend the first hours of the morning marking papers, enjoying the warmth and quiet of my classroom. My brother plows the schoolyard with the orange Kubota tractor. I let my mind wander, imagining the thrill of floating down a mountain slope on my snowboard in this fresh powder.

At ten o'clock, kids start to pour into my classroom, their eyes big and their voices excited and frantic.

"They arrested Dad and took him to jail. They shoved him into the back seat of the cop car."

The teenagers tell me their animated versions of the story after the little ones go to their own classroom. My brothers and sisters will not be getting much schoolwork done today.

In English class we discuss the Charter of Rights and Freedoms and read online articles that call for the government to deal with the issue of Bountiful. Then, taking advantage of a teaching moment and live passion, we start brainstorming our research into an essay outline on the green chalkboard. Our thesis: why enforcing Judeo-Christian marriage law in a multicultural country like Canada is unconstitutional.

"This is Canada," I reassure them. "Nobody cares about polygamy, actually. The government just has to show that they are doing something to deal with polygamy because they have an archaic law they have to deal with. There is a lot of pressure on Canadian law enforcement after they raided the Warren Jeffs compound in Texas. They have to do something to ensure they are keeping people safe. Dad's arrest is a symbolic gesture to start a review process."

I try to reassure them and feel that what I'm saying must be mostly true. After all, this is Canada in 2009. Men can marry men; women can marry women. Poly families are becoming accepted. Lifelong monogamous marriage is more the exception than the norm—divorce rates are more than 50 percent. The idea that the government could prosecute polygamy in our current society seems bizarre if not laughable.

Two police cars had pulled into Dad's driveway that morning with lights but no sirens. They cuffed him in front of his children as they were leaving for school in the fresh snow, put him in the back seat of the car and took him to a jail cell in Cranbrook. Later in the evening, after they have processed his papers and taken his passport and my dad has posted bail, he is allowed to go home on restricted terms.

Dad is told later by a news team that they were tipped off that his arrest was happening that morning and would have been there to film the whole show had there not been an avalanche closure in Kootenay Pass on their commute from Vancouver.

The family's anxiety rises and ripples into the community. What will happen if Dad goes to jail? Some of the American mothers have their residency status based on expensive international study visa programs. Others have been denied access into Canada when their visas have expired or when their countless attempts at immigration have been denied for one reason or another. Without Dad having a passport, the family will be split up by the border. What about church and community life? Would this all be over now? Dad figures out most of the financial end of things for the school and runs the fence-post mill, which employs a few dozen people. If Dad ends up going to jail, what about the mothers? What about other polygamists? What will Canada decide to do with polygamists?

Dad and I disagree on where polygamy should fit in the legal system. He argues his right to live in polygamy is protected under religious freedom and he says his family and polygamy have always been about living his religion. He believes his family is connected to him through God and religion has everything to do with the fact that he lives and believes the way he does.

I, on the other hand, feel that decriminalizing polygamy is a human rights issue. I am adamant that criminalizing a family structure or relationship style puts vulnerable people within that demographic at risk as it makes them unlikely to seek services if needed.

⍟

Finally finished my practicum, I am ready for commencement and graduation with my bachelor of education, and I am awarded the distinction of valedictorian for the graduating class of 2009. I know that's a good thing but when I google what the distinction actually is, I am beyond honoured for being recommended by my professors.

The university makes a grand event of it. I am finishing my practicum in Canada, so I can't attend most of the associated hoopla. My picture is on the university website for a month and my husband and I are invited to a private dinner party at the university president's home. The new president of the LDS Church, Thomas S. Monson, is also a special guest.

The next day, ten thousand people gather to support the grads in the big T-Bird stadium. They leave my parents' names off my bio announcement and my father can't cross the border to see the first of his children to receive a university degree.

I want to be hopeful that we are close to being able to change the story.

The media coverage this year is incessant.

⍟

In the summer of 2009, *National Geographic* contacts my father to do a "fair" story. They have a reputation for being responsible storytellers. Dad gives them my number and tells me he is "assigning me this little project." For several months my husband, children and I are deeply involved with an eager crew of three who follow us around our lives for a week at a time, gathering our story.

Neil, Olivia and Michelle are fascinated that I have finished my degree and am moving home with my large extended family. According to everything the world has been told and believes about Bountiful, an educated woman should be getting as far away from this place as she can.

"Why are you returning with your children to build a house on the family property to teach school and have more children?"

I tell them that I've lived in various towns and cities in BC and in Utah. I've raised little kids worried about busy highways. I've experienced isolated parenting without much support of family and friends.

I talk to them about family and community and my idealism about growing up in a social environment where people know their neighbours and children play outside. A community school, I believe, can be a centralizing force that grounds people around common values. They follow Sam and me to look at the location for our new house and hike with us to swim in the river. They even come to film me setting up my classroom. They give us a camera to keep for a few months. They tell us to film our everyday lives and they will send us a digital copy for a family keepsake.

Over the six months, we share openly about our heartache of these last few years, about losing family through the division in the church. We share our own struggles to make big life decisions, and to grow together and support each other as husband and wife. Despite feeling that these people have become our friends, I start having distressing dreams of the humiliating way they will portray my family. I'm anxious and concerned that we've made a huge, irreversible mistake.

I sit the three of them down finally. I know these people have a job to do; they have to create something that will sell. In no uncertain terms, I tell them the conditions under which they can talk about my husband and me. We have worked hard to create this life for ourselves. I am a woman working to build a life and career. We know we aren't perfect but we aren't naive, simple, stupid or hypocrites.

In the end, they do a fair job with their story and I never hear from them again. I am still waiting for the family keepsake footage they were making for me.

Momma Bears

The next time Mother and I set up a meeting and drive to see Sue, we are successful. It's March 2010. She and Ben bring their children and a beautiful homemade feast to share with us at the park. Brittany, who is now seventeen, has decided to make the trek with us this time. She hasn't seen Sue in almost a decade, so with a van full of cousins, we make a trip of it and check out Mount Rushmore and the Black Hills.

Susie's little boys pull a cardboard box out of the back of the truck. They have a live chicken to play with at the park. The kids chase it and laugh as it hops and flaps around the playground. I've never thought of taking a chicken to the park but Sue says her youngest son thought it would be fun. He chases it up and down the slides and laughs hysterically as it flaps and squawks.

At the picnic table, Sue brings out coolers and boxes and lays out a spread of pulled pork from hogs she raised and butchered. She made the barbecue sauce herself with her applesauce and tomatoes sweetened with honey. All her breads, including the cinnamon rolls and the waffle cones, were made with her organic sprouted wheat and sweetened slightly with honey. She's made all of her cheese herself, she says, handing each of us a thick wedge of vacuum-sealed mozzarella to take home. She gives us bags of string cheese and cheese curd and buns and muffins to enjoy on our drive home.

"Oh, wow," I comment. "That block of cheese would cost twenty dollars at the grocery story."

"Oh, really?" she says. "I haven't been to a store in over four years. I have no idea what things cost anymore. We just order what we need through our storehouse."

Brittany was only five years old when Susie got married and hasn't seen her since she was about eight. Now, seeing Brittany grown up and walking with her arm around Susie is astounding. We've always told Brittany how similar she and Susie are in their mannerisms, the way they look and walk. Being the middle sister who adores them both, I've longed for this moment of completeness, having the three of us together with our mother.

Sue tells us she is home-schooling all of her five boys. Starla and Kayden play with their cousins. They are shy at first but quickly overcome the awkwardness when their grandma pulls balls and bats out of her car.

Out of a box of ice, Sue pulls out a pail of homemade ice cream and serves it on her waffle cones. When we can't eat one more bite and have tried to squeeze in more stories so the afternoon doesn't end, Sue and Ben say it is time to go. We snap photographs and hug goodbye, feeling the strange foreign worlds we will each return to. Sue does seem as though she is quite full and possibly content in her world of little boys chasing chickens and fresh wholesome food. Mom and I comment on this as we walk around Mount Rushmore and explore the Black Hills Caverns before getting back on the interstate to head home. "She seems pretty good," Mom says.

"Yeah," I acknowledge. "But she's a fierce momma bear. I think her stability will depend on whether her boys decide to stay in the religion. It'll all be fine if no one tries to mess with her kids."

CALLING CONTRADICTIONS

I suppose most daughters, as they grow up, must learn that their parents don't always know best and are, in fact, flawed humans just like everyone else. I find this lesson particularly hard when my father is either a very publicly respected or ruthlessly criticized man. Many people in the church consider my father a prophet; others see him as a wise counsellor. To the Warren Jeffs group he is the most wicked man on earth, and to the media he is a rapist and a pedophile. Knowing my father well and working closely with him, I've determined to create my own relationship and opinion of him. I don't doubt that my father is an inspired man, and mostly he is a pretty good dad. Up close and personal—and especially now that I'm an adult, a parent myself and a burgeoning feminist—I've struggled to separate his spiritual role from my dad's very human nature.

In truth, my father is like two men and the contradictions between them, as well as the way he deals with conflict, can make him a frustrating man to work with. One is an academic with progressive ideas and a creative mind, but the other is a crafty, self-made businessman. He rises early and works late and wants others to as well. He avoids conflict by simply not being present for it or by preaching a sermon or giving a history lesson about the old days.

It isn't until the spring of 2010 that Dad makes a decision that really makes me question the very basis of Mormonism. He decides to take another eighteen-year-old wife. It's been ten years since the Split. In the last couple of years, I've been working closely with my dad at the school. Although we don't always see eye to eye as I wrestle with making changes to school operations, I feel that, after so much time together, I really get him. But I'm not prepared for this.

Father has taken care in the years since the Split to teach his family the lessons that were taught by the old brethren about the correct way for families to enter into the sacred ordinance of plural marriage: a man should not take another wife without the consent of his wives. Five of Father's wives left during the events surrounding the Split; one of them came home, and no other women have married him. Most of the mothers say the family is big enough. They are in full swing raising a household overrun by teenagers and they feel they can barely take care of what they have.

But now young Adeline has told Dad she wants to marry him and he is going against his own teachings in marrying this woman even though some of our mothers are adamantly opposed to it. To everyone's surprise, they announce that they will marry just after Adeline's eighteenth birthday.

The whole situation is contentious. It's hard to watch the mothers struggle through their emotions and anger. Most of the older daughters and wives feel Dad is going directly against what he said was taught by the old brethren: a marriage union should include the consensus of the wives and the husband. All should give their blessing.

Several of the mothers go to Dad, voicing their questions, and they feel that he dismisses their concerns. The older daughters watch their mothers struggle with their unanswered concerns and decide they need some answers. They will go to Father to express their concerns. He tells them, "She is the one who wants to do it. Go talk to Adeline."

Instead, they come find me.

"You have to talk to Dad about this," they say. "He listens to you."

I think about it. I have been working with my father for a few years now and we do have a pretty open dialogue that most people don't have with him. I've felt comfortable seeking his counsel over the years when I have spiritual questions or moral conflicts. I feel it is a philosophical discussion I'm willing to have with him.

"Explain these contradictions for us, Father," I query. He tells me that when a girl is inspired to marry a man and she has kept herself pure and clean before God, then that man has a responsibility to marry her.

In my past experience with these talks, we deliberate and discuss and I take the information to mull over and see where it fits. But what he says now explicitly opposes what he told me when I'd asked about my own inspiration to marry just over ten years before. I wonder if he's caught himself in his own tangle of principles.

"Why did you tell me no when I told you whom I felt inspired to marry? What makes her inspiration so different from mine, Dad?" My argument is more rational than emotional. "When I was sixteen, I was pure and clean before God and I told you I was inspired to marry a young man, and you told me no, that God had different work for me to do, so you married me to Sam instead."

He listens, surprised, then smiles. "Your husband is a good guy. You are lucky you married him," he says.

"Yes, Father," I respond. "I am happy I married Sam, and Adeline will be happy in ten years if she doesn't marry you."

He's irritated at my jab and I don't care. After a pause, he says, "Go talk to her if you want to. She is the one pushing this, not me."

✈

I don't know Adeline. She's almost a year older than I was when I got married, so I try to put myself in her shoes. When she decided to marry Father, she was determined to win over the mothers. She went around to each of the moms' houses and told each one she would help them for a day. They all had different reactions. Some were welcoming, some reserved and some told her in no uncertain terms she was not welcome to marry their husband. I've got to give it to her: she's got guts.

It's just stopped raining and a group of the girls, most of them just younger than Adeline, decide it will be less uncomfortable for us to take her for a walk. Mother Marlina accompanies us—I assume to protect her if necessary. Some of the girls are pretty fired up. "What kind of seventeen-year-old could possibly think being married to our dad could be any fun?" they ask her, incredulous.

I try to steer the conversation into more neutral territory and appeal to her sense of reason. "If you are inspired to be in Dad's family," I ask her, "why don't you go get yourself some education so you can have a good job to immigrate to Canada and a useful way to contribute to the family and support yourself? If God has inspired that this is where you will be for time and all eternity, it will still be the right thing to do in two years. You'd be showing the mothers that you are committed to supporting yourself. I bet they would feel differently about you then."

It begins to rain lightly as our shadows extend in front of us and the ball of the streetlight is now at our backs. "You've seen polygamous families your whole life; we know none of this is going to be a surprise to you," I continue. "You know the reality of a big crazy family. You know all our mothers have to work to help support themselves. How will you do that if you can't get a job in Canada?"

My fourteen-year-old sister Sara asserts her two bits: "If one of our mothers leaves because you are so insistent on joining the family, we will always see you as the reason our mother isn't here anymore. There isn't one of us who would choose you over any of our mothers we already love."

I'm impressed that she is able to hold her own on this rainy walk with her future daughters. She presses forward as if what we've been saying has slid over her like rain off a duck's back. "I've prayed about this," she says. "I've prayed long and hard about this for four months and this is what I am going to do."

"Four months! Four months?" I blink, not even trying to hide the judgment in my voice. "I've thought longer about buying a new pair of shoes." I stare at her. Suddenly I realize just how young seventeen is, a simple sheltered child with no understanding beyond instant gratification, no thought or planning in this pivotal life decision. I think back to my marriage ten years ago and think about the developing brain. I had been sure I was ready for adulthood. Now I'm just angry at the adults in Adeline's life who I'm sure should be protecting her from making this decision. I'm angry at the church for creating the space and the mindset for this kind of thinking. And the group of us are pretty angry at our father for not standing up for our mothers and for going along with something that looks as if it will pull our family apart. To me, their upcoming marriage is an example of everything that is wrong with polygamy and the church.

✎

Adeline turns eighteen and they get married. Some say it is as much an act of defiance as it is conviction to live a sacred principle. One of our mothers leaves the family with five of her children and moves to the United States with her new husband.

The family feels rattled. Hurt feelings come with ripples through the family, calling up questions about the values of the church and religion and leadership and Mormonism. I'm asking ever-deeper questions about what my own values are around this practice of plural marriages and even about what it means to be a Mormon. Watching my father's wives and daughters struggle with keeping their feelings and keeping the peace, I can see generations-old patterns of women suffering for the decisions of men.

One of the mothers says to me, "It wasn't that he was getting another wife that was upsetting. I already share my husband with many other women. I don't think him having one more wife is going to change our relationship. It was the way they went about it that really hurts."

Dad has married twenty-five women in the church, always under the directive of the Prophet. He says he had no more to say in those marriages than his brides did. They all believe fully that it was God's direction in their lives. The families they have created through their marriages, they all believe, are inspired and blessed by God.

This last season of God's blessings leaves these families all feeling as if they've just gone through a hurricane.

A Bird in a Popcorn Popper

I continue to fret about my dad's decision to marry Adeline. It prompts me to examine my feelings about Mormonism and my own marriage at seventeen. One top of this, fruitless months of trying to conceive are an extra worry for my husband and me.

The conflict in me runs much deeper. I want to have a baby. In the same frantic way I'm trying to meet the requirements for our school accreditation, I'm trying to conceive this longed-for pregnancy, but at the same time I'm noticing the almost subconscious fear about the loss of my identity and freedom that I connect with having a baby.

Finally, I sit down and ask myself, "What am I afraid of?" In my previous pregnancies, I was a young, uneducated, teenage, polygamist girl with no voice and no money. Now I have a bachelor of education degree. I have travelled in seven European countries, gone skydiving, received honours and distinction in my studies and been valedictorian of my university. That has to mean something! I have a car, money and a retirement plan. None of those things will change if I have a baby.

Sam and I are building a new house on the property in Bountiful, trying to sort out a balance for family life and work. We've worked our butts off for the last decade keeping up a mortgage, doing home renovations, going to university and raising kids. My husband works long hours as a machine operator in forestry and is mostly gone all week. I spend many nights alone with the children. In reality we've created separate lives.

The prospect of having another baby makes us look at our marriage. I want to see what it is like to have a partner to share it with. He talks about retraining or getting a local job. We talk about being home more with our children and doing things as a family. I bring home as much money as he does now and provide all the child care. I want him to be home more. I want a family life. He tries, does the extra driving, only to fall in bed exhausted. His work gets all of his best hours and on weekends he just wants to rest. By the end of my week teaching grade three, driving kids to lessons and coming home to have dinner with a seven-year-old and a nine-year-old, I feel like a bird that has been in a popcorn popper. We struggle to find things to do as a family that we both enjoy so we can imagine we have a life together. He works hard and the lifestyle of a machine operator takes a toll on his health and body. For me it starts to mean just more laundry, dishes and an extra lunch to make each day. We are both sure we want another baby and are trying to get pregnant. I feel like I've already raised two kids by myself. It would be great to share it with someone this time.

⚘

So far 2010 has been a rough year for Dad and me. Not only have we disagreed about his marriage to Adeline, but we've been butting heads in our organization of Mormon Hills School. I've scoured the guidelines for independent schools to learn policies and processes for accreditation. We've put our heads together planning and scheming how to build programs to meet government requirements. I've worked as vice-principal of Mormon Hills School and a full-time teacher, so most of my administration duties take me well into my after-school hours. As superintendent of the school, Dad has continued to make ambiguous decisions about things such as dress code, whether the students should or shouldn't dress up for Halloween or if we should take certain holidays off.

In June he comes to the school one day with an announcement that school will end three days early for some reason or other. The teachers and I have meticulously planned a big end-of-year hoopla but now we scramble to get everything done and do a shoddy, hurried job of it. I am furious.

The next Sunday it comes up and I call him on it. We hash it out in front of a couple of his wives. I tell him he had no right to come in and make those decisions because he doesn't work at the school. I tell him flatly that he can make suggestions to the staff and we will decide because we are the ones who do all of the work to make things happen.

I tell him it feels as if he doesn't value the work we do at the school. Getting kids to value school and their education needs to start with the parents. "This is too damn much work and our school is too important to our community for you to undermine what we are trying to do to make school engaging and meaningful," I tell him flatly.

My father harrumphs and waits, and then he gets up and leaves.

⚘

About a month later, we have another discussion about school. We disagree about something and then quite suddenly all the anger and frustration of the last few months comes out in a roar I've never witnessed from my father. For ten minutes he yells angry words at me. I do my best to yell back but I choke up and through my tears the best I can do is tell him I am putting in my two weeks' notice. I won't work for him.

"Good," he says. "You don't respect me. You don't value me. You directly defy me."

I am stunned, in shock. My family are tactfully passive-aggressive in conflict but fortunately there are so many of us that it's easy to avoid people we don't want to see. When we are angry at one another, we keep it locked inside and stew and fester for ages, years even, or until we forget about it. We don't yell it out and work it out. We do surprisingly well for the number and temperament of our family, but if it explodes, there is a slammed door three seconds later. Maybe this is a residual effect of the church-prescribed "keep sweet" teachings we were programmed with. Or maybe Blackmores have always been this way, though I can't imagine my seafaring great-grandfather bottling up his temper.

I fuel up my Pontiac Grand Prix and drop my children off at my mother's for the weekend. My father's words sear my brain as I replay them over in my thoughts.

A long road trip and a map are the only therapy I can think of. I think how little my father actually knows about me. How can he say that I have no respect for him and don't value him? Every decision in my life—from my marriage to my career—has been because I have honoured and respected my father.

People are easily replaced in his life, I fume. He doesn't need to take the time and effort to repair our relationship. He has sixty-seven daughters. There are plenty more where I came from. My anger burns with the tears that run down my face.

Father says every person is important in the sight of God. He stands up for the underdog and has spent his life serving families, taking care of widows and the elderly and bringing people into the faith. All my life he has had time for every struggling teenager whose parents were at their wits' end. Now he cannot see the value in the people who have spent their lives working by his side. Why can't he reach out to his own family? It hurts to watch my siblings struggle in their relationship with Dad. To Dad, obedience means love. How could these be the actions of an inspired man?

I'm walking by the ocean in Oregon when my cellphone rings. I'm happy to hear Jake's voice.

"Just come home," he says. "We all know Dad can be hard to deal with sometimes, but we need you. Come do it for us, and the kids. We appreciate you; the kids need you."

"Fine, I will come. But I'm not working for him. He doesn't care about people."

I am struggling in my marriage. I am struggling with religion and the rules. Truth is, I am struggling with life.

Just a few weeks after I get home from the coast, I stand in our small bathroom in the cabin. It's September and outside I can hear the sound of the wind gently blowing the fall leaves. I hold my breath as the little pink line creeps across the tiny window.

GOODBYE, GRAMS

I'm pregnant. I go to sleep with flutters of excitement, imagining what my future will hold.

The next morning I weep into the palm of my dying grandmother.

I really believed that Grams would pull through yet again. When my aunts call to tell me she's taken a turn for the worse, I leave my class and run over to her house. People have been in and out all morning. While others are saying their goodbyes, I am making a list of promises to God if he will just let her live a little longer.

I want to tell her about my baby. Selfishly, I want her to make my father and me be friends again.

Whatever the deal is with God, he is wherever Grams is. What used to be so clear to me is now all just so confusing. I have been so drawn into my own life that I have not organized her picture books as I had promised. She'd asked me to sew her a new dress.

She leaves us in the golden hours of that September morning. Her eyes hazy, she gasps for breath and I cling to her hand. My aunts are standing around her, touching her, caressing her, encouraging her. "Go be with Daddy now, Momma." For one last moment, she looks right at me and her eyes are clear and she knows I'm there. Then she goes back to the hard job of dying. She slips away into another land.

How many times has she asked, when I help her roll over at three in the morning to use the bedpan, "How do you die?" How she has struggled in the last five years, feeling trapped inside a body that will not do what it has always done.

The last years of her life's service were her most difficult. Her family provided her with twenty-four-hour care. We all worked together, patiently working though our differences, to ensure her needs were met. We came together in our love and care for her. I can't imagine what will happen without her.

I cling to her and weep bitterly.

I am betrayed by her death and the crumbling of a world that promised to support me. I rage internally at Susie, who has not seen our grandma in over nine years because she is living in a secretive religious compound in South Dakota. What one visit with Susie would have meant to Grandma.

I spent a full day and a night each week with my grandmother for a year. The last months especially, whenever she saw me, she would ask about Susie. "Where do you think Sue is?" she would ask for the millionth time. I know she loved me and appreciated what I did for her, but I could never be my patient older sister. Susie and Grandma had been so close before Susie's church-directed marriage had taken to her the US, and then her and her husband's obedience to Warren Jeffs took her even farther from us. It's already been so long since that lingering hug I shared with Sue. I shudder remembering that day in church at conference in Colorado City and the certainty I had that I needed to leave. Even then, it was so hard to leave Sue and so many others whom I loved, whose company had been so vital to me when I felt isolated and afraid in new motherhood and in my in-laws' home. In the few letters I have written over the years, which I have no idea if she received, I coaxed, pleaded and begged her to come. Just for one visit. It would have meant the world to Grams.

Now Grandma is dead. My sister doesn't come to the funeral.

Linda comes to help me gather pictures from everyone to put into a slide show for after the funeral. We walk into my grandma's house and some of my aunts—the ones who were in the Warren Jeffs religion and haven't even come to see Grandma or help with her care for years—have Grandma's big hope chest out in the middle of the room with the albums and journals spread out on the floor. They tear the pages out of the old wallpaper scrapbooks to give the pictures away. They each have a few of her journals. I want to scream at them to stop but I am held by lessons of my youth not to cross my matronly aunts. Sure, she was their mother, but she was everyone's grandma and no one is entitled to her stuff, least of all those who let their religion be a reason they barely spoke to or visited her in the last five years. We all shared her and no one has the right to tear apart and own her things. Her photo albums should be put into a special place where we all can have access to them. One of our greatest pastimes as children was looking through Grandma's books and reading her old journals. Now, her precious books lie around the room as shredded as her family. I gather up whatever is left and make a special place in the school library where everyone can access them.

With many people pitching in, I work through the funeral preparations. Her family was split in two by the conflict in the church. Some people talk of trying to do two funerals for her so both factions have an opportunity to pay their respects. She worried a lot about this in her last years. She would say, "Are they going to fight over me after I'm dead? If they can't come see me when I'm alive, they don't need to see me after I'm dead."

In an amazing collaboration, our family puts aside our differences for a day and everyone rallies together to prepare the unfinished hall for the biggest funeral any of us has ever known. Family members who had not spoken in nine years hug and cry together. I hug my father, wishing there were some way to fill the canyon between us.

The service avoids the topic of religion and focuses on Grandma's amazing life of service, selflessness and love. For one day we focus on what we have in common rather than our differences. It is Grandma's last gift and lesson to her family.

During the funeral, my aunt reads a letter Grams wrote to her daughters and granddaughters on how to be a good wife and mother:

> Memory has asked me to write. For some reason she thinks I'm a good homemaker. She wants this written for the girls. She loves you all very much, as if you were her own. Please don't disappoint her by thinking you are smarter than your father and mother. Respect them, help them, and please try to be a person with sense and self respect. I too am counting on you.
>
> How to be a homemaker, where should we begin? Have you picked up your coat? Gather up your boots and put them where they go. Keep your room nice and clean. Can you have your clothes in your drawers? Are you able and do you do your own washing? Can you mend your own clothes? If you can honestly say yes, you just might be able to be a good homemaker.
>
> You see, once you say, "I do," you are no longer one of the children the mothers need to raise. YOU are no longer a girl that your husband needs to raise. YOU need to look around you and see what needs to be done without being told.
>
> Whatever you do during the day, make certain that the toys, books, and everything is gathered up before your dear husband, the father of the house, comes home during the day. Don't let him come home to a mess. Even if you are living with his folks, clean up for him. Make it

special. He works hard; he doesn't deserve to come home to a mess. You, yourself, be home. Be ready to be a comfort and a help. What man wants his wife to be out for a walk with her girlfriends when he comes home?

Be careful about your door yard. Do not allow every living thing, or dead to be scattered about your yard. Be mindful of coats and shoes and socks and mitts, have a place for these things and they certainly must be under control. One woman didn't know where her spoons had gone, and on my way in I counted ten. Quilts, mind you, drug out in the dirt are soon garbage and pillows and rugs. Where should I go now ...?

As Grandma Mem reads on, my grandmother's words tear at me. I can hear her voice so clearly through this letter. It's as if her voice is embedded into my DNA, the fibre of my being. I can feel my innate determination to please her, to design my life in a careful and godly way. I can feel the commitment I made long before my marriage to be "a comfort and a help" to my husband, family and community. Her letter makes me want to be right, to do right, makes me feel frantic and helpless that I'm failing as a wife and daughter. I am stricken and angry at her passing and grieving my own crumbling world.

"Grandma," I want to weep into her coffin, "why did you make me like this? Why did you raise me to believe that my highest calling is to be a servant? Everyone needs something from me and I can't do it all. I'm making a mess of it and hurting the people I love the most."

From the depths of my grief, my mind diminishes my powerful, nurturing, wise and amazing grandmother to a simple, stupid, polygamist woman who knew nothing of equality and being liberated.

She was a victim of circumstance and her times, my mind reasons. If she had had the opportunities of being a modern woman, of travel, of education and a social life, she wouldn't have been stuck caring for a million people until she died in her chair. So many things she wanted to do were left undone because she spent her last good years baking bread and spending her money on lunch goodies for the boys, instead of travelling across Canada as she had always talked of doing.

Her biggest regret—my biggest regret—is that we never organized to take her across Canada before she had her stroke. She always wanted to drive across in the fall, but we waited a year too long.

Why, God?

It's October 2010. Starla is nine now, Kayden seven. School accreditation is in two weeks. I throw myself into a frenzy of work. It's the government inspection of our whole high school program. Several teachers' salaries hang in the balance. If we pass our high school program, my grade-twelve students will be the first class in our community to graduate from our school with BC's Dogwood Diploma since 1994. My formal schooling ended when I was in grade ten. I went directly into our community workforce for a year before I married at seventeen. I became a mother one month after my eighteenth birthday and my son was born before I was twenty. The world didn't end, as the religion had promised it would, and upgrading our education has been a challenge for most of us. I am resolved that if we are to have an independent school, it will have a government-certified high school.

Uncle Merrill and Uncle Rich were both principals with years of experience working with the Ministry of Education. They both tell me there is no way we will pass this inspection and we are crazy for trying. I think we are crazy not to try. I believe I know how to do it. Dad must believe me too. "Go for it," he encourages.

We pass. Together with our hard-working team of skilled educators passionate about the education of our kids, we pull it together. The inspection team for independent schools approves our program for the 2010–2011 school year. Mormon Hills School is a K–12 Dogwood-certified school, meeting the same graduation requirements as any other school in the province. Our students now leave the school with the prestigious Dogwood Diploma recognized by universities all over the world.

☙

With the triumph of the accreditation still fresh, I find I still can't get away from the feeling that I am working against a ticking clock. I must do all the things I won't be able to do later on in my pregnancy. I play hockey as much as possible because soon I won't be able. Slowly, I allow myself time to acknowledge the little life growing inside of me, to think and dream of our new life. I imagine the joy of a baby in the house—my children doting over their little sibling, the baby giggling as we play together. In my mind's eye, I picture the line of family photos as each year "our baby" takes centre stage. My heart flutters that, finally, after eight years of hard work to prepare for this, I am going to have another baby.

Sam and I decide not to tell our kids, friends and family until we are twelve weeks along. Our focus is to get our house done. Now that we have a baby on the way, the house is top priority. It will be so much easier working on the house with the baby not born yet. I am determined. We will move in by the end of May, two weeks before the baby is due; phase two will be done by Christmas. It's a season to celebrate!

God has a different plan.

One Friday, when I am eleven weeks pregnant, I have my kids at the dentist at eight in the morning. I get them a ride home with Grandma Alaire so I can pop in for drop-in rec hockey for a quick skate before going to the high school to substitute teach for the afternoon. When I get off work, I am tired and crampy. I stop to grab some groceries before I head home and slip into a hot bath. I call Sam to pick up the children from his sister's on his way home from work.

And then it all ends. I think of Grams's words, "I'm youth, I'm health, I'm strength"—my body does not agree. My baby is gone. My dreams and prayers drain out of me and are replaced with questions.

Why, God? What have I done? Are you punishing me? Why couldn't my body sustain life? Was I careless, not taking every precaution? Why don't I get to have a baby? I sit in the bathtub, my tears running down my naked body and mixing with the inky blood turning my bathwater crimson. I had faith in a future and now it's gone. Alone, shaken, I let the grief sink deep into my body, and finally, I have time to cry.

I tell myself it is a blessing that I haven't told anyone, especially the children, about the baby. Now, I won't have to un-tell them. Only my mother and my husband and close sisters share my pain. I hold my head high for the rest of the world to see.

DECAY

The miscarriage is long, messy and draining. For three long weeks, my body tries to cleanse itself of the rest of the fetus. There are few things I've seen in my life quite as gross as an infection of the uterus, and I'm a farm kid. I feel as if I am rotting from the inside out. I lost more than just my dead baby.

Some couples going through trauma see the pain of the other and it becomes a cement that binds them more deeply. My husband and I share a deep loyalty, a long tradition and story and a passionate physical connection, which we define as a happy marriage. In truth, our inability to communicate our deeper hurts and longings has created a marriage in which we both feel quite lonely.

In the lengthening shadows of that snowy November, nature finally makes its peace with my body. I square my shoulders, put on my new pair of tight designer jeans with their gaudy sparkles on the back pockets, a low-cut shirt and extra eye makeup. "Well, babe," I say to my husband, "if we aren't going to have a baby, let's get drunk and go dancing."

We go to his work Christmas party. This will be our first time just going out drinking together with friends. This last year I've gone out a few times with my school or hockey friends when Sam offers to stay home with the kids. Tonight I've decided alcohol will be just the therapy we need. I wonder if I can dance my way into feeling like a woman again. We have a "fun" night, going out to the bar after the party, shouting over loud music at our friends and getting jiggy on the dance floor. My husband tells me the next day that I embarrassed him by dirty dancing with my cousin. I am incensed he would say that. Why didn't he step out to dance with me?

In desperation, we decide to call "a break," whatever that means, from our almost eleven years of marriage.

One week in, doing basically what we have always done, him going away for the week, me going through the motions of kids, school, hockey practice, homework, laundry and meals, we stare at each other. My emotions flatline. In my head, I can hear the monitors beeping. A week of not talking has not fixed us.

We decide to separate for a month. Since we aren't talking to our kids about our separation until we can decide what we are doing, we feel we are sparing them unneeded pain. We hold it together for a week to get through Christmas. My husband says he will take the kids to his sister's for New Year's.

Every New Year's has been with my big loud family doing games with the kids, playing board games, shooting guns and banging pots and pans at midnight. I can't face the questions I would be asked if I went alone. I call some friends from Utah who are spending New Year's in Phoenix and fly down the next day for a four-day, alcohol-fuelled mental sedation and party break. Stories fly that I have gone to hook up with a guy I liked as a teenager.

When I return, it doesn't matter what actually happened, my husband is done. Our marriage didn't need a break; it has run itself out.

Dreary weeks follow, alone, not knowing what to do or who to talk to. This is a new experience for me. I feel like a failure on so many levels. I feel rejected and abandoned by my friends and family as I hear snips of what people are saying. I have spent years dedicated to these people; I step outside the lines once and everything I've done means nothing.

I am broken.

With a paper, pen and calculator, we separate our eleven years of material belongings dollar for dollar. He takes the motorbike and I take the horse. He takes the truck and I take the shell of a house. We promise we will stay friends and support each other on our journeys. We didn't choose each other but we have grown in love and made a beautiful family together. We know we created something together that is special and we both feel protective of that. We have experienced more love, passion and life than many people get in a lifetime. What we are doing just doesn't work anymore.

I look at Sam and my body aches for his strong arms and gentleness, the hugs that wrap me in warmth and safety. I miss our family, cozy nights on the couch and rides in the truck to find a hot spring or a hidden lake to paddle our canoe.

There is a sea between us and I feel I will drown if I jump in. Worse still, I don't want it to get ugly and mean and messy. I love him too much for that. I know I'm not okay.

When we finally sit the kids down to talk to them about it, I tell them I have something important to tell them. My eight-year-old son says, "What is it, Mom? Are we going to Disneyland?"

I turn to their dad.

"Sam, when are we going to Disneyland?"

I don't tell anyone about the miscarriage or my marriage breaking up. I go to work and come home. The students know something is wrong but they let me have my silence.

Here I am, a young, attractive, capable woman in my twenties. I have my own money, my own house, my own car. I can book a ticket to Timbuktu if I want to and fly there tomorrow.

I am a free woman by any feminist definition. Yet the ache of loss gnaws deep, as if someone were twisting a knife stabbed into my gut. I miss my husband who has been my best friend, I miss the family we created together, the dreams we built. I miss the unborn baby I barely had time to love, and all the dreams and future that come with the creation of a new life. I miss my grandma. I miss my dad, and I miss me.

Finally, after a long month of true loneliness, I corner Sam.

"Where are we?" I ask him. "I'm so tired of being this sad." I realize that whether we are together or not, I care what he thinks and how he feels. We give each other permission to be happy.

"I'm Broken"

Breathing in a different kind of courage, I push into February 2011 with too much enthusiasm. A few close friends even comment that my exuberance is alarming. But I refuse to worry. It's a new year, new light. The sun is returning, bringing with it flowers of hope, breathing life back into my body. My health is returning and I imagine I'm being quite Zen about my situation. I'll make lemonade. I devour self-help books and start playing my guitar again. The possibilities of new adventures glitter like tantalizing jewels on the surface of snow. I spend an entire weekend planning. I will travel—volunteer in international programs, teach overseas, learn to scuba dive, take my kids to explore the world. Suddenly I see only a world of endless choices and opportunity. I have my life before me. At twenty-seven, for the first time, I feel truly free to make my own choices about my life.

I also have time to write! I remember telling my mother the most wonderful thing I could imagine would be having a whole day where I could just write uninterrupted. Now that I have it, I don't know what to do. When Sam has the kids on weekends, I wake up in the morning and have only myself to feed and dress and entire days to fill with my own interests and pleasures. From Friday night to Sunday night I float in an ambiguous space with no identity, no house to build, no husband to spend quality time with, no kids to enrich. One weekend writing, listening to the voices in my head, and I determine there are plenty of other things that need to get done first.

I begin planning my spring and summer. Go to Hawaii with my kids, a trip to Mexico with friends, go back to Oregon. Meet people. Go dancing. Take more surfing lessons. My sister Nesta and I put together the details of a backpacking trip across Australia we have been dreaming about for years. This time I'm really going to go! I feel manic with excitement. My mother has soaked up a lot of my tears these last months and when I tell her my travel plans she is cautious but supportive. I wait for the spring and, with it, my adventures.

❧

In the meantime, it's still winter and my school has booked a ski trip to Kimberley Alpine Resort. Conditions on the hill are good, packed, with a few icy sections. With a free supervisor ticket, I spend my day taking as many runs as I can to keep an eye on the students.

On this particular day, I feel closer to God than I have for a long time. I feel, maybe, the God of my childhood, the kindly old white man with a long flowing beard and grandfatherly love for me, is smiling, reaching for my hand, and loves me still. Carving the hard-packed, groomed snow, I fly and float off the knolls and catch air that I imagine will float me into the cloudless sky if only I had a larger scarf.

Over a hundred kids on the hill and everyone is having an amazing time. I've learned lots of new techniques this year. I tag along some runs with my son and his friends racing on their skis and do some runs trying to keep up with the high school boys as they hop and twist over each jump and side trail. I even land a one-eighty. I'm proud of my progress.

I'm high on the crisp mountain air and stunned by the beauty of the changing light across the Rockies as the tree shadows get longer through the later afternoon. The speed and the adrenalin are addictive and I'm eager to get a couple more runs in before the lifts close. My run is going perfectly. I'm floating off the tops of the hills and moving with the ease and grace that only birds must know.

I wipe out coming off the last big hill. There is a familiar blur of snow and force, but then my board cuts down into the snow, sending my body on a trajectory. A chilling crunch and a stab of pain knifes through my body.

I am directly below the ski lift. Every kid in the school must have passed above me while I hollered and moaned for help. "Mrs. Roundy, are you okay?" they call from above.

"I'm not okay. I need help." Finally, a medic comes with nitrous oxide. Oh, glory, the sweet release of being lifted from that agony for a gentle wander in the clouds on this beautiful day. Emergency rescue people have a place in heaven and so does nitrous oxide. I am secured gently into a sleigh and taken down the hill.

The X-ray reveals the tibia and fibula of my leg are severed in a nasty twisted spiral break and the tibia is broken down into the ankle socket. Surgery. The doctor uses plain, clear words: he can bolt it all back together but he will make no promises. But I'm a dancer, I climb mountains, I argue, as if that will change the outcome.

It hurts. It hurts like hell. I thought morphine was supposed to make me feel good.

✒

Six months, the doctors say. But I'm supposed to leave in three.

"You won't be going backpacking in Australia this summer, my dear," my mother says as she wipes the hair back from my forehead. Her tears taste as salty as my own. What hurts the most is having these little shards of hope, my dreams, my courage, ripped away from me.

My mother holds me while I bawl. "I'm broken."

I lie in the hospital bed, counting the clock ticks so I can push the button and tell the nurse I can no longer handle the pain. The drugs wreak havoc on my frazzled nerves. My mind is overwhelmed by how pathetically my world has fallen apart. The girl on a mission, the girl with a plan.

I can barely sit up on my own. I need help just to breathe.

Six months, they say, but they are not sure. What the hell kind of joke is this? Is God a sadist? For the next five days, that seems to be true. My whole world comes to a painful, grinding halt. Sixteen screws and two metal plates will hold the bones in place while they heal.

Turns out I am allergic to morphine. They are increasing my dose. My body burns and itches. I am acutely anemic from the miscarriage the month before and I ingested fluids during the surgery, so I develop severe pneumonia from not breathing well and my reaction to the morphine. It takes a shift change and a new nurse coming in who takes one look at me and says, "This girl is not okay."

I am quickly moved to the ICU. They roll me for a CT scan of my lungs. In my delirious, disoriented state, I try to explain to the tech he is making a mistake taking pictures of my lungs.

"No," I try to explain. "I broke my leg. You should be scanning my leg."

After the surgery, I am helpless and overwhelmed. The first person on my mind, as it has been for the last eleven years, is my husband. I call him. He sits with me in the hospital. I need him and he is familiar and patient. He checks on me, brings me snacks. He brings the children. Kayden has his lucky birthday while I'm flat on my back, sucking oxygen through a tube.

I am grateful to my husband for showing up despite our separation. He is a good man. But I also want my strong, calm father to come wrap me in a big hug as he has always done, to remind me that everything in the whole world will be okay and that he will always be there to love me.

"We'll skate it off," I can hear him saying when I banged my knee ice-skating. I can hear his calm directions telling me to "lean into the next turn" when he took me for my first night ski in Kimberley. My dad and I are farmers, poets and writers. Back then, I thought love and approval were the same thing. Truth is, his disappointment hurts more than my shattered leg.

Five days in the ICU, I wait for him.

He doesn't come.

🞂

Deeper than I have ever known, into the murky depths of the dark well of pain I go, far enough that my mind gives up. I wallow in the inky blackness of pain, broken bones, broken dreams and promises. I lie in a crowded hospital bed with my dead baby, my dead grandma, my abandoned husband and my angry, disappointed father. I wake to blinking lights, oxygen tubes and monitors in my darkened corner of the ICU.

It's five in the morning. My mother, who has just delivered a baby at the hospital, is sitting beside my bed, holding my hand, with a bowl of fresh cold grapes in her lap. We sit in the dark, tears rolling down our faces, as she feeds me grapes one at a time.

Somewhere there is a superhero out there. She gave her good strong O-type blood to me. Two units. She is a courageous goddess of light. I can feel her life force pouring into my body. As I watch her strong red cells carry hemoglobin and oxygen through the narrow tube in my arm, gratitude replaces the pity that had taken hold in my heart. I keep some of her DNA.

🞂

After a week at my mother's, I decide with stubborn determination it's time to head home. I wake up to two feet of snow. I could have stayed at my mother's house in Cranbrook with central heating, but I go home to my cabin. My eight-year-old son and ten-year-old daughter will help me keep the fire burning. My kids need to go to school. My students have government tests in a week, and my dogs need someone. I have ice grips on my crutches, and I plan to teach from my wheelchair.

I think about trying to get well, but it's hard. I miss so much about my old life. I used to be an early-to-bed, early-to-rise kind of girl, more interested in house reno projects with my husband, early hockey practices with my brother and the kids on Saturdays or slipping out for a sunny hike or a day of snowboarding. Occasionally I enjoyed beers and dancing with my friends, but before my divorce this really was a rare indulgence.

With no husband and my old family life disrupted, I flounder for what to do. Months ago we promised my little sister Hanna we would take her out dancing for her nineteenth birthday. As amazing friends can, Linda shows up to my house unexpectedly, helps me dress and curls my hair. "Grab your crutches, girl," she says. "We are going dancin'!" I adore this woman and can't imagine what I'd have done if I'd lost her in the divorce. Right now I am thankful she never became Sam's second wife.

It's a therapy of sorts, I suppose, pushing my body and heart past their limits. I'm not spared the judgment and pity of family and friends. I already know being drunk on crutches in a circle of sisters is a strange way to express grief, but when the sun comes out on a tantalizing spring Saturday in the Rocky Mountains, I make good and sure I'll be flat on the bathroom floor with a swollen leg and a pounding head to dull the pain of missing spring.

✈

On a windy April afternoon, I call my children to come in from playing floor hockey in the top of the Old Barn with their friends. They talk excitedly, sniffing their drippy pink noses as they come in from the chilly spring air. We sit together to eat our criss-cross potatoes and roasted chicken legs as they tell me about their game. The day has been warm enough to lure people into their yards to start spring cleanup after the snowmelt. After so much turmoil in my heart, it's good to have a full day of hard work. I still limp but now, dirty and tired, I feel a rare sense of calm.

We are enjoying our dinner and one another's stories and begin discussing what to watch for a Saturday movie night. Suddenly, my little brother Darrel bursts through the door yelling, "The Old Barn is on fire!" We look out our window; a hundred yards away, flames leap into the sky from the back of the barn.

Sirens are already wailing in the distance and people are gathering on top of the hill. By the time the trucks arrive, there look to be about a hundred people gathered with more showing up. We watch in shock and awe at the sight before us.

As I stand with the growing crowd on the hill, I think about how much the Old Barn has meant. About my days as a child, running and playing with my cousins. I think about the conflict between my father and the church during the Split. The familiar silhouette of the Old Barn has stood patiently in the little valley against the mountain since the beginning of forever. It's always been a symbol of our grandfather. It's been a symbol of home. At the top of the hill, some voices are exclaiming in shock and sadness. Some kids are crying. People are taking photos, telling stories and hugging. Kayden is bouncing around with a pack of little boys, so I wrap Starla in the blanket I grabbed as we hurried from the house. Out of the dark, her little cousins Jenna and Stella wiggle in for the snuggles and warmth. We watch, worried that the leaping flames might be blown toward our little cabin. The front of the barn is still untouched and I can easily picture the Old Barn from my childhood with grey cedar shingles in lines from the ridge down to drop off at the hip where the joists connect. There is ancient, peeling white paint on the siding and one lonely door sags on worn-out hinges on the second-storey window. As the events in our family unfolded, the Old Barn was always there, a silent witness to our story.

The crowd thins. I stay until the mighty beams fall and the tired roof collapses into burning rubble. The coals glow into the night.

3

WANDERING BUT NOT LOST

2011–2018

GOD SITS WITH ME

The Old Barn is gone. I collect a few long spikes from the ashes that I imagine I'll craft into a memento someday. A month after the fire, the guys bring a dump truck and track hoe to clear up the rubble. The clean, bared concrete where it once stood looks much smaller than I would have thought. One evening I stand quietly on my front porch. I'm surprised that I can hear the creek running. There are no lights, no people, no noise. Just an emptiness that is echoed by the first spring call of the crickets along the creek.

The emptiness haunts me. I'd like to put together a small bag and wander wherever my feet take me, but my children keep me grounded and my devotion to my students keeps me going back to teach. The years pass by. I ache for different answers from the ones I used to believe. I know neither Mormonism nor my marriage held all the answers that I crave but I miss their familiarity and comfort. I know that my teaching career and even motherhood is not all I want out of life. I look for purpose in new places.

I get my licence to sell life insurance. I eagerly start the training program to solve the world's problems through mastering the financial system, and it's here I meet Amber. As I devour books on investing and financial planning, I find I'm peeking over at Amber and leaning in a little more when she speaks. She's tall and angular with a sharp sense of fashion and short, flaming-red hair. She moved not long ago from Vancouver and then met and married her second husband here in Creston after her first husband died. She's quick and smart with a quirky sass and idealism about her that I admire, as if I'm watching my worldly big sister whom I'd like to become.

I hope that financial literacy and a good portfolio are the secrets to freedom and joy. I attend workshops and trainings and rah-rah events of the rich and famous. It's Amber who invites me to join the Brave Heart Women's tribe. We have a local chapter that meets regularly, and I attend retreats and women's gatherings in California. I feel certain healing and releasing personal and generational trauma must be the ticket to freedom and joy. I go to Vancouver a lot. I attend drum circles and meditations, festivals and gatherings. Perhaps giving up traditional stability and travelling around Central America in a camper van could be the way to find freedom and joy.

Each trip away is a weekend here, a week or two there. Then I come home. I wander, but I don't believe I'm lost. I pick up my kids from the daddy-grandmas-aunties network collage I have created and go back to my log cabin next to the mountain.

Though we're divorced now, Sam and I continue to co-parent our two beautiful children. I fill my days driving kids to their hockey practices and dance lessons. I organize concerts, recitals, community socials, camp-outs, hiking trips, weddings, graduations and hockey games. My mother is my homing beacon. She holds me gently when I need a place to land and gives me lots of room with no judgment. Mother has a revolving door with food in the fridge and a bed made up for the extras passing through. She continues her busy midwifery practice and always has a full house with my sister Brittany, her two foster daughters and friends and family. I don't see my dad much.

Often I find myself wanting to be almost anywhere else, but I have a stubborn determination that I'm not going to move away until there is something inspiring calling me to another place. I'm not leaving my home and my life because it's too hard to be around my own family. Over the years, when people have left the religion, they've created other lives and have had little to do with the community. Sometimes I feel ostracized by my family and I struggle with feeling like an outsider, but this always strikes a chord of fight in me. This isn't about religion: this is my fucking family. If I let the old ways crowd me out, there will just be a string of siblings crowded out after me. If I should belong to anyone, I should belong to my family. If I should expect to be accepted and to live in peace anywhere on the planet, I should expect it at home with the people who look just like me. How can I ask for world peace if I can't even find peace here?

❧

In my teaching at Mormon Hills School, I share with my students the wonders I have seen and the places I have explored. I teach kids to write strong arguments and well-structured essays. Over the next few years, my former students keep me updated on their post-secondary marks. We have an almost perfect school completion rate with all of the high school students from Mormon Hills School graduating with the provincial Dogwood Diploma the next few years. Their success is a triumph for us all.

I now own a television and I watch TV series and movies. I get stacks of documentaries and nature videos from the library to watch with my kids, but I don't watch cable television. When I do see advertisements, I am perplexed when I see popular culture that perpetuates gender stereotypes and oversexualization of women. I'm diligent to teach my daughter empowering feminist values in big and small ways, encouraging her to not have oversexualized dolls like Barbie and Bratz dolls. With my nine-year-old and eleven-year-old, I'm carful to observe my own habit of having a gender division of house chores and activities. Both kids go to hockey practices and gymnastics. As they get older, we have conversations about double standards and sexism. But when my kids go to their aunt's house, they get sucked into TV advertisements and they come home with lists of things they want me to buy, from sugary cereals to toys to a new car. They talk about feeling criticized by more conservative religious family members who comment on their clothes and values not being right. I roll my eyes in frustration and wonder to myself if anyone anywhere feels they are making their own decisions. After so many years of being told through the media and well-intended outsiders that I've been brainwashed, I've become hyperaware of which decisions and values are actually mine and which have come from "brainwashing," including my purchase of one-hundred-dollar designer jeans. When otherwise-kind people use their religion as a justification to criticize children, and TV commercials are making all of my children's decisions, I ask myself, Isn't this all just brainwashing?

✈

Following Dad's arrest, the Crown determines it can't prosecute on the charges of polygamy, so it drops the charges and returns Dad's passport. There is no precedent in Canadian history as to how to proceed, and no judge is willing to hear the case. In 2011, the justice system puts the law on trial to see if the law, written in the 1890s, is still constitutional.

I argue that when Canada and the United States criminalized polygamy, they created an environment that attracted fanatical religious extremism coupled with an environment where secrecy is essential for people to live their religion: the perfect storm for potential religious abuse.

For a year, the Crown subpoenas witnesses and specialists on polygamy, spending millions of taxpayer dollars to determine if the law is constitutional the way it stands. Dad decides there is no point getting involved in the process. I follow it closely and think it could be positively impactful to have a few educated women speak openly about their experiences growing up and living in polygamy, but I honour his wishes to not get involved.

I'm hopeful that, with a modern perspective and educated professional minds working to update this 120-year-old law, polygamy will be decriminalized, as these changes would allow law enforcement officials to focus on abuse and harm prevention and would provide women security to seek services when they require them without feeling they are putting their family at risk of repercussions from the law.

But alas, after months in court with expert witnesses testifying about the constitutionality of the 120-year-old polygamy law, the Polygamy Reference is rewritten with very few amendments and deemed to be constitutional.

I had been so hopeful that this process could make some real positive changes to empower the lives of women living polygamy. From legalizing same-sex marriage to recognizing the legal rights of polyamorous families, people having more rights and recognition has always moved toward more safety and protection for vulnerable people within that demographic.

I also feel frustrated knowing that, going forward, people living polygamy will continue to hide their lifestyle from law enforcement and vulnerable people will still feel like and be treated as second-class citizens when they need to seek services. Criminalizing polygamy ultimately makes women in this lifestyle more vulnerable.

﷼

I spend a season as a self-taught student of *The Secret*, studying the laws of attraction and retraining my thinking to manifest the life I want to live. I feel certain that if I can think it, I can create it. This, I decide, will start with a positive attitude and motivation. If there are universal laws and truths that control this crazy spinning ball floating through space, I reason, they should work every time, all of the time. Like gravity. These are the conversations I get to have with Amber. I'm fascinated by the way she is able to follow the tiny threads of my very specific ideas and then provokes me gently to see if that is really what I think or not.

One useful thing about the concept of the law of attraction is that there are no shortcuts. What goes around comes around. The way to live in a good world is to create one, and the way we live in peace is to create peace in our own lives. In the church, hell is waiting for people in the next life but can be avoided if a person repents and gets dipped in water between now and death. I feel inspired by the contrast of esoteric spirituality, which asserts that heaven and hell are of my own creation and by my own choosing. It appeals to me that it doesn't include the arbitrary judgment of an emotional god. God just is. When I first hear Ghandi's words "Be the change you want to see in the world," I repeat them again and again.

✿

Designating myself the master creator of my own life starts me on a journey of discovery that began with digging into the financial world. Somehow I'd imagined this would be the ticket to freedom, but what I find is a fear-based culture using all the same scare tactics as religion, just motivating the masses to buy financial products through pushing the fear of aging and poverty rather than hellfire and damnation. My take-away from my years doing debt consolidation and retirement planning for people is that there are many useful tools and products available to navigate the social agreements we have in Western culture around debt and money, but the sales and marketing strategies use all the same angles as the Mormon missionaries. They both promise prosperity, family and community if you do it, and loneliness, poverty and abandonment if you don't.

Next I delve into being a student of self, healing and mindfulness. I dabble in Buddhism and meditation, hoping to find a way of living that is motivated by something other than just fear.

In every circle I find myself in, I hear people talking about community in a way similar to how we always talked about building Zion, the New Jerusalem after the Second Coming of Christ. It's a beautiful idea that people could create a world of harmony where everyone would be known and could know their neighbours, put aside differences and work toward a common goal.

An emotional and easily angered God who picks favourites seems far too fickle to be in charge of much, and an old-white-man version of God who curses people with dark skin when he is angry and disappointed in them seems completely irrelevant. I'm looking for answers to the big questions. What is or who is God? What are we doing here? What does it mean to be free?

I dream; oh, how I dream. I fall in love, many times, with hundreds, maybe thousands, of people. I fall in love with courage, with humanity. I fall in love with the planet!

I join women's spiritual healing circles. I go on healing retreats and do healing work with shamans, hold hands in circles and gaze into the eyes of all colours and ages of women. I want to create peace in my own life. I wonder about what peace could look like for the world.

❧

In the summer of 2011, I assign myself a spirit quest and spend ten days driving and hiking up and down the West Coast, looking for God. I've been to many places, looking for God, moving quickly, sometimes trying to sit still. I find myself meditating on a cliff overlooking a bay in the south of Saltspring Island. I ask, "If I am not my mind, what am I?"

It's easy to separate my spirit from my body. This was taught to me as a child in my church lessons and I understand this easily from connecting intimately with prayer. "But I will certainly vanish into dust," my mind argues, "if I am to release my ego's frantic grasp on my mind's identity."

Beyond me, the Pacific Ocean sparkles in the mid-July air.

"If you are not your mind," my ego argues, "you are an idiot. You just spent forty thousand dollars to educate that mind. Now you are trying to tear it away and throw it to the wind on some hippy-dippy whim. You were valedictorian of a graduating class of thousands of people. You are a debater and an academic. If you are not your mind and your thoughts, your story and your knowledge, you are nothing."

I watch the waves in the water. I hear the birds lighting on the cliffs. I see the rich reds of the arbutus trees leaning into the air. In the pure stillness until all the world stops, God comes to sit with me and gently gives me a nudge. "You are your heart, silly."

Barrel of Monkeys

It doesn't take much coaxing when my almost nineteen-year-old sister Brittany insists that going to the Shambhala Music Festival is what we need to experience together. She has just returned from nine months in India. We've discovered I don't need to act like her mother anymore and we are excited about just being friends.

It's been a year since that day God sat with me near the arbutus trees on Saltspring Island. That day I remembered something from my childhood that I didn't even realize I'd forgotten. That day I found my way back into my own body and life and sank my roots into my Mother Earth. I was reminded that I know God.

Still, each day, my mind struggles to understand the pain of the human condition. I continue to walk around with as many questions as answers. I wonder about what we are doing here and what it truly means to be a woman. I continually remind myself to stay high-minded and nurture my optimism for a healed and peaceful world.

Brittany and I have already been in the lineup for seven hours. A beaded dream catcher dangles from the rear-view mirror in my sister's red, dust-covered 1994 Ford wagon, which she calls Irene. I'm excited and nervous to be on the road to Shambhala.

Shambhala represents all the big taboos that most parents warn their children about: sex, drugs, rock and roll and, in this case, electronic dance music. I'm a divorced schoolteacher-momma from Bountiful. I could easily have painted a big sign on my car that said Mid-twenties Life Crisis, if that is a thing. I am too cautious and prudish even to have a proper mid-twenties life crisis though. Alcohol is really my only drug of choice and isn't allowed at the festival. I'm prepared to "do" the weekend sober.

"I'll be doing research," I say, knowing I sound snooty. "It will make me a better teacher," I rationalize, as much to myself as to any of the raised eyebrows. I shake my head, thinking of the rumours I've already heard my family have told about me since I divorced my husband. If I did even half of the things people have accused me of, I'd really have some self-judgment to work through, but their pointed comments sharpen my determination to experience this festival as the responsible professional I'm committed to being.

Thinking of my query to God on the cliff over the ocean, the question comes to mind: If I am not a teacher, what am I?

Everything I know about street drugs I've learned from the colourful accordion-style pamphlets sent to schools by government programs as part of the mandatory curriculum for the grade-ten unit on health and drug prevention. The little sheets lump them all together and make them all sound equally bad: marijuana, heroin, ecstasy, psilocybin, LSD, ketamine and crack cocaine. I don't have a stitch of personal knowledge of any of it but I do know enough to know that some are worse than others. It seems like a really important topic not to get wrong. Even young people need to have the information to make choices. As a young person, I was never faced with any of these questions, but I know our kids are navigating a whole different world. I tell myself that if I know the challenges and the temptations of these places, I will be better able to speak to youth from an informed place and to help guide them to make better choices when they find themselves facing peer pressure or wanting to experiment on their own. We can't protect kids from everything. We need to give them the tools to make healthy decisions for their own lives.

✸

Curiosity, yes. Adventure, yes. Sparkles and costumes, yes. Four days of dancing to live bands and electronic music, yes!

Perhaps this is the nirvana so many seek. Perhaps it is the act of gathering with the intention of connecting, putting differences aside, opening our hearts and minds and just being together that is the act of knowing God. Ten thousand people share a space on this piece of land for a weekend, generously offering food and gifts to one another. They welcome another. I frolic; I actually dance from stage to stage around the festival. I smile at the irony as a piece of scripture shows up in my mind: "For where two or three gather in my name, there I am among them" (Matthew 18:20). Certainly there are at least a few of us gathered here to know God. This is the least expected of my Shambhala discoveries: the familiarity of the gathering and the open-heartedness of sharing a love for art and music. People have travelled long distances to embrace brothers and sisters who are meeting for the first time. We are pre-bonded by a belief that we share something deep and personal and that we have a sacred something that sets us apart from those who are not fortunate enough to gather with us because of limitations of either the mind or the body. It's not unlike the church conferences of my youth, where families would travel for hundreds of miles to gather for three days of festivities, music, dance and prayer. We would spend weeks preparing new clothes, sewing conference dresses and preparing delicious spreads of food, plus long days of cleaning, gardening, landscaping and preparing for guests. All the boys would come home from the work camps and crew houses. It was a time of rest and celebration and an active time for youth to mingle with like-minded families of the faith to make connections that might lead to marriages. We congregated around food, prayer, music, dancing and entertainment. The mass exodus, saying goodbyes and the long treks back to the rest of our lives, left us tired in body and exuberant in soul.

I rise refreshed each morning of the festival, eager to take in the sunny yoga class and the guided meditation workshops led by masters of the art. Afternoon speakers and workshops include some heavy warnings about global warming, rising oceans and extreme weather conditions as well as corrupt corporations. Monsanto and pharmaceuticals are taking over our food production and our health-care system. Even these warnings carry some of the same gut-heavy tone of hellfire, damnation and end-of-the-world warnings when God will wipe the wickedness from the face of the earth. We must stay alert, educate ourselves and prepare for a pending crisis: they cue the warnings that give me a familiar old knot in my stomach.

I notice my sister lying on her back with two dozen other inanimate bodies loosely clumped in a circle, surrounded by four large gongs. It looks as if someone spilled their Barrel of Monkeys and forgot to pick them up. The cool grass is welcoming as I join the perimeter of the circle. In my body I feel the flicker of anger still hanging on. I barely let myself notice, but there is a pang of resentment for the years that fear hung over my youth, the need to always "keep sweet" and the constant preparations for the time of the destruction that made it so urgent for girls to marry and become women so young. I glance at my sister Brittany. She is free and confident, radiant in her own skin. I remember her as the little baby I helped raise while I was still a kid myself. I was a mother when I was her age. Her life is already so different from mine. I practise my mindfulness breathing and try to find my way back into my body. As I breathe out the anger, the gong vibrations wash over me.

ᴥ

Somewhere in the midst of all the beautiful chaos and music and people of Shambhala, I meet Joe. A Kiwi boy, a world traveller from New Zealand, he met my friends in Vancouver through a couch-surfing meet-up site and together they made the trip to Shambhala in the mountains of the Kootenays. When Brittany met up with friends, I wasn't sure I'd love hanging out with a crew barely older than my high school students, so I was set to do a low-key, mature-adult version of the festival alone, watching other people's creativity. Instead, I find myself lounging in my friend Deep's hammock, listening as he and Joe discuss politics and spiritual practices and books and ideas. Joe's wit and charm engage me as he explains the philosophy of cradle-to-grave business models, which in practice would assume responsibility for all people and environmental effects of the whole scope of a product. He is a policy analyst in New Zealand working on his law degree and out for a three-month sabbatical around the world. After an afternoon of playful banter, I'm fairly certain there is nobody else like New Zealand Joe in the whole world. He dances when he walks, hugs and sings with strangers. He gives and receives gifts easily and is the first to offer assistance wherever he sees a need. He has skills too; he's good at fixing things. He works with his hands like a country kid. The life of the party, a trickster and a people magnet.

We bebop through the festival as if we've always lived here and get others to join us as well. We show up inside a teepee in a well-lit corner to join a small group sitting in the sand. We share our names, stories and songs. We do workshops on acroyoga, hula-hooping and walking a slack line, write notes for the wish tree, swim in the river, climb trees and look endlessly at art and vendors. We dance until we can't move, sleep for a few hours and then dance again. All around me, music, sounds and beats blend until nothing separates me from the festival. The journal I imagined would fill my time stays closed. I take only a few pictures.

I think of my sister and the youthful exploration I never had. Mother and teacher though I am, I let myself relax into a carefreeness I imagine must be close to hers.

✏

"We've got to be up for the last sunrise," Joe tells me. After an hour or two to warm up and rest before the sunrise, we venture into the dewy blue morning. A few stages have shut down and the tone of the music has changed to a light, upbeat reggae somehow remixed with pianos and horns. Those walking around in the early morning light are vibrant— their costumes and sparkles are in disarray but pure light gleams from every face.

Monday's sunrise is the ceremonial gathering of those who are truly driven by the love of music, dance and people. Whatever challenges people brought in from the outside world have been left in the dirt on the dance floor. Open hearts, joyous laughter and pure light and love are all that remain.

All packed and ready to leave, Brittany and I meet Joe and Deep in the crawling snail's-pace exit line. Joe is debating whether to take a ride to Vancouver or stay a few more days in the Koots and hitch to Van City later. After Shambhala, Joe will be on the road to Burning Man, before heading to New York and then Europe for two more months.

"I'm gonna stay," he calls to Deep and tosses his pack into the back seat of our car.

I squeal at my sister in excitement: "We've got ourselves a Kiwi!"

Five days later, my kids and I drop Joe off at the ferry in Kootenay Bay so he can hitchhike back to Vancouver, where he will secure a crew to take the trek to Burning Man.

As we splash on the pebble beach, Starla, Kayden and I watch Joe step onto the longest free ferry ride in the world. The forty-five-minute ride might just as well be to the moon. I can't imagine a world where I never see Joe again. I've never met someone with so much courage to imagine and dream. There is so much raw humanity distilled into that one compact expression of a man. Never have I felt so much permission to just be me and express myself without needing to dim my light for fear of offending someone. He waves from the deck for a long time as the boat turns, gaining speed across the deep sparkling lake. I want nothing more in that moment than to be going with him.

❧

I look down as my phone alerts me that I've received a text message. "Meet me in New York." It's the last week in August, only two weeks until school starts, and three weeks since I last saw Joe. I've dreamed of going to the Big Apple. It feels reckless and spontaneous to imagine going.

I work day and night to prepare my classroom and buy what my children need to start another year of school. I don't even know which airport he is flying into but I book a flight to match the day he said he would be going to New York City and send him my itinerary. I drive six hours to Calgary to catch my flight, and with my one carry-on-sized bag, I arrive at JFK airport on time and intact.

Coming into arrivals, before I can even begin to orient myself to find the subway, I hear a whoop. A dusty top hat with Amelia Earhart goggles atop them is prancing toward me in the crowded airport! I scream and drop my bags and we dance, hug, kiss and laugh.

"My plane landed only an hour ago," he exclaims. "I got off and checked my emails on an airport computer since I lost my cellphone in the desert. I came right here!"

Magic! Somehow, the universe brought us together.

"I reckon that's how it is when you follow inspiration. It's travel magic." The way he says it, I doubt there could have been any other possible outcome.

⟡

New York is a portal to the whole world. Just being in this city makes everything feel possible. Joe and I walk down streets crowded with generations of stories stacked into the brownstone buildings of Brooklyn. We book a room at a guest house run by a feisty, motherly minister. She tells us she spells God with two o's. "I go to the church of Good."

It doesn't feel like chance to be staying with this lovely humanitarian of the Brooklyn Society for Ethical Culture. She is one of those timeless women with wild curly grey hair who know age is irrelevant. She moves up and down the steep stairs easily in her flowing muumuu dress with sparkles in her eyes that tell of her love for humanity. The furrow in her brow and her well-sunned skin speak of a front-line worker who knows that the real important stuff in life, like birth and death, is messy.

Over our coffee each morning she shares stories of her work in Haiti, bringing relief directly to people who have experienced disaster. Most often, she tells us her work becomes that of connecting and coordinating relief workers from organizations such as the Red Cross with where the actual need is. "Usually," she says, "the challenge is listening and knowing what people need more than it is just making soup."

Over our coffees, yogurt and blueberries, in the narrow courtyard behind her family's fourth-generation, three-storey brownstone townhouse, she gives us a mini-workshop on her Technology of Participation work, there beside her sunflowers.

On Thursday, Joe meets up with an old friend. I spend my day alone wandering through art galleries and museums and reflecting on the art history course I took in college, pleased that I know a little about most of the artists and styles. I imagine I live in a world where this is what I do on afternoons in the most multilingual city in the world. I sit in coffee shops and talk to pleasant strangers. They say it's obvious I'm not from here.

ᛒ

We burst into the shaded brownstone street. Joe laughs and takes my hand, skipping down the steep stairs and dramatically opening the ornate black iron gate. The street in front of Community Be Good Guest House looks like a movie set. We laugh about whether to burst into song and dance or skulk along in the shadows, keeping an eye out for crime.

We explore Wall Street and Times Square and take the ferry to get a close-up of the Statue of Liberty. We rent pedal bikes, ride along the water and visit the South Street Seaport Museum. We eat barbecue in Chinatown and take a romantic stroll through Central Park. It's hard not to compare this tired little swatch of nature with the beautiful natural wildernesses we come from, but we stay in the spirit of the experience and buy ice cream. We go window-shopping and try on expensive furs in a shop in Manhattan, and we view the city from the top of the Empire State Building. On our last day in the city, we take a train all the way out to Queens to the quiet beaches and try famous East Coast fish tacos. We pop into an eclectic jewellery shop. I buy a little amber sun pendant and Joe surprises me with a silver claddagh ring since his family is Scottish. We end the night sipping fancy martinis at a late-night jazz club and slow dance as the lazy saxophone noodles into the night.

ᛒ

Joe catches his flight today. My flight leaves in the morning. Joe must jump on his overnight flight from LaGuardia Airport to London. He takes my hand as we walk toward the subway station from the coffee shop where we drank our last coffee together. After a long slow kiss, we look into each other's eyes full of hope and promise. I dare imagine that I love this man. I feel as if we've known each other since way back and that he knows a part of me that no one has ever known. I let myself dream of a world we could create together.

Again he leaves me, his pack bobbling as he disappears into a subway stairwell to catch an airplane for the old country. I just stand there on the sidewalk as the busy Brooklyn life goes on around me. This time I'm certain that the universe is in on an elaborate scheme that brought us together. I'm not going to question it. I don't know how or why but I feel like anything is possible.

✈

I smile as I feel the wheels hit the runway. Already, my thoughts are at home. Five hours from New York, I land in Calgary for a six-hour drive through the stunning colours and jutting peaks of Banff National Park in September. At this moment I picture the beautiful free body of my little sister with the light shining from her eyes and the courage and curiosity I've given myself permission to share because of her. At home, the bright faces of my children getting ready for the first day of school, as they do every day, remind me that I have the perfect job, the perfect life. We bang on the bathroom door telling each other to hurry. My daughter and I comb our hair together in our small bathroom as she fills me in on friends, dance lessons and her favourite audiobooks. My son snuggles on the couch in a blanket until the last possible moment when he needs to put his shoes on as we run out the door, grabbing backpacks, homework, lunches, keys, phone, glasses.

New Zealand

My winter peacoat goes into my second piece of luggage. I'm still not the minimalist traveller I hope to become; one might think I was moving to New Zealand rather than planning on touring around the North and South Islands for a month. It's the end of December 2012. After a busy family Christmas with the kids and Sam at my mother's house and the myriad of parties and events of the season, the kids will stay with different cousins for a week at a time to go to school and will go to their dad's on the weekend.

I met Joe in August and bought the plane tickets in October, but it feels like much longer. Nervous anticipation pulls at my stomach during the seventeen-hour direct flight from Vancouver to Auckland. I barely sleep. It's a long time to sit and think. I'm flying to the other side of the planet, seeking adventure but also seeking my future. I'm going to a place that has taken up so much space in my childhood imagination from the many stories of my grandfather's church mission, his work among the powerful, warrior Maori people and his conversion to fundamentalist Mormonism.

On Grandpa Ray's two-year mission in New Zealand with the Maori people, he learned their language and customs. Dad says that when they coaxed Grandpa at a gathering, he would break into the fierce tribal war dance of the Maori; with a whoop and an intimidating warrior yell, he performed a *haka*. He learned Maori songs, and reportedly he baptized many people there into the Mormon faith.

The Mormons did a good job of showing how similar their faith was to traditional Maori culture and were successful converting and baptizing whole communities. I was interested to learn that the Mormons had made more of an impact on the Maoris than the Catholics had.

My father would often tell a story of Grandfather on his mission, preaching to some of the old Maori polygamist brethren, many of whom had been converted in the early days by missionaries sent out by the Prophets Brigham Young and John Taylor to carry the sacred teachings of the gospel to the four corners of the earth. These early Prophets and elders had sworn to uphold the sacred teachings of celestial marriage and never let this practice leave the earth.

My grandfather found himself facing a fiery devout elder who had four wives. Young Ray Blackmore related to him that Wilford Woodruff, president of the LDS Church, had signed the manifesto under the direction of God. This agreement with the United States government stated that Mormons would no longer practise polygamy to open the way for Utah to become the country's forty-fifth state.

The elder rose to his feet, challenging my grandfather to go read the Doctrine and Covenants. "You are telling me," he boomed at young J.R. Blackmore, "that God would have me abandon my wives, not claim my family and hide from my principles to receive the blessings of man?"

Grandpa Ray said he had no response for him; he too felt perplexed that God would have taken this sacred principle off the earth when the Prophets had committed their lives to protect it. He combed the early scriptures and teachings to try to explain and understand for himself which of these conflicting teachings was correct.

John Taylor, the third Prophet of the Mormon Church, when asked to sign the manifesto, had famously held up his right hand at the pulpit; those present said a glowing countenance came over him and his voice shook the building like thunder when he said, "I would have my right arm torn from my body before I would sign the manifesto."

Even in memory, these stories strike a gallant image. I recall their telling and retelling and the conviction I felt that we must also be the ones to protect this sacred teaching. My grandmothers and aunts spoke with passion about how beautiful it was to live plural marriage and how blessed we were to carry forth "the work." At a young age, I too felt their fervour and conviction. I too imagined I would live the principle some day. I saw the way many of my mothers and aunts loved their sister-wives. Grams always said how she had adored Grandma Aloha. Even after the Split, my husband and I discussed what that lifestyle would be like if we were to choose to live it. I've seen it lived and I've seen it happy, but I've also seen the holy hell of it.

I sit staring out the window. Joe and I have expressed our intentions of building a life together. I have half-grown kids. I can't be the one to move first—when they are older, for sure. We don't know when or how, but I know any pursuit of life with this man will be one heck of a journey. He talks easily about his experiences with polyamory and a poly-lifestyle, which he says is quite common in liberal Wellington. "I reckon it's not that different from your family," he muses. I reckon he is right. How is it that different? Considering the commute for our conjugal visits, it seems like a practical choice for us.

✺

My thoughts return to my grandfather and what it must have meant for him in the 1940s in southern Alberta to decide polygamy was a lifestyle he felt called to follow. When Grandpa Ray returned home, he inquired in earnest to the stake president and many of the church leaders in Alberta. Grandpa's oldest brother, John Blackmore, an astute academic and Member of Parliament, also supported fundamentalist Mormon teachings and was in touch with the brethren from Utah but never lived polygamy.

Utah had committed to eradicate polygamy from the state. These men had sworn to keep the sacred practice of polygamy and celestial marriage alive. They pledged to not let a year go by without a child being born into the priesthood work.

Many of the elders of the church had a family or two in hiding; often they went by a different last name. Fathers' names were kept off birth certificates to avoid detection by the law. Great-Uncle John's oldest son, Herald, and his youngest brother, Grandpa Ray, began travelling to attend these meetings, where they felt they were finally being taught the fullness of the gospel. They felt a kinship with these men who dedicated their lives to keeping the sacred teachings of the principle of plural and celestial marriage alive, regardless of the hardships they might face.

✺

Back home in my mountain valley, where my grandpa brought his family to a place of refuge on the ranch that became Bountiful, I met a wild, adventurous Kiwi man. He was raised by a community of earth-loving hippies on the South Island, and his eyes still carry the spark of idealism for a better world. When we walk together, the world is small. When I met this man, I knew I'd met a kindred flame. We share passion for people and place that I already know is a rare treasure in a cynical and wounded world. "Wait until you see where I'm from," he says by way of explanation. "Then it will make more sense."

While he has captured my heart and my imagination, somewhere I know I signed up for New Zealand a long time ago.

I'm frazzled and feel less than attractive after the long flight and sleepless night. At the Auckland airport, I change from my jeans into a sundress. After a wander down a jungle-lined trail to the domestic terminal, I board the smaller plane to Nelson Bays loading from the tarmac. I look around, feeling I might see a chicken on this crowded domestic flight full of families carrying miscellaneous items and tourists flying south from New Zealand's largest and bustling international urban centre.

I didn't realize how nervous I was until I saw Joe waiting in the vine-covered pagoda that is the arrivals terminal. He's holding a long-stemmed rose and a bottle of wine in his hand. Joy, relief and excitement flood through me—for just a second I wonder if I thought he wasn't going to be here. I drop my bags and we embrace, jumping up and down. We have a long passionate kiss that reminds me why I came to New Zealand, and he carries my bags past the smiling travellers who've shared in our reconnection.

I can barely believe that I'm here, he's here. I can't stop touching him. It's real; he's real!

🕊

Beautiful Nelson Bays, New Zealand.

"This is going to all make so much more sense when you see my home and meet my family," Joe says as if answering my questioning thoughts. Our mothers are both midwives and our fathers both founders and leaders of intentional community projects. On opposite ends of the world, we both grew up farm kids, riding horses, cutting trees in the bush, driving tractors, cliff jumping in fast rivers and camping. We are each the product of the community that raises a child. Joe grew up near Nelson, New Zealand, and I near Nelson, BC. The similarity ends where Joe is an only child and I am the fifth child of my father's 132 children.

Joe pulls the car off the winding road in front of a rustic old boathouse. A wedding is being prepared in the quaint heritage building where his family owns shares in the restoration project.

"Grab your bathing suit," Joe says, as if that's the only information I need. He moves quickly, going inside as I dig in my luggage. I pride myself on my adventure preparedness skills. I pull a handful of strings and fabric from the front of my suitcase. Ducking to the port side of the boathouse, I do up the strategic ties under my sundress. I smile, thinking how funny it would be if I stepped out in one of the long swimming dresses of my youth. Joe would get a real kick out of watching me jump off the boathouse deck in layers of fabric. It's been a few years now since I shed the dresses in favour of smaller and smaller bathing suits. To be honest, I prefer the clothing-optional beaches of the West Coast. I'm hopeful this is a thing in New Zealand.

Joe peels off his narrow-legged hipster jeans and polo shirt. Climbing onto the sturdy wooden railing, he whoops and splashes dramatically after plunging twelve feet to the salty sea below. He comes up and waves for me to follow him. I hold the beam above me for a steadying moment and to let my glowing December-white skin feel a tickle from the sun before I dive, gracefully slicing the water beside him. Salty kisses, warm Pacific waters, smooth skin—we playfully climb and splash like a couple of kids, as happy with our own good fortune as we are with each other's company.

Above the steep, low mountains, the sun slants lower across the narrow bay. Sleepy sailboats are tucked in like ducks with their heads underwing. Joe's right. The mountains do feel like my beautiful home in the Kootenays. I watch as he pops the top off the Akarua sparkling rosé. Water drops shimmer like pearls on salty skin. The last few stressful months leading up to this trip have left me on my thinner side of curvy, and I look sexy in the stringy straps of green and purple fabric. We lean against the wooden railing, quietly sipping from long-stemmed glasses, soaking in the golden glow off the still harbour. The warmth of his body beside me feels courageous and hopeful.

⚓

After a late evening of drinks and greetings, I will myself for the 4:00 a.m. wake-up, determined not to miss a thing. "Uncle," a rough Maori man who was a dad figure to Joe during his youth, has decided to take us fishing. Joe brought one of his uni mates for the South Island New Year's party and holiday adventures. The four of us will be an adventure crew for a few days. All of our supplies stacked in Uncle's small Jeep, we head out.

Thoughtfully, Uncle saved me the head meats of the day's catch, the eye and the "sauce," the gooey bits from the brain and guts, which moisten the meat as it sizzles on the barbecue. Joe jokes easily with his family and winks at me across the room. Uncle lightens up with a few drinks, enjoying the spoils of the day.

He starts teasing Alex, a soft-skinned city boy with a baby face. "Have you ever kissed a hog?" Uncle asks him. Uncle grabs the sides of Alex's face and scrapes his spiny whiskers from his jaw to his eye. Alex screams; his face is bleeding as if he did a face plant on asphalt. Tears stream down his cheeks but he keeps with the "fun" of his South Island hazing.

"Welcome to the South Island, boy. We gotta toughen you up." Uncle slaps him on the back. I blink. Such rough play is certainly not unfamiliar in my family of hunters and loggers, and as a kid I was on the receiving end of plenty of teasing. But now, similarly to when I was young, I notice there really isn't any way for this poor kid to save face or escape Uncle's torture. At this moment, I feel relieved to be a woman.

Spring storms have washed out a road and Joe gets a message that the New Year's party is relocated to the drier, California-like hills of Christchurch. We pile like sardines into Uncle's old four-by-four Jeep in the late afternoon. "You can sleep on the road," Joe assures me.

I'm keen to ask Uncle on the car ride if he has ever heard of my grandfather, the singing, yodelling, roping cowboy missionary. Uncle is busy driving and his answers are clipped and short—I'm always unsure if I'm understanding all of what he is saying—but he responds, "Blackmores, yeah mate. I know Blackmores. Lots of Blackmores round here in the South Island."

Joe has said the same thing. When I told him about my grandfather who spent two years travelling around, living with and among the Maori people, preaching the gospel, learning their language, culture and traditions and baptizing many into the church, Joe says, "Maybe your grandfather wasn't such a good Mormon boy after all. Maybe you got a whole lot of Maori cousins running around in New Zealand too."

His words ring as blasphemous to the pure image of the larger-than-life grandfather who was untouchable by the temptations and seductions of the devil. I notice that I immediately want to defend my grandfather's good name at Joe's inference that he could have been anything other than the devout man of the faith I knew from our childhood mythology. I'm half asleep, curled up in the back seat next to Joe with our bedroll for camping tucked around us. I let my imagination mix with my dreams and wander into an alternative tale of my grandfather ...

A forbidden love between the tall, handsome, grey-eyed Mormon missionary and an amber-skinned Maori princess. A secret tribal ceremony, as her father would not join the faith and she determines that she must. A child that he planned to return to claim when he was released home from his mission. Knowledge of the marriage and the child would have broken the conditions of his missionary contract and resulted in a dishonourable release from his mission. Before he could return for his family, his chocolate-eyed sweetheart died tragically in childbirth, which always seems to happen in these stories. My imagination continues narrating this saga, which is not dissimilar to other Mormon missionary stories from my youth. My grandfather's attempts to contact her family resulted in threats from her father. Grandfather was never able to claim the child, and because of his broken heart, he never told his family of this secret love. Continuing to follow his calling to serve God, he married a devoted Mormon farm girl to start his family.

There was plenty that might have pained my grandfather's heart, but imagining him having secrets with a past and regrets somehow softens the edges of the long-suffering, devoted man of God that my childhood mind created out of what I thought I knew about my grandfather. I knew him only from stories but still cared deeply for his approval.

I snuggle next to my boyfriend, who is sleeping lightly beside me. When my father talks about his last year with his dying father, his stories are thick with love and emotion and a bond I know he still feels. He carried so much devotion to continue his father's work in the community and to help finish raising his father's family. I wonder how well that seventeen-year-old kid really knew the heart of his fifty-seven-year-old dad. I imagined I knew my dad. If he had died when I was seventeen, his memory would have been set next to the martyrs and saints of old. For the first time, I ponder these two men as mere mortals, no greater, no less. I imagine them having anger and jealousy and lust and pride. I set beside them their accomplishments and their passion and dreams and their stories as I know them.

I ponder their blood running through my veins. I know the fire of having dreams burning inside you when your world has nowhere for them to go. I know what it takes to stand for what you know is right and good and true, even when you are being told it is against God. I know what it feels like to take a stand to create your own life, even at the risk of losing friends, family, community and home.

As we bounce down the highway with the radio playing to the hum of the Jeep motor, I realize I do know these men. I wonder if there is room in their way of thinking to ever know me.

✒

In a suburb of Christchurch that miraculously survived the desolation of the earthquake a few years before, another of Joe's uncles has a bachelor pad in a corner of a concrete bunker of a building. He owns a collection of vintage cars that take up the next two floors down. He's working on a few pieces. One is on a hoist. Parts and tools are heaped and in lines along the floor. He beams as he talks about engines and torque and horses running.

Here, I meet Joe's father. His strikingly similar facial features and a cheeky smile are shadowed by darker eyes that look like those of a man who has known disappointment. Joe has told me lots of stories and I'm eager to badger him with questions.

In the seventies, New Zealand became a sanctuary for pacifists and draft dodgers from around the world. New Zealand was cheap in those days. Idealists, alternatives and hippies came in droves to find another way to live and work together. They imagined a world where people and community made war and government irrelevant. Joe's dad was a visionary and leader who put his whole heart into building the world he imagined. With a few others, he financed some property for their growing community. They tried to be smart about it, he says. They worked out terms of agreement but mostly they trusted each other.

It went really well for several years, he tells me, but he's looking toward the thick hedge as he talks. Work was secured with the landowner and they all worked to pay the remaining cost of the loan. It all ended in tragedy and betrayal when one of the men had an affair with the landowner's wife and left with the money they needed to pay the mortgage. The community was divided by his disloyalty. They continued for years more, but they never recovered.

I can hear the bitterness in his voice. "There is precious little to be gained in that kind of life," he says, not necessarily to me. "Work for the man. Get yourself a pension. Reap the benefits of your own work. People will just use and use you, then stab you in the back when they've got what they want."

I want to argue with him that people are mostly good and that there is so much beauty in community. I want to glean from his insights. "I'm sure you learned a lot. What advice would you give to others who want to create community?"

He scoffs. "Don't do it." His tone of betrayal and resolution remind me this isn't the time to impose my naïveté and idealism. Four decades ago, he and his crew must have sounded just like Joe and me, eager and ambitious. They thought nothing could stop them from building utopia.

I think about my grandfathers, dad and uncles who carried a similar kind of vision for community. I think about ways my childhood was utopian. I think about the ways in which it was not: about the babies who die too soon, about the mothers and fathers who leave their families, about the tensions between families when religious beliefs become divided. I know that living with other people is rife with complexities.

Joe talks about his childhood similarly to the way I do. We both grew up with a pack of cousins who roamed between their aunts' houses, rode horses, did farm chores and escaped to the bush in their free time.

I sip a beer across from the hardened, worn-down man whose disappointment sounds just like that of any one of my uncles. The man beside me, his only son, is as fine a product of a life as I've ever seen. I think about my cousins and siblings and the lifestyle our parents created for us growing up on the ranch. I wonder if perhaps his project was actually more successful than he gives himself credit for.

◆

Joe and I rent a car, and the next week is a tiki tour around the South Island with many stops to pull out the chilly bin and cook up a spread with an unsuspecting auntie or cousin, all of whom have taken some part in raising this wild South Island Kiwi. None of them are warned of our coming but we are welcomed with eager open arms and no hesitation to make up a bed in a spare room, a shop or shanty, and to cook up the traditional traveller's meal of whatever we have brought, combined with whatever they have on hand. Each meal is a surprise feast we share, connecting with family and telling stories.

Parliament has just passed legislation to adopt the traditional name of the South Island, Te Waipounamu, "the waters of greenstone." We drive over the mountains to the Gold Coast and then south on a winding highway that edges steep cliffs dropping dramatically to the thrashing waves of the wild west coast. We stop at each swimming hole, hike to hidden rope swings and jump off bridges into clear rivers. We float inner tubes, spelunking through the blackness of a river cave, and stare up at a starry sky of glow-worms. Joe comes out of a small shop with a greenstone pendant in the shape of an adze. "Wear it for strength," he tells me.

We return the car and board the ferry to cross the strait toward Windy Wellington. Joe returns to work and I buy a multiday pass to the Te Papa museum to brush up on the history of the British Commonwealth and Christian manifest destiny. It's a familiar, brutal story in which Indigenous people pay a heavy price for European ambition.

Joe teaches me to sail at the Wellington yacht club. I grip the rope with white knuckles, tacking and ducking as he calls out and the two-person yacht skips wildly across the windy bay. As the high-summer sun dips toward the silhouette of the South Island, I think about my family back home, where the nights are dark and long this time of year. Hand in hand,

Joe and I stroll along the waterfront to see *The Hobbit* in the theatre where Peter Jackson and his cast held their movie debut.

With an hour to spare, Joe steps into a shop and grabs what he says is an exceptional bottle of wine for a special occasion. Next to the harbour, we sit with our backs to a shipping crate, sharing the sunset and drinking from the bottle—a vintage far too fancy to be consumed this way. I absentmindedly tap my knee against his leg as the warm wind plays at my hair and the light fabric of my skirt. The moment is bittersweet. This will be the third time we've said goodbye. This time I wonder if it will be the last. I'm slated to travel alone for the next week through the North Island. I'll just wander as the wind blows me and make my way north to Auckland, where I will catch my flight home.

We joke and laugh easily, keeping it light and real. We don't say what we both know is true. Joe has a good life here. He is quickly working his way up the corporate ladder. He is set to have the life and luxury his parents didn't have and weren't able to give him. I have my kids, and I'm not convinced I would do them justice asking them to give up the home and community they have. I have a lot of questions about the world and what I'm supposed to do here. When I ask the question "If I am not a mother, what am I?" I can feel that motherhood has never been an identity that defines me, but those kids have been my greatest joy and raising them is something I definitely want to get right. I'm not willing to trade my time with them for any man. Not even Joe.

"They will be grown soon enough," I tell him finally. "I'll be thirty-six when my daughter is eighteen. I'll still have plenty of time to take on the world after that."

⁊

Te Ika-a-Maui, "the fish of Maui," as the Maori call the North Island, is a steaming landscape of geothermal hot springs and volcanic lakes with an active tourist culture. I bus north from city to city, whitewater rafting and soaking in mud baths. Contented sheep dot the steep rolling hills, busily growing the fine merino wool Kiwis love.

Near Rotorua, I attend a traditional Maori cultural sharing and feast hosted by a proud patriarch and his family. The guests walk through the geothermal geyser that Maori communities were built around to harness the thermal heat of the hot springs for cooking and for heating their homes in winter.

An elder walks along behind us. I hang back to talk to him. He explains that his family have been Mormons for several generations and shrugs as he says most of the young people don't care for it much anymore. I ask about my grandfather, Ray Blackmore, the Mormon missionary. He nods assuredly. "Blackmore, yes, lots of Blackmores in these parts, especially of the Maori."

I'm puzzled. He straightens his broad shoulders and explains, "In the old days when the missionaries were here converting Maori families by the hundreds, there was a lot of pressure by the government for the Maori to take last names so they could get official ID. It was common for the Maori to take the last name of the elder who baptized them into the church."

✒

Giddy with excitement, I buy a ticket to take a tour boat to White Island. Today I'll walk on an active volcano and see the breath of Mother Earth. From Whakatane, the pristine waters of the Bay of Plenty are the bluest blue.

I strike up a conversation with Hayden, the handsome bronzed shipmate who is cheerfully talking to travellers and serving warm towels and puke bags to those who are already seasick after only a short distance over the rolling waves. He moves easily around the rocking ship on his steady sea legs. He points and the ship slows. It's a circling sperm whale and calf. After guiding for more than ten years, he says, he will soon have his skipper's licence. Next time it will be him at the helm, he tells me with a grin. He speaks of the sea and the changes of this living, breathing island with unusual reverence. On the days the sea is too rough to take travellers, he walks on land and wishes he were at sea.

He takes me to sit on the starboard side to let my legs dangle under the railing. The water leaps toward me as the ship hits each wave. I'm astonished when a pod of dolphins appears to surf the wake just a length beneath my toes. The bright sun glints from their sleek bodies as they dive and play.

Meeting Hayden-of-the-sea, I think of the stories of my British great-grandfather, William Morrish Blackmore, who spent his formative years at sea scrubbing decks and climbing masts. I smile remembering what feels like long ago, when my cousins and I relived the gallant tales of our great-grandfather as we climbed the layers to the Old Barn, the ship I grew up on. We walked beams and swung on ropes to drop into the hay below.

In awe, I walk through the sulphuric steam and bubbling pits around the orifice of the great volcano. "What would we do if it erupted?" I ask, teasing him for a response. He laughs easily with the confidence of his knowledge of the island.

"Well," he says, laughing, "it's never happened. Those machines would warn us. But I guess what we would do is run for the sea."

Before my people settled and began farming the land, they were nomadic clansmen who roamed the moors of England and voyaged across the sea. It feels familiar to have the earth under my feet and the wind in my hair. Remembering that my ancestors shared my restlessness to see beyond the next horizon reminds me that what it means to be a Blackmore is not written for me, but determined by the story I will write and the legacy of my life. I carry the wandering blood of my ancestors. Looking out at the sea, I understand a bit more the heart of my great-grandfather.

After bungee jumping in Taupo, I make a last-minute decision to change my travel plans and return to Wellington. Joe's friend Alex, who travelled with us in the South Island, will pick me up at the bus station to surprise Joe. Rushing to catch the last bus south, I beg the driver, who is loading the last bags, to stall for me while I purchase a ticket. He shakes his head, tagging my suitcase to stash below. "Damn, you are lucky," he says. "There is one empty seat on this bus. These trips are usually sold out weeks in advance." He moves another passenger so I can sit behind the driver's seat. For the next six hours, he gives me the bus driver's version of New Zealand socio-politics and economics.

Instead of Alex waiting for me in the airport, Joe is hiding behind a column and jumps out as the wheels on my suitcase are clipping over the uneven lines in the concrete. The moment I see him I know I made the right decision to come back for a final goodbye. I'll spend my last night in New Zealand with my sweetheart. This goodbye doesn't feel so dramatic.

With a bag in each hand, I shake my head and laugh at him as he playfully kisses me on the nose before I turn into the airport. I feel sensible and worldly, having accepted that he's kind of perfect right here in Wellington. If I just go home now, he can stay like this, at least in my memory. We don't need to drag each other back and forth and spend all our money to figure out we were both supposed to stay home in the first place.

I fly home to a snowy Canadian January with my kids in our cozy cabin with the green tin roof. My wood stove crackles as I make dinner and help my kids with their homework. I laugh to myself at one of a million memories with Joe and realize I wouldn't be surprised if he showed up at my house next week or never. I actually just like the world better because he's in it.

DOUKHOBOR MUSEUM

I stand in the kitchen of the Doukhobor museum of Brilliant, BC, near the Castlegar airport. I can't believe I've already been teaching for four years. It's the spring of 2013 and I'm on a class field trip to visit Selkirk College with students from grades ten, eleven and twelve. We've toured the Keenleyside Dam, which was built in 1968, flooding deep fertile valleys and creating the Arrow Lakes to hold back water on behalf of the United States. Visiting the heritage village of Brilliant is also of much interest as my students have researched Doukhobor history.

Our guide is a round-faced, grandmotherly woman with a wide smile. My students warm up to her quickly as she rambles on telling tales of her family and culture. She's impressed with how informed my students are and relates in animated detail the harrowing history her people endured as devout followers of the faith.

These rambling houses would hold up to five families and don't look dissimilar to the one I grew up in, with long wooden tables and benches in the communal kitchens and meeting halls. The grandmothers would sleep in the kitchen near the warming ovens to keep the fires burning and start the baking early.

The Doukhobors refused to give up their traditions and send their children to public school. The government of British Columbia decided to assimilate this band of Russian-speaking, borscht-eating pacifists. In true colonial style, the government forcefully took their children and packed them away in a prison-style residential school. The first raid on their children took place in 1953, the same year as the Short Creek raid on the fundamentalist Mormons in Utah.

A small group of Doukhobors, the Sons of Freedom, rallied to stop this oppression. Naked protests, including men and women, were staged outside the school prison walls, strategic power outages were caused by blasting electrical power lines and a government building was burned, followed by naked marches through the middle of town.

"Yes, they took us for only five years," the motherly tour guide tells my group of students, children of fundamentalist polygamist families. "But it was enough to sever the generations. Our fathers were sent to prison. The children were off at the residential schools. Growing up, many of us felt ashamed of our parents, our traditional dress and language, and wanted to just be normal. Mostly our culture is lost to our descendants. The government broke us."

⟡

Dad's arrest, and polygamy being illegal, is alive in each of my students' minds. Several of my little sisters hang back as we are leaving and share with our guide, their now confidante, their own personal harrowing stories of watching their father be taken away in the back seat of a cop car. The one-and-a-half-hour drive home over two mountain passes is sombre. My sister Elsie talks about one thousand people going to jail for three years simply for walking through town with their clothes off. Children were taken to a prison school for five years just because their parents wouldn't teach them English.

"What if that happens to us? Why was Dad arrested for having more than one wife, when most of the world can sleep with whomever they want? If children can't be taught by their parents for five years, of course they will lose their faith. What would happen to our family if the children were taken away?" Her anger and youthful sense of rightness and wrongness is raw, but the fear and uncertainty she conveys settles in the group.

"That was a long time ago," I console them. "This is the twenty-first century. Canada is a progressive, liberal country. There are many good laws and systems to care for children and families and human rights. Dad was arrested on a 120-year-old law. The government is stuck with a law that is a relic of Judeo-Christian ideals."

I continue with what I feel is the truth. "In Canada, we believe that the values of one sect cannot dictate the laws of the land. The Charter of Rights and Freedoms guarantees every Canadian the right to religion. There is no way this kind of thing could ever happen again in a modern Canada."

⟡

I struggle because I know Dad doesn't deserve to go to jail for living his lifestyle according to the faith and tradition he was born into. I realize a large part of my anger with him is because his choice to marry Adeline was breaking up the family, and he was doing it in the name of the inspiration of God. The family was reeling over their marriage, which contradicted what he had told us about how a man should take another wife.

How could he do this? After the split with Warren Jeffs and our struggle just to maintain some connection as a family, it felt so wrong. My own bitterness chokes my heart. I feel so let down by him. He had no right to teach me to have a strong moral compass, think for myself and have hopes and dreams, but then have no room for me in the world when I needed to stand up for them.

I know he will never approve of my choice to leave my marriage. In our church, a priesthood marriage is for time and all eternity. According to the faith, God will require me to burn in hell forever as I have broken the most sacred of vows—my marriage covenant with my husband.

Throughout my life, my father's approval has always been of the utmost importance. He was an inspired man of God; thus his was the same as the approval of God. I always dressed a certain way, did my hair a certain way, spoke and behaved in a way befitting a woman and mother in Zion.

These days I dream often of moving away, of moving to Vancouver and starting a new life. But knowing I would be running away and wanting my children to have connection to family is what makes me stay. I know that wherever I go, there I will be to work through my struggles. I want to move toward something, not away from something, not away from my family. When I travel to Shambhala, when I go to New York and to New Zealand, I am searching for meaning, for adventure, for distraction, but also for clarity. No matter where I am, I discover that I still long for my dad.

As a child, it bothered me that all my friends had their own dads and they still got to share my dad because he was the bishop. I want the dad who told me the great legends of my larger-than-life family heroes. The one who could sing any song and strum along with his three chords on the guitar. The one who showed me birds' nests and helped me keep them secret. The one who wrote poems with me and told me we were going to be famous one day. The one who helped me get my first hockey equipment and who taught me to ride a motorbike. The one who was proud of his smart, pretty daughters. The age-old Blackmore stubbornness means my father and I will very likely go to our graves angry and silent.

I realize you don't stop needing a dad when you grow up.

⁌

One night I get a call from Starla's aunt telling me her kids showed her a Snapchat of our thirteen-year-old Starla and Jenna drunk at a party at a boy's house in town. Horrified, I drive to find them, and we spend the next week fighting and crying about boundaries and safety and grounding. I hold my own babies and I know it would be impossible for me not to love them. I let myself remember how much parents love their children.

Ironically, I realize that if I don't consider the religion as a factor, my dad and I are both angry at each other for doing the same thing. We each made our personal, potentially selfish choices at the cost of people we love.

For two years I believed that my father didn't love me because I felt he would never approve of me. I withheld my love from him because I thought if I loved him, that meant I approved of what he was doing.

How wrong I was to confuse approval with love.

⟩

A few weeks after my visit to the Doukhobor museum, I am at the meeting hall setting up chairs for our school graduation. Father is across the room with his now twenty-year-old wife. I busy myself with the chairs, ignoring them. My father walks all the way across the shiny tiled hall toward me. "Mary, come here. I want to show you something."

He speaks as if we have been conspiring on a project, not like these are the first words spoken between us in well over a year. I follow him into a side room where he has been wiring some outlets and now has it ready for drywall. We walk around the room while he shows me his work. I comment appropriately and he leaves. As I line up chairs in the echoing hall, I realize my dad is really trying. This is him reaching out to me, his apology of sorts, and him inviting me back into his life. I take this little tour of his handiwork for what it is: a peace offering from my dad.

BURNING MAN

Burning Man has been on my bucket list for a while now, so it's an easy decision when my friend Deep calls me from Vancouver. "I've found two Burning Man tickets. Do you think we can pull this off?" We have a week to prepare for a festival that most people take a year to plan for. School will start for me the day after I return, so I also must prepare my classroom before I leave.

Deep and I meet in Portland and then drive down together. I'm taking my turn driving as the landscape opens into the Nevada desert. I'm thinking about Susie, who I'm sure is only a state away in Utah but may as well be in another galaxy. Deep and I arrive in the dark, find a little corner to tuck in our modest camp and head out to explore our new home. Black Rock City is laid out in a large C with streets going out like the spokes of a wheel sectioned off like a clock with "the Man" exactly in the centre.

The principles of Burning Man feel oddly similar to the principles of the United Order that the fundamental polygamist Mormons practised. The United Order loosely followed a communist value system and everyone was expected to jump in and help out. I was raised with a high value placed on working for the common good, which is still important to me. And these days, I kind of like the idea of "dedicating all that I have to God." We fully believed that dedicating tithes to the church and offering generously to our brothers and sisters was the path to achieve a life of true prosperity and abundance.

❧

Dressed as a stealthy tigress, I slink across the playa. I climb up a ladder and crawl in the back of an art car to find a group snuggled up on some large cushions. I join them to share warmth and stories while the mutant vehicle drives directly into a slowly lightening sky. To our surprise, it stops and the side of the car opens. Out come enough tables and chairs to host high tea for the extended royal family. As the strands of first light trace playful fingers across the playa, electric swing music brings a swirl of white-clad dancers in Victorian ballroom gowns, coattails and pintucked trousers. We join the party to sip coffee, eat crumpets and dance the sun into the sky.

The next night, I'm walking through the high playa at 2:00 a.m., digging in a little extra to keep going. From out of nowhere, in the middle of the desert, someone hands me a hot grilled cheese sandwich, dripping with cheese and crunchy. I savour every morsel.

❧

"About thirty minutes before sunset" had been our agreed time to meet in the cozy Heart Tribe lounge tent near our camp. A gale of powerful wind hits. With fellow Burners, we take refuge inside an art installation. Finally deciding I can set the wind at my back and make my way back to camp, I fasten my gear and seal my goggles over my eyes, tightening my bandana across my mouth and nose. My Winnie-the-Pooh backpack bobbles behind me as I pedal my trusty ten-dollar thrift store bike with a wicker basket wired between the handlebars, hair and streamers flying in the wind.

Waiting for Deep, I enjoy some refreshing yoga stretching on the dusty mats. From out of the swirling dust appears a stocky man with a youthful face and wide shoulders ducking through the hanging curtain door. His bearded face is serious and earnest. He is wearing a fur hat with earflaps and a long, heavy fur coat. He looks like he could be one of the coureurs de bois, the French fur traders who helped settle Canada and forge relations with First Nations people.

He's engrossed in his storytelling, one hand held over a large, smooth, triangular pendant that hangs over the centre of his chest from a strip of leather around his neck. He speaks of the visiting alien prophet who selected him to be a keeper of the relic. His eyes include me in the conversation, so I move over to listen more closely. The heavy smooth stone has been tested, he says, and is proven to not match any stone known to earth. On each side is a surprisingly detailed machine-engraved stencil depicting scenes of aliens. The first is some kind of battle scene and the other is a long line of aliens carrying their dead or injured and waiting to board a disc-shaped spaceship. He explains that he has just left his meeting with the visiting alien prophet, who came to Burning Man searching for reliable keepers to safeguard these relics. Emphatically he tells us that there were originally two thousand of them but some were found and confiscated by the evil American government, who said they would put them into a museum but are actually conspiring to keep them from ever being connected so the prophecy can never be fulfilled.

The alien prophet emphasized to this young man that one day all the relics will again come back together. Each one carries part of the key that holds the secrets to life and a peaceful world. When the time comes and they are united, all will be revealed to humanity and then our years of suffering and pain will end. The governments that have oppressed people will fall and the earth will know freedom and peace. Tonight, he has been anointed by the prophet as a keeper and has now been entrusted with the relic.

"I will know when the time is right," he assures us. "That is when it will be time to gather."

Just as he's concluding, Deep appears through the shifting door, wearing a brown bear hat with small alert ears that look like they are made to go with his brown skin. He wears bohemian attire that looks playful and comfortable. As Deep and I walk into the evening, I ponder the tale and the conviction and passion the relic keeper carried in his words. He spoke with the heart of a man who has at last found meaning, hope and something to live for. I never considered questioning his story. It all may have been just a beautifully crafted and curated art installation. For today, at least, the alien prophet is as real as he needs him to be, and the coureur de bois, keeper of the relic, anointed by the alien prophet, is as real as I need him to be.

As we walk into the dimming light, my mind turns to my Mormon family and all the years of my life living by the directions of the Prophet and serving as God's chosen people to prepare for the Second Coming of Christ. I muse at the similarities my story shares with that of this burly idealist and his resolution to help usher in the end of suffering. My sister Susie is out there living in another desert, following another tale given to her by a man or perhaps an alien calling himself a prophet.

Deep and I run to catch up and leap onto the back step of a toddling art car, a colourful shoe that has somehow gone missing from a giant clown's tickle trunk. Glowing green aliens run past in a hurry to get somewhere.

ARRESTED AGAIN

The Crown has found a judge who is willing to hear Dad's case. His lawyer tells him there is a warrant out for his arrest and the police set up two roadblocks on both main roads going into town. Dad drives his pickup through Riverview in Lister, which winds through the Lower Kootenay Band reservation, and he drives right to the police station and turns himself in.

"I wasn't going to give those suckers the pleasure of arresting me again," he tells us later.

It's 2016, seven years since the original arrest. The buzz and the media flare up all over again.

※

I usually know there has been another development in the media version of the Bountiful polygamy drama when someone comments about it as I'm going about my life.

Only weeks after Dad's arrest, my kids and I are headed to Vancouver Island to see their aunt Brittany, who is now studying nursing at the University of Victoria. In Greenwood, we stop for a bathroom break and ice cream. Disappointed, we notice it is after five o'clock. The sleepy historic main street is closed for business.

"It looks like your only option," I tell Starla, whose urgency is showing in her face, "is to go into the Royal Canadian Legion." I inquire in the dimly lit billiard hall, where two older gentlemen sit at the bar.

"She can't go past the bar," the bartender asserts hesitantly.

As I wait, one of the patrons asks where we are from. At the mention of Creston, he immediately starts in with the familiar question: "What do you think they are going to do with that Blackmore and Oler problem?"

In these situations, my answers depend on how I'm feeling. Occasionally I feel like provoking the conversation. Sometimes I actually share my thoughts and identity. Sometimes I play the part of the passive general public.

Today I've got a minute. "Well, I'm a Blackmore." I introduce myself, cheerfully shaking his hand. "Winston is my dad. These are his grandchildren."

The man at the bar introduces himself as Bob.

The gentleman on the bar stool beside my friendly inquirer harrumphs a few times. Under his breath he says no one should have that many kids and continues listening intently while not making eye contact.

"You see," Bob says, "for me, it really isn't about polygamy. If a man wants to deal with that many women and their emotions, he's got my blessing. What I've got a problem with is all the abuse. What makes me mad is Winston having all these women and not taking care of them. How can a man take care of so many women? And that's not even to mention the children. You can't tell me," he continues, "that all of those women are married to Winston Blackmore and having all of these children because they want to."

I listen and nod along to his genuine concern for human well-being and his reiteration of what two decades of media sensationalism have created out of the story of my family. I don't have the time or interest to debate with Bob today. So I smile good-naturedly. Maybe it's because Greenwood looks like a scene from the Old West or because I'm talking to this friendly old cowboy in a bar, but I put my hand on his arm in a theatrical gesture and speak in a southern cowboy drawl. "Well now, Bob, you, my friend, have just asked the million-dollar question. It sure beats the heck out of me, but them old gals ain't a pack of dummies and they keep sayin' they love my old man. I think at some point ya just got to believe them."

My sixteen-year-old daughter and fourteen-year-old son look at me with a mix of humour and horror and quickly remind me we need to get going.

I secure my handbag across my shoulder as I prepare to leave.

"And besides that, Bob," I continue more seriously, "if this is about abuse, he needs to be charged with abuse. There is no evidence of abuse under the definition of the law. And as far as his kids go, my father has at least forty adult children and we mostly really like our dad. I know people who have only a couple of siblings who talk about their dads like they wouldn't hesitate to throw him in front of a train. That's gotta say something. And if ya ever get a chance, you should meet him; he's quite a sparkly fella. I bet you and he would get along."

❧

The next weekend, over our mashed potatoes and gravy, Dad tells us his version of this second arrest. I don't go to many family or church events these days or even know about what's going on most of the time, but my relationship with my dad is something we've both worked at. This has been a really hard few years for him.

"Come on, Dad," I half tease him. "Take one for the team. As a spectator sport, this would be a lot more interesting if we actually got to see how it ends. Let us find out what they *are* going to do with polygamists."

He scoffs, offended that I'm arguing for the wrong team. "It's not you who has to give up your passport and go to jail. Sitting in the grubby little jail cell was very sobering. The little cot was sticky and gross and the toilet needed scrubbing. I would have happily cleaned it if someone had brought me some cleaning supplies. I'm not going to jail," he says emphatically. "I have no idea what these numbskulls are going to try to do with me. I would rather spend all my time working and spend all my money not going to jail."

I really can't fault him feeling this way. When he turned fifty-seven a few years ago, Dad was the age his father had been when he'd died. That year Dad was obsessed that he needed to get his life in order as he felt this might be the year God was going to call him home. Each year since, he's expressed gratitude that God has given him one more year to make fence posts and hay, one more year with his wives and one more year with his kids. I can see that the thought of spending even one year of that time sitting in the "grubby little jail cell" is almost more than he can stand.

For Dad and his family, this whole thing is starting to feel like a witch hunt. I can see why they are losing faith that this was ever about the review of a law to better protect people and prevent "harm to women, to children, to society and to the institution of monogamous marriage," as it has been revised to state in the Polygamy Reference in the Criminal Code of Canada. I'm confused about why multicultural Canada is so protective of the "institution of monogamous marriage." With a failure rate of 50 percent, I'd argue that it is currently a failing institution. I'm not for or against monogamy any more than I'm for or against polygamy, or gay marriage for that matter. I just think people should get to choose whom they want to love and create their own definition of family. I don't think the government has any place here.

I certainly don't agree with everything my dad has done. I still struggle with how I feel about Adeline. But here six years later, I applaud her for working her way through nursing college. For all I can tell, she's as happy as a pig in mud and loving the weird life God inspired her to live.

I've argued with Dad that he is being paranoid when he goes on about religious persecution and powerful people in government who are making his conviction and jail time their personal vendetta. Now I'm beginning to think he might be right. I'm pretty nervous for him. It's looking like he might end up in jail.

➹

While spreading butter on his fresh dinner roll, Dad explains the legal process of why he was arrested the second time.

"Wally Oppal was the guy in government determined to see the law crack down on polygamists. Oppal hired two of the lawyers who had been used in the trial on the Polygamy Reference to do more research into section 293 of the Criminal Code to determine if the law would withstand a constitutionality challenge. These lawyers, Doust and Peck, determined that it would not. Still, the Attorney General appointed Wilson, who had me arrested again the second time." Dad pauses his storytelling as my younger sisters serve dessert, a scoop of fresh ice cream with bottled raspberries and juice poured over it, plus a warm homemade cookie on the side, a Blackmore family favourite.

Joe Arvay, Dad's lawyer, challenged the government for prosecutor shopping, which is illegal, but the judge struck it down.

As we are finishing up our dessert, Dad continues. "I had my lawyer offer Mr. Wilson that I would plead guilty to living my religion, which included polygamy. He told me to stand mute, and the trial began."

Our dinner plates are smeared with extra gravy and a bit of leftovers. About twenty of us push our chairs back and remain hanging around the tables. Only a few people get up to start clearing up the dishes.

Among our moms and Dad's adult children and spouses, we have a lot of practical skills. We are nurses and teachers, farmers, machine operators, business owners and tradespeople. We are an effective group if you need to get something done. But this is a different kind of problem, and besides gathering resources for financial support or just sitting here to listen, we don't really know what else to do.

➹

Even curious observers of the process are all asking the same question: How does the government seriously plan to prosecute polygamous relationships? A concerned friend of mine has been following Dad's case. She is in a committed poly-family relationship and tells me she is concerned with how decisions concerning this case will affect and set a criminal precedence for other non-traditional poly-family structures.

The way the 2011 Polygamy Reference is written, any person having one legal marriage and another committed relationship is living in polygamy, which is a Criminal Code offence and punishable under the law with a maximum five-year jail sentence. I know lots of people who fit this family structure description in and out of the church whose lives and children will be legally affected by this law.

Here, seven years after my dad's first arrest, I still feel that the criminal system is misdirecting its efforts if its goal is better protection of families and preventing harm. The polygamy law does little or nothing to protect vulnerable people who might find themselves living in polygamy and, I would argue, has not discouraged people from living this lifestyle, as no one in Canada has been prosecuted under this law since 1890.

This law does the opposite of protecting people: it actually creates a more at-risk demographic by making it necessary for people to lie about their marital status and hide their lifestyle from health service providers, law enforcement and even their friends outside their trusted community.

Polygamy has been illegal in Canada for nearly 130 years, but cultures of poly families continue to survive despite its criminal nature. People choose a polygamous or poly lifestyle for a whole gamut of reasons, including religious beliefs. The cultures of secrecy and insular communities have been made necessary and perpetuated by the criminalization of a family structure people believed was fundamental to their faith. Secret marriages and families are a direct result of a Euro-Christian mandate by the Canadian and American governments to criminalize the polygamous family structures of Mormons. The Canadian law written in 1890 originally stated "Mormon Polygamy" until the wording was changed in the 1950s.

Women living in polygamy have lived with the fear that if they seek services, they will put their husbands or themselves at risk of prosecution and their children at risk of going into government care. These are not imagined fears as many have seen family and other communities live this experience.

If a polygamist family structure were legal in society, those who practise it would have access to the same resources and support systems as the rest of society and fall under the same regulations concerning common-law entitlement and child support when a marriage breaks down. This would create a safety net for the vulnerable people in this demographic to access health and wellness services as well as advocate for their families without feeling like they would be putting family members at risk of criminal charges. Additionally, this would give community services and law enforcement the avenue to focus on harm prevention rather than getting hung up on the criminal nature of the family structure.

Furthermore, eliminating the need for secrecy takes power away from potential perpetrators of abuse, such as Warren Jeffs. He took advantage of the legal need for secrecy and used it as a tool to manipulate vulnerable people under a pretense of protecting the sacred. A culture that is saturated in secrecy and religious dogma is not protected by anti-polygamy laws. People living within the culture are made more vulnerable because they are less likely to seek counselling, health services or even friendships outside of their community because of fear of exposing family members and loved ones to repercussions from the law. Removing the need for secrecy would remove a crucial layer of oppression on the vulnerable people within polygamist relationships.

I sit back and watch my family. We sit for a few minutes in silence. This part of the drama has always been in the background of our lives, sometimes louder, sometimes barely thought about at all. My brothers push back from their chairs to get back to their lives. There are trees to cut and logs to haul and money to make and bills to pay. But we have each other; we may be misunderstood by the world but we are family and we are here for each other through thick and thin.

WOMEN'S BODIES

It's been five years since Sam and I divorced. I've wondered if the thrill of airports and faraway countries would lose its sparkle after a while, but it feels like the opposite is true. As I venture farther afield to foreign lands, music festivals, spirit quests and workshops, my hunger to learn, experience myself and more deeply know God only becomes sharpened. These journeys have also informed my widening understanding of feminism and the places that women occupy—or are allowed to occupy—in their communities, their families and their own bodies.

In spring 2015, Linda and I visit Turkey. I try to check my prejudice before I arrive. "What if you get beheaded by a jihadist?" was my cautionary goodbye from friends as I left. I'm determined to go with an open mind. The train from the airport is full of sharply dressed men with polished shoes and sleek, black, sculpted hair. Pressed together in a crowded train car, I shuffle my pack. In the tight space, a tall man behind me lets his hand rest on the side of my breast. I stiffen, surprised, and turn so his hand falls away.

Linda and I spend days exploring the streets, combing through museums and drinking pints of Tuborg each evening on the rooftop patio overlooking the Bosporus strait with the silhouettes of the mosques' spires outlining the stunning Istanbul skyline. I look for women to talk to, which proves to be more challenging for an English-speaking traveller on the tourist route through Turkey than I would have thought. I want to know how the course and dialogue of the feminist experience has differed in this part of the world, shaping the minds and thoughts of women in a country where women didn't spend a decade running the factories and institutions while the men were off at war and then get sent back to their houses and domestic responsibilities.

Two young men approach us as we are walking across the tulip-covered Sultanahmet Square. In calculated English, they tell us they study at the university and ask if they can walk with us to practise their English. Getting a chance to ask questions and learn a few Turkish words feels like a good trade. We order tea at a shop overlooking the Blue Mosque with its striking gardens and bustling square filled with tour buses and selfie sticks.

"Women have rights here," Sud, the more outgoing of the two, confirms with confidence. "They can own land and go to school."

"Where are they?" I ask. Women are noticeably absent from the workforce and more noticeably absent from the social life in restaurants and bars as well as trains and public spaces.

"Women and grannies like to stay home," Sud assures us and they both nod. "They have house parties and eat in the backyard with the grandmas and babies."

"Well, what if they want to go dancing?" I ask pointedly.

"They are allowed but they just don't want to," he affirms.

⚭

At the hostel, Ammon is unusual because he has spent eight years in the United States travelling for business, which is really the only way to get a visa. He gives us some insights into our experience of the assertive men we navigate in the markets each day.

"Turkish men have this idea that Western women are easy and promiscuous, especially travellers. They would never treat a Turkish woman in this way or her daddy and her brothers would cut them." He makes a snipping gesture like he's using scissors.

A woman at the hostel tells us her travelling-in-Turkey trick and Linda and I both start wearing a ring on our left hands, which works wonderfully.

Linda and I conclude that, pleasantly, we don't feel unsafe here, just cautious of grabby hands. Turkish men have a curiosity and forwardness that feels juvenile compared with men in Western culture. They seem opportunistic rather than predatory, like drunk Canadian men can be. We master good eye contact and firm noes.

I'm still curious what the real lives of these women are like. Ammon tells me he is a feminist and attends women's rights rallies, which he says is not common for men here.

"Do many women go to school to get a university education?" I ask him. "What about women who want to have a career?"

He laughs. "Yes, women go to school, but women have a good life here. That is not needed. It isn't the struggle life for women here like it is in America."

I think about my friends keeping up with career and family and bills. I don't disagree with his statement. I think about my "struggle life" back home in Canada. Then I also think about getting my own paycheque and having my own credit cards and buying my own plane ticket to Turkey.

Divorce in Turkey is still rare, but Ammon describes a case from the local news that followed an ongoing court battle for a woman who experienced violent long-term domestic abuse. This was a rare case in which the woman was awarded her house and her children and charges were laid against her husband.

He says, "Many people blame religion but beating your wife is not part of Islam. We must stop this kind of violence. Slowly, this is changing."

I hope Ammon is right. I know the story of men hiding behind religion and using it as a justification for abuse. Abuse is everyone's problem. Families and communities, I believe, are the front line of protection and are accountable for keeping their vulnerable people safe, but when they fail, government and laws must protect people from abuse.

I think about Dad being arrested in 2009 on charges of polygamy. When the law was put on trial in 2011, the prosecution was challenged with proving the harm that polygamy causes to women and children.

I know how hard it is to break from long traditions in which heavy consequences of heaven and hell and eternity are deeply ingrained. I remember how hard it was for my brothers and me when Mom asked Dad for a divorce. In our way of thinking, she was breaking the connection our family had to one another in the afterlife, our eternity together. That felt like a high price to pay for temporary happiness on earth. I ponder that maybe this is why in some religious contexts people can have confusion around what equates abuse. Set next to the punishment of hellfire and eternal damnation, a little thumping around probably seems insignificant.

Recently here in Turkey there has been a push toward more traditional Muslim values, which argue that the troubles of society stem from forgetting the old ways. This sounds very familiar to me. I can hear my old aunts and uncles proclaiming the importance of remembering the long suffering of the old Prophets and leaders and all they had stood for. Grandma Mem said often, "There is nothing uglier than a woman who swears." I remember Uncle Mac warning my father that he needed to better safeguard the virtue of his daughters. Frequently he cautioned that our dresses were too tight and our hairstyles showed vanity. We had to work like boys but we couldn't cuss like them. Our clothes needed to be modest and functional for hard physical labour but somehow we had to be feminine. We had to think and prepare our hearts for marriage but never become indulgent in fantasies about the men we would wed. We had to be sweet, helpful and nurturing, but never self-righteous or bossy—heaven forbid the world should be cursed with an angry, bitchy woman. Oh, what shame that would bring on our families! We had to keep our bodies and our minds strong and pure that we might bear the sons and daughters to build the Lord's army.

It's easy to see religion as the enemy. After watching my community struggle to release the mental grip of the Warren Jeffs regime, here in Turkey I shudder to see institutionalized systems seething with religious dogma. My Western sensibilities echo passionately for the separation of church and state, but with my background, I also have some room for compassion and even understand the comfort of a culture of deeply internalized religious beliefs.

The others hanging around the conversation have gone to bed and Ammon leaves to finish cleaning up the restaurant and finish his work. I drink the last of my beer standing at the railing, looking across the dazzling skyline of Istanbul with the silhouetted spires of the Blue Mosque.

In fall 2015, six months after returning from my travels in Turkey, I get an opportunity to attend a community development conference in Toronto that is being hosted by Tamarack Institute and the fabulous Paul Born, whose work I've been following and studying for a few years. The week of the conference is everything I need it to be. I am thrilled to see an opportunity to sign up for a writing workshop with none other than Mr. Born himself. He's from a Mennonite heritage, and we connect through our stories and talk about our shared passion for inspiring and helping communities to thrive.

I'm pleasantly surprised to discover my last night in the city coincides with the Nuit Blanche art festival. But as I'm wandering downtown, I come across a pro-life demonstration across the street from Union Station.

I notice some people wearing "Vote Conservative" buttons and Conservative Party leaflets being handed out. I try not to debate this topic. I've engaged in sociology classes or commented on social media, but more closely when it has affected the real lives of people I love.

It stands to reason that women actually having control over their own bodies is the direction we should be headed in a free society and I feel very cautious about the idea of having more laws in government controlling a woman's right to her own body. Still, I am not prepared for this scene.

Expensive, glossy, colour printed posters of mangled and mutilated human fetuses are being marched across the street by well-dressed university student evangelicals. Piously, a young woman opens with "Do you believe life is sacred?" It's a sales hook to get me to stop long enough for her to unleash her well-practised script.

I stand looking at her for a minute with my brow furrowed. "Think of what you are asking a woman to do." I delve into the dark end of the spectrum. "What about rape victims, socially marginalized citizens in poverty who have turned to prostitution, the homeless or the mentally ill? If a woman knows she cannot provide her child with any kind of life, is she not choosing from a place of desperate compassion?"

She answers with exaggerated disbelief, as if the simple solution should have been clear to me. "We aren't suggesting women in these situations should keep their babies." She pauses to let me catch up. "They should give the baby up for adoption. There are many families who can afford a baby and would love to give that baby the life she couldn't. Life is sacred. A child should have every chance at a good life."

I'm taken aback by the naive simplicity and near cheerfulness in the way she makes this statement.

I blink and don't even try to hide the judgment in my voice. "You want the government to force women to have babies they know they can't raise, so someone else can have the joy she can't afford herself? You think that it is an easy thing for a woman to give away her child?" As I speak, images from "A Modest Proposal" by Jonathan Swift come into my vivid imagination, and for a moment this feels like an elaborate conspiracy to get the struggling lower classes to give their babies to the wealthy who can't be bothered to have their own children. I shake my head and look at her directly. "Now what kind of a woman would do that?" I walk into the bustle of the street crossing, the clamour of Union Station folding into my thoughts as I pick up my pace to catch my train.

I leave them feeling gut sick. How have we taken this intimate personal challenge some women find themselves facing and turned it into an ugly, polarizing political debate to rally the morality of our youth and smear into a campaign for votes? I settle into the clatter and rock of the train car as I think of a quote I read by an old Canadian midwife: "Only a woman knows if she has enough love to give life." Tonight I add, "And maybe we could just trust her."

✤

In spring 2017 I visit Amsterdam and go to Red Light Secrets, the world's first museum of prostitution. I consider the contradictions, beauties and dangers of living in a woman's body as I wander the museum. My audio guide informs me that in the Book of Genesis, the wiles of the first Biblical prostitute, Tamar, were praised when she cunningly outwitted her father-in-law, Judah, who was the grandson of old Father Abraham. Through thoughtfully curated installations, visitors listen to the personal stories of the ladies of the night. Many speak of their profession with pride. Visitors can sit inside of a street window to see what it feels like to be watched by passersby on the street. As a young woman I always felt I was being watched; even if no one was around, God was always watching. I stayed pure and sweet.

I think about women, our bodies, our rights to our bodies. The ability to say yes and to say no and to have culture, laws and enforcement to make those yeses and noes actually mean anything, whether it is being a "sex therapist" or marrying a person who is also married to someone else. I think of the experience of being a woman in the world and how drastically different being a woman can be depending on where you are born.

As I'm looking for my number on the passing buses, I'm thinking about how confusing and potentially harmful it is to have laws controlling what we do with our bodies and how we love. It feels clear to me as I settle into my seat, watching the lights of Amsterdam go by, that the only role for governments and laws to play when it comes to the body and the heart is to prevent harm and abuse. When we have culture and systems that provide real choice, let a woman do whatever the fuck she wants to do with her own body.

My Thirty-Fourth Birthday

It's May 3, 2017, the morning of my thirty-fourth birthday. I sit on my front porch. I'm lost in thought, watching the spring sun slanting across the vibrant green meadow at the base of the Skimmerhorn mountains. Both my parents are in court today. My dad is charged with practising a polygamous lifestyle, which is illegal under the Criminal Code of Canada. My mom has been subpoenaed as a witness for the prosecution.

I imagine the scene being played out in that sterile courtroom as a TV drama for the entertainment of the public. In my mind's eye, I don't see them as my parents but rather as the media portrays them: my father's charisma and earnest nature comes across as self-importance, and my petite mother's sense of duty appears vindictive. Both are characters the media has created, two bitter and disgruntled people, worn-out victims of a life that is presented to the viewer only to be pitied or scorned. I've stopped watching the news.

⁂

My dad's hair is almost white now and his hairline is receding, making him look so much like the black and white photos of Grandpa Ray that hung on our living room wall. I'm not sure when his hair changed colour. It's his round face, square jaw and wide smile I see reflected in my own face. We both wear glasses. He and I have a complex relationship but I'm always happy to see him. Jake and I often remark how, even when you are mad at Dad, by the time you have spent an hour with him, he's got you so stoked about his next project that you forget all about it. He's careful to look professional when showing up for court, so he's traded his tan vest for a black tie and a sports coat. He quickly buttons the top button when he's walking so his belly won't hang out, he says. He is not a tall man but his broad shoulders and stance take up plenty of space in a room.

Since the Split, when my father went from the beloved "Uncle Wink" to what Warren Jeffs designated him, "the most wicked man on earth," I have observed and found myself defending my father. The man is a lot of things, but I really think what you see is what you get. He has a weird habit of thinking out loud and he gives truly thoughtful, reflective answers to any question you could think to ask. He's a pilot and a farmer. His favourite clothes are his Carhartt jacket, his leather ball cap and his sturdy leather boots. He's an old cowboy at heart and, I'm sure, still imagines himself singing and yodelling through the meadow, riding his favourite horse, even though I can't imagine when the last time was he got on one. He's patient at unexpected times and is the most skilled and thoughtful minister, caring for families during the really important parts of life when you need that calm fatherly presence, especially when families have to bury their dead. Over the last decade I've seen families who've scorned my father and shamed and hated him, but upon the death of a child, he is the first one they call. His generosity and skill in caring for grieving families and putting together funerals are remarkable.

➥

My pretty mother gets more and more fretful in the days leading up to her testimony. She says she has to review evidence in her file from past hearings, which includes listening to dreadful old interviews with every "um" and stutter glaring at her. "It's terrible," she says.

Before the Split, my mother was the beloved "Aunt Janie" of our community. She delivered the babies and cared for the sick. She worked as community social worker and family counsellor. She was generous with her money and her time and frequently offered her services and resources for free to those she knew were struggling financially. She spent her snips of spare time building lavish flower gardens and giving dance lessons to the girls in the community. She's always encouraged women to walk for their physical and mental health.

Walking and gardens have been her sanity, she says.

➥

The dancing stream that runs behind the Old Barn just beyond the mountain is the same one that captured my childhood imagination and is also where my parents played when they were childhood playmates. Mom and Dad rode horses across this valley when they were a young couple, and this is where their babies grew up, squished mud between their toes and saddled their horses.

In my imagination I see them together, just the two of them with their three sons, before our mother shared him with other women. They knew their family would grow and their love and home were meant to be shared. Their strong sons grew; other women joined their family. I came along as their fifth child, only six months older than my brother, my father's sixth child. From the time I knew the world, I lived in a house full of women who wrestled out life together: my grandmother, my three mothers, my aunties and my older cousins. My uncles lifted me onto their shoulders for piggyback rides. Each evening we circled the big dining room table, arms folded and heads bowed in gratitude, smiles and laughter served with stew and Grandma's fresh bread.

How did we get from there to here?

✜

I imagine my mother as she takes the stand to answer a series of questions about her time with my father, her ex-husband, as well as her time in the church and her role as a caregiver for the family and community.

She is a beautiful woman whose natural disposition, I'm sure, is to be quiet and thoughtful. But a long life of shouldering a heavy responsibility, caring for a large family and being a voice for women who didn't have the courage or skills to be their own, has left a furrow in her brow and a curve in her shoulders, which she is determined to correct with yoga.

I picture her straining as she recounts memories of family tragedies, my father's poor decisions and unkind and even cruel treatment of sensibilities from the past, whether in the name of the church or plain bad judgment.

✜

"Twenty-one days in BC Supreme Court to prove I'm a polygamist," my father says in exasperation and shakes his head. "I have never once denied that I live my religion and love all of my wives and children. Seems like to me these guys don't have enough to do. The part that really bugs me is I've got to work at night to get all of my logs hauled after sitting in court all day. What a waste of time," he finishes.

I don't even bother to read any of the news reports about Mom's testimony or Dad's defence. We've been through this many times before. I'm not interested in what he said or she said in court. I've been a careful and attentive witness to their lives. Ultimately, this will be just like the last time my parents went through this. We will work through all seven stages of grief and slowly we will be okay again. Right now I'm just on the mop-up crew.

"I feel again like I have leprosy," my mother cries at me. "None of the family will even talk to me."

"Just give it some time, Mom," I reassure her.

Even before their divorce, back when I was a teenager, I knew my mother disagreed often with my father. It was hard to be in the middle as they asked each other to be and do more than they could. They were, however, both very careful in what they said about each other in front of their children. I've always appreciated that she never tried to taint the way we loved and respected our father. Even as my father and I have struggled through our own relationship, she doesn't add fuel to the fire.

With the summer heat raising our temperatures and our full life never breaking stride around us, we gather our hurt feelings and keep celebrating birthdays and weddings.

✦

Birthdays, for me, always call up a time for reflection. I've called myself a feminist for a long time now, and since I've been on my own journey to know God, it has brought me to look at myself in the mirror with a desire to understand the woman I see. I've witnessed how my life and challenges have been so much different than my brothers'. They are good men who work hard, but their paths have been much more direct and in their own control. I'm actually very similar to my brothers and my dad. Often I've thought about how much easier it would have been for me had I been a man in my community rather than a woman.

I look out to the meadow, which has opened into a yellow blanket of dandelions as the sun came out. I think of Grams's lessons to be "a comfort and a help" to my husband and how burdening this assignment felt to me as a young woman. This many years later, I don't disagree with her. Being a comfort and a help to your spouse is good advice. But now I like to imagine Grams giving these same lessons to the men in my family.

I'm thinking about arranged marriages, about polygamy, choosing the relationships you want and love, and the ridiculousness that the government should have anything to do with any of it. My parents didn't choose each other and neither did Sam and I, at least not at first. I know from experience that love grows in proximity, shared experiences, shared values, shared goals, shared wins. It did for us, and I've always felt what we created together was a beautiful example of partnership and marriage. We spoke easily of how innocent and natural it felt to learn and develop together our physical connection and intimacy, which opened into a creative and expressive love life. We shared awe in watching our love evolve and deepen through our years together.

I never do this but today I let myself just think about Sam and wonder, What if things had been different? What if our baby had lived? What if we finished the big house and raised our children there?

I loved my husband even when I knew we could not be together anymore.

For us, separating felt like an act of compassion. I had too many questions about the world and how things worked. I knew that what I needed to learn and do for myself probably wasn't going to fit into any clean lines.

Through our decade-long marriage, I grew to love that man so intensely that many times I felt I would be willing to give up everything else I wanted to experience in this life so I could be his wife.

One day, several years after we had broken up, I was yet again trying to convince him we should give our relationship another shot. He laughed a little to soften his words but they still stung. "The thought of trying to make you happy scares the shit out of me," he said honestly.

Tonight, I smile gently, thinking about his words. For a long time, I let it hurt my feelings. I wasn't asking him to make me happy, I said. I just wanted him to love me for who I am. I wanted it to be okay to be all of me.

I take a deep breath, enjoying the warm smell of sunshine. I know I'm where I want to be, living a life that feels more every day to be designed for me. Sometimes the thought of trying to make me happy scares the shit out of me too, but I'm doing it.

PEACE IS NOT PASSIVE

The week after Dad's sentencing hearing, there is visible strain in family interactions. Conversations stop suddenly and there are awkward changes of topic for my sake. At school, my little niece gives me a hug with tears in her eyes. "I'm sad," she says, "because I don't know what to do. Annie said Grandma Jane wants to make Grandpa go to jail and she is making up lies about him to tell the court so Grandpa will have to get locked up. She says Grandma doesn't like Mormons or God so I don't think I can talk to Grandma anymore and I'm really sad."

After school I stop at my sister's house and ask her what's going on, as I've also had a strange conversation with her mother. Our mothers were close friends and sister-wives who really loved each other, so this surprises me. Now I am really concerned.

"Yeah, Mom is really upset. Just a few weeks ago she confided in Mother Jane, and she just feels sick that Mother Jane could take what she said and use it in court against Dad."

I call my cousin Mir. I'm not good at keeping up on the gossip circles at the best of times but it makes sense that people aren't sharing their anger toward my mother with me, sparing my feelings. With so much collective anxiety, it feels like the family is imploding with tension and scapegoating after the trial.

Mir fills me in on the details. "I heard your dad say himself, 'She's made it clear that she is no friend of ours.'"

I remember the way my dad used to talk about my mother, about how she was the smartest, most beautiful girl, about being classmates growing up together, about him praying that he could be a good enough man that he could marry his sweetheart. Now my mind flashes through this old dogma of enemies of the priesthood and enemies of the family. We have a long history of bonding best while defending against a common foe. Maybe this comes from our Mormon pioneer heritage. When someone yells "Circle the wagons," at least we know what to do.

⁘

"What the hell is Mom trying to do?" my brother Joe says. He's loading his horse trailer. I cross the barnyard between our houses and he leans against the side of his pickup truck. We debate the third-hand versions we've heard about our mother's testimony of the this and the that of our dad's current scrutiny under the law.

"They are going to go after her sons next. Does she want Peter and Hyrum put in jail? Like Dad said, if she doesn't want her family to talk to her anymore, she's really doing a good job of it."

I can feel the anger boiling in my blood. "Joey, they are divorced people acting like divorced people. You know why they're mad. They are mad because of a lifetime of being asked to do the impossible and they've both failed. They've been through a lot together and they've been plenty shitty to each other. We need to just let them be mad at each other. It is nobody's business to turn this into the next split in the church with Mom as the next enemy of the priesthood. This is bullshit. If we've got to blame someone, let's blame the government, or if we need to be mad at someone, let's be mad at Dad. In my opinion, he should have pleaded guilty two years ago so no one had to go through any of this. I argued with him to just let the system decide what they are going to do with polygamists. He is the one who is the polygamist and maybe he should have just gone and sat his ass in jail instead of dragging everyone through the last two years. Why would he even bother to appeal it?"

I pull out my phone and text my dad. "Dad, I'm sorry you are feeling hurt right now but this has to stop. You do not get to talk about Mom this way. This is between you and her and has nothing to do with the rest of the family. Her grandkids do not need to feel like they have to choose between their loyalty to their grandpa and their love for their grandma, whom they adore. At this point in her life, her kids and her grandkids are her whole wide world. This is cruel. She is mad at you, Dad. Not the family."

To my surprise, not ten minutes later, my dad rides over the hill on the white Yamaha four-wheeler that his kids and grandkids bought him for his sixtieth birthday.

"What's this, sweets?" He holds up his phone.

I'm digging in my garden, transplanting petunias. I'm still worked up from arguing with my brother. Dad leans forward on the handlebars. I take a few deep breaths.

"You have never heard me criticize your mother," he says. "I don't criticize any of my kids' mothers, no matter what any of them say about me. I love all my kids and I love their mothers for helping me raise them." He says it often and it's true. He doesn't criticize his wives or ex-wives but he sounds a bit too long-suffering in his statement, and I'm still mad.

It's rare for any of us to just have it out in a face-to-face verbal confrontation. I've worked hard to rebuild a relationship with my dad but this feels big and important, like something pivotal is about to happen and I need to try to stop it. "Dad, Mir said herself you said in a large group of people that Mom is no friend of our family. Dad, Mom is mad at you. She has plenty of reasons to be mad at you. But you don't get to make this be about the church or the family."

"Why would she bother saying she had never wanted to marry me? What's the point of all that?" He gets emotional when he says this to me, and I can see she got in a punch into some of the soft bits in his heart.

✸

One of our moms went to the sentencing hearings and faithfully sat in the gallery and listened to the whole thing. She came home saying most of what Mom said was a pack of lies. She relates the gory details to the mothers, the kids and the neighbours, each hurtful dig and detail splattered that day in court.

I go over to her house to talk to her. "Lies," she says, bursting into tears. "And just as she was going on the stand they gave her the option to opt out of going on, but she did it anyway. She didn't even have to do it. She isn't the only who was hurt here. This hurt our whole family, especially the mothers. This isn't just about Dad either."

"Right," I respond. I'm not nearly as sensitive as I should be to her pain. "You and the moms can keep your hurt feelings until the day you die. You lived through all these years and you've earned your trauma, but you don't get to give it to the kids. This has nothing to do with the kids, and we don't need to gift our children with a generation of prejudice that has nothing to do with them. Just leave them out of it. So I do have a problem with what you are saying, especially in front of the kids."

I'm exhausted, wrapping up my family triage. I go home. I'm still in momma-bear mode, hackles up and adrenalin coursing through me. I can't shake the feeling that something really bad almost happened to my family and I shudder at the familiarity of it. I shake my head at the stupidity of how we pass our prejudice and hatred onto our children, and watching my family do it is unsettling.

✸

As my children fall asleep in their warm beds in our family home that evening, I'm thinking about Aunt Debbie. I'm thinking about her desperation, her courage, her fear and frantic determination to save everyone from the suffering she experienced. I think of the way her words added to my own struggle growing up, and the way, in her war against abuse, she was turned into the enemy by her own family. As I'm falling asleep, I think about a Margaret Atwood quote: "War is what happens when language fails." If communication is the ticket to world peace, how can we build peace on earth when we so easily confuse our own caring family with the enemy?

On July 24, 2017, my father is convicted of polygamy under section 293 of the Criminal Code of Canada.

FAMILIES, NOT FELONS

The emotional and financial drain on my father's family these few years takes its toll. Two of my father's wives, who have education degrees from Canadian universities and meet all the requirements to immigrate under the point system, have been denied their immigration because my father's name is on their children's birth certificates. There is a real cost to them putting their livelihoods and work on hold, as their temporary work and immigration visas expire. One of them is deported back to the United States in the middle of the school year and has to pull her children out of school so they can be with her. She isn't able to cross into Canada again for a year. Dad is stuck on one side and the mother is stuck on the other side.

"Why does the government hate our family?" my eight-year-old sister Julianna asks me one day, her concern evident on her face. That's a hard question to answer, whether as a big sister or as a teacher. I'm determined not to perpetuate the fear that is so real to most of these kids and their mothers. I answer with less conviction than I used to as I tell the kids this is a process the government must do because they have a law that polygamy is illegal. "Well, it seems like they should just change the law so our family isn't illegal," she states matter-of-factly.

I encourage her sense of justice. "Well, sweetie, when you grow up you can become a lawyer and help fix the laws that don't make any sense. People made them and people have to change them. That's the only way to create the world we want to live in."

I'm as curious as the next person about what the government sees as a solution to Canada's "dirty little secret." What will Canada decide to do with polygamists?

"When it feels like the whole legal system is against you and there is prejudice at every turn, what can I do?" Mother Zelpha rants in frustration. "I've done everything right to be here legally and I'm made to feel like a criminal and second-class citizen. I want to go back to school to be a lawyer. I hate feeling powerless and that my voice doesn't matter. I'm so angry. When I got married and moved to Canada, I really thought I would at least be able to be a person. I paid international student fees for seven years of schooling. I have done the time and process. I deserve to live here."

I listen to Mother Zelpha and I feel her frustration. I don't agree with everything my father has done but I don't believe that the government should define what a family can be.

⚘

May 17, 2018, is our father's sentencing hearing. Several dozen of us take the day off to support our father in court. With fifty or so of my siblings planning to attend the sentencing hearing to show our support for our dad, we have a quick family meeting. Those of us who have public and professional lives in the larger community decide it could be helpful to be proactive about the message we want to send from our family to the media we know will greet us the next day. This part is always nerve-racking for me as I know some of the things said by energetic, defensive youth can make terrible sound bites for television and newspaper.

We agree to keep our message short and clear. My sisters Elsie and Marissa pick up some brightly coloured poster board and markers from Staples. Hanna, Elsie and I step into an open room at the courthouse to make our boldly lettered signs for our media photo op sporting the words "There is no cookie cutter for family" and "Families, not felons."

Siblings crowd together and on shoulders. Anyone watching can see the true love this group have for one another. Watching and taking photos, I feel comfort knowing the outcome of this day will not change that.

We squabble lightheartedly as only siblings can over who gets the red cushioned seats in the inadequately small BC Supreme Court room in Cranbrook. We surprise even ourselves with how many Blackmore bums we can fit bench-style with gaps between each chair. "Balancing a third of a butt cheek on each chair and the rest to open air," Dayna whispers, forcing us to stifle our giggles. The overflow goes to a downstairs room.

In between sessions we hang around in the hot May sunshine. In the courtroom the prosecutor and defence attorneys compare past cases, grasping for a precedent of a similar crime someone was ever convicted of under the Criminal Code. I'm intrigued with the process as they bounce back and forth, arguing specifically for evidence of the "harm" polygamy is to society and the appropriate punishment for this criminal offence. It's evident that all three lawyers know they are grasping at straws. I find myself thinking about the two hours on the phone I spent with Aunt Debbie last night. She told me she is following Dad's sentencing. I was interested to hear the genuine concern in her voice while she was talking about my dad. She talked about how to best support the family and how to access counselling through victim services. She told me that experts have estimated the Crown has spent over sixty million dollars trying to prosecute under the polygamy law since the police first started to review allegations of polygamy in Bountiful in the early 1990s. She talked about "our family" and that it was very important the children didn't have to keep being afraid of the police. I agree with her about that: it feels so important to somehow break this cycle of fear, which for me now is so unnecessary. I think of my own childhood and the cloud of fear that hung over my idyllic days of sunshine and mud and homemade pudding. It was a very real fear of the police taking children away from their families and dads being put in jail for polygamy. That fear was perpetuated by religious conviction about the wrath of God and the Great Destruction, fear that felt so real that if I didn't make it to heaven, I would lose my family and all that would be left for me would be a fiery inferno of eternal damnation and burning in hell.

I sit here in the small courtroom, patient and attentive as always, listening, analyzing, supporting. The lawyers dogmatically reach at a precedent. Suddenly I feel far away. I'm watching them play their game and listen to the judge. I realize no one here knows what they are trying to accomplish. This thing we call the justice system has so many flaws and loopholes and has little or nothing to do with seeking justice. It's a display of power and egos and winning and losing, and all of these highly paid, powerful people know it. I've spent more than a decade of my adult life defending and justifying the right I believe people have to define their own families. I have been interviewed, posed for photos, organized my time and been ridiculously accommodating because I've said I value the role of the media in a democratic society.

I'm just so goddamned over it.

My mind turns to that summer day on Saltspring Island. When I close my eyes, I can see the waves lap against the rocky shore and the slanting sun turning the red of the arbutus trees to a blazing gold. Somewhere, even in this courtroom, there must be God.

CHILD BRIDES

On June 25, 2018, Dad is sentenced to six months' house arrest. He can leave his house from 8:00 a.m. to 6:00 p.m. to go to his place of work six days a week. On Sundays he can go between the church and home from 10:00 a.m. until 1:00 p.m. His sentence will have been served at midnight on Christmas night.

This summer I notice my freedom with a bit more gratitude as I drive up bush roads looking for obscure trailheads and sleep on sandy beaches on Kootenay Lake. I cross the border into the US as often as possible, just to enjoy my passport. My kids are growing up quickly. I'm finding that having older teenagers is a good stage of parenting. Starla, Kayden and I take a road trip to the red mountains in Utah. We tour the national parks, hike to hot springs in slot canyons, camp in the desert and rent mountain bikes. Starla is a new driver. Her dad and I buy a grey all-wheel-drive minivan with studded winter tires from the neighbours. She will be safe, even if she's not very cool. Having kids who can drive gives us a whole other level of freedom as parents.

I'm also thankful each night that Dad is sleeping at home in his own bed. He says he's never slept so much in his life. He's one of those old guys who wakes up at four in the morning and thinks he's wasted half of the day if he hasn't hauled a load of logs by eight. I help him get his computer set up right so he can work on his book. I think he's the happiest when he is writing regularly. I enjoy his 6:00 a.m. phone calls and the excitement in his voice when he just has to read me another chapter he has been up since two writing. He reads them aloud to me as I stretch in my covers, waking up for another day. He's a skilled writer and reads in his good preacher voice. It's been a long time since my dad read me stories in bed.

My dad has got a lot more raising to do and my big brothers have told him in no uncertain terms that he has no business dying any time soon. "Plan on twenty years from when that last baby hits the ground," they've told him. "There ain't no way you get to leave us with this."

We have clumps of family within the big family. We do things in small groups, in medium groups, with the grandkids, with the sisters, with the R girls, with the M girls, the married girls, the big girls, the cowboy brothers, the stoner brothers, the kids who snowboard and the kids who hunt. We have brothers and sisters who play hockey, enough to make two hockey teams and play each other. A bunch of the kids play guitars and we all love to sing our little hearts out. We've got hipster rednecks and a few of us my brothers call hippies. Almost all polygamist kids know how to work well as a team to get a job done.

With Dad now serving his sentence, getting enough rest and spending more time than ever with the people who love him, a collective sigh passes through my family. We'll be okay.

❧

I get an email from a reporter at the *Salt Lake Tribune* saying he wants to meet with me.

He writes, "How do you feel about being a child bride?"

"I'm a 35-year-old schoolteacher, president of the Trails for Creston Valley Society, a writer and a community activist. I don't identify as a child bride," I reply, feeling a bit cheeky.

He forwards me a copy of his "child brides" list. I'm surprised such a thing exists. A flood of emotions comes over me as I read the names of mostly my cousins who were married under the age of eighteen between 1990 and 2006. Some of them I have not seen for thirteen years. Susie I haven't seen in seven years.

How do I feel about being a child bride? I give his question some real thought as I chop veggies for a stir-fry for dinner.

He's persistent. He'll be in town working on another story and he'd appreciate if I could contact any of the other girls on the list who might join us. He'll buy us dinner.

I invite my two closest friends, promising them a free meal at our favourite restaurant in town. I promise them wine. Mir and Mandy are not naive to the drill. "Nothing's free. What do we have to do?" Miriam digs.

"Come on, it will be fun," I coax with my line that makes them roll their eyes. "We'll drink lots of wine and tell stories about being child brides. How could that not be a good time?" A surgical nurse and a senior insurance sales rep, they raise their eyebrows and blink at me. "This will be different from the time I took you kayaking and you lost your keys in the river," I promise Mandy, who still likes to chide me for taking her to dangerous places.

"Why don't we buy our own food and then we can talk about whatever we want?" Mandy chips in her witty and very logical response.

Nate, the reporter, is accompanied by Jacki, a zesty photographer from Vancouver who works for *Vice* magazine and whose presence is very helpful as Nate seems a bit too preoccupied to be social. Jacki is our age and we talk easily about life, our careers, families and hobbies as we sip white wine from a local vineyard, which pairs perfectly with the evening special on the patio at Real Food Cafe.

Nate interjects occasionally to steer the conversation back to his child-bride agenda. "Tell me how you feel about being child brides and how it has affected your life." He's direct about what he came to talk about.

Each time I am taken off guard. I realize this is something I don't really think about.

I had adult responsibilities for at least a year before I was married. I was an oldest sister all my life, caring for children and taking a responsible role in our big family similar to that of my mothers. I drove a crew truck and crew to work every day to a post mill for a year. Marriage was the natural next step for me, as it was for all of my friends. Together we moved into and through our roles as wives and mothers, supporting each other. We had a place in community as we started our new families. We were supported and valued as important contributors in our world. We planned camp-outs and girls' nights together even when we each had a baby or two tagging along. I got a school bus licence at twenty-one so I could borrow a vehicle big enough to take all of my friends and their kids to the lake. We were ambitious, energetic teen mothers, just as our mothers and grandmothers had been.

Actually, those preschool years, when my babies were all mine, I remember very fondly. It was simple and clear. My husband was a good friend and companion. He went to work and came home each night. He was a good support and provider. We each knew what to do and we did it. We felt our little family life, community life and work were the whole world. If I hadn't been married, I probably would have been doing dishes at my dad's house and working in a post mill.

Like our parents before us, we were living out the natural patterns of the culture and traditions we had been born into, celebrating the seasons and cycles of life as our ancestors had done. As a young person, it never occurred to me to want something different. I loved the life of family and community I had grown up in, and I wanted that same connection to family and the land for my daughter and son.

As I sit across from this man, I can feel the edge of anger getting my attention. I notice my emotions as I imagine the sensationalism of how I assume Nate the reporter will write his story about the struggling lives of the "child brides" twenty years later.

I sit and think about my female friends. My "child bride" friends have experienced about the same divorce rate as my town friends who chose their own husbands and married for love. I don't feel one group is particularly more successful financially or happier than the other. Each demographic has experienced a healthy dose of mental illness, death, divorce, car accidents, abandonment and sexual assault. It turns out it takes a lot of doing for a woman to get to forty regardless of the world you grow up in.

It's been a long road these last twenty years and I'd say we've experienced our share of disappointments and tragedies. For a group of women pushing forty, we've got some life under our belts. Our children are mostly grown up and now we are looking at the world from a different perspective.

For us, stepping into adulthood wasn't this vague grey area of trial and error, propping up and falling down, but simply a clear and practical step across the threshold into our new lives. Our hopes and dreams and interests unfolded as our families grew and new opportunities and challenges came our way. While this journey has been no walk in the park, I do feel gratitude for the care and love of the people who raised me.

I think of my own children, who are now seventeen and fifteen. Their lives are so different in every way than mine was. I encourage them to have their own opinions and invite them to argue with me when they think I'm being unfair. I've been careful to provide guidelines rather than rules and ask them to feel what's right and wrong for them. I've been the mom who shows up to the party and tries to regulate the alcohol and hands out water and food and drives kids home. I've helped them set goals and save money. I flew my children to Mexico to go backpacking, stay in hostels, hike Mayan ruins and learn to scuba dive. My children steeped their childhood imaginations in Fablehaven and Percy Jackson tales rather than sermons of destroying angels and burning fire from heaven.

I've gathered up my daughter off the bathroom floor when she thought the world had ended because of cruel rumours spread around her high school. She said she needed a new school and a new life. "It's your fault, Mom," she wailed. "If you were more strict, this never would have happened." That day, I thought she was right.

I've been a teacher working with our youth for a decade. At times I feel like I've stood as a human shield between our kids and a heartless world as they've reached out their feelers to find their own way. I've watched as our youth have tipped over into drug and alcohol addiction and I've cheered and supported as they've slowly crawled their way out of it. I've celebrated every graduation. I've gone with them when they were in trouble with the police, their girlfriend's parents or their own parents. I've driven them to the emergency room and their counselling appointments and sat with them when they were on suicide watch. I've talked and talked and talked to our kids about healthy relationships, healthy sexuality, consent and not mixing alcohol and sex.

But how do I feel about being a child bride?

When I notice the defensiveness in my voice as I'm talking to the reporter, I take a deep breath and sit quietly for a minute, listening to the women beside me providing a buffer for me with their lighthearted storytelling, being gracious dinner dates and giving thoughtful, reflective answers about raising children who somehow became almost adults far too quickly.

I challenge myself that in this man across from me, so committed to his story, there could be an inkling of genuine concern for the actual well-being of the women on his list.

I challenge myself to really answer his question—if not for him, then for me. How do I feel about being a child bride? As far as my kids went, I loved being a young mom. My kids got me up early for morning hockey practices, motivated me to celebrate every holiday and event and to be active in community life. Everything feels urgent when you measure the passing of time by your children's lives, and social injustice is impossible to ignore when you see it impacting your children.

From my mid-thirties, I can see that there are lots of ways to live a life. Potentially there are harder and easier ways to do it, but I'm less convinced there is a right and a wrong way.

When I think about the true harm to me through my life, it doesn't feel like it was my marriage. Regardless of my age or how Sam and I married, I still feel very lucky to have known and loved and raised children with that man. Maybe, if anything, I have some resentment that the conditions of our life were such that we couldn't have made it more our own.

When I challenge myself to be honest about the harm done to me, whether directly or indirectly, I guess it feels the most true to say it was abuse of power even more than religion, although the context of religion is how it was justified, both in and outside of the church.

And when I think about the feminist fire, it feels relevant that these positions of power were mostly held by men, whether in the media, law enforcement, religion, family or just tradition.

For our dinner conversation, I sensor my sharp tongue as the wine flows and our conversation gets more direct. Giving this man in front of me a good public shaming and holding him accountable for what I consider abuse by his profession really would bring me no joy.

What if positions of voice and power actually exercised responsibility equal to their privilege? What if we had a culture so keen on preventing harm that we trained ourselves to not get caught up in the drama and put our energy and resources into true strategies and solutions for a safer, more equitable society? What if we just called out abuse when it was sitting in front of us?

I'm thankful to Mir and Mandy, who help me keep our conversation with Nate the reporter mostly lighthearted, despite my directness.

On the restaurant patio, a bottle of the fragrant local Skimmerhorn Winery Ortega between us, the four of us women give him a bit of friendly ribbing, ganging up on Nate about his "child brides" list.

"I didn't make it," he tries to defend himself.

Several bottles of wine and hours of stories later, we say our goodbyes.

About a month later, we are back at the restaurant for dinner. The waitress brings us the unpaid tab.

I roll my eyes as I pay the bill. "I was really hoping he wasn't going to live up to my expectations. Mir, how do you feel about being a child bride?"

Shaking her head, she says, "Used."

I Am Not a Mormon

With Dad a month into serving his sentence, I don't think he minds one bit that he has to be in his office by six o'clock on a Saturday night and that his sons get to take over the responsibility of hosting the church social for conference weekend. Mother Edith plays the familiar waltzes and two-steps Mormons have been dancing to since before forever. They say that even as the Saints were crossing the plains heading out west, they would set up camp and do the Virginia reel, the Chicago glide and the Danish finger polka out under the stars.

The church is scrubbed and packed with smiling faces on this rainy summer evening. Saints have gathered from high and low for a weekend of connection and prayer around food, recreation, church and social activities. I've persuaded my children to dress up in their nice going-to-church clothes and come with me to the conference weekend social.

Every year I teach my high school students the traditional Mormon folk dances in our PE classes, along with other styles of dance from hip hop to country swing. Community socials are a lot of fun. The girls have an array of outfits from formal ball gowns to slinky fitted dresses and the boys are really getting into their buttoned-down fashion, complete with bow ties and shiny dancing shoes. I so enjoy seeing the kids rock their confidence on the dance floor.

I sit next to a handsome new guy. As I don't know him, I assume correctly that he is from one of the polygamist community groups in the United States and has travelled a long way to gather with like-minded people to share connection and inspiration. In the last decade, ever so slowly, different polygamist communities have been sending out their feelers to get a sense of what other groups are doing. Some are curious about religious interpretations of doctrine and looking for others to reorganize the hierarchy of a church administration of some sorts, but most are visiting for more practical reasons. They are looking for potential partners for their growing children so they may marry and raise families in the faith.

This guy's name is Steve. He is about my age. We quiz each other, trying to sort out a general sense of where the other fits in the widening network of polygamists from Timbuktu to the United States and everywhere in between.

Looking across the dance floor at the many hair and dress styles, I comment on what an interesting and diverse group we have become. He responds that he enjoys the diversity in his community in Missouri as well, with people representing various Mormon factions, including mainstream LDS, Jack Mormons and non-believers.

"Where do you fit in?" Steve asks me.

I pause a moment, feeling out his question as there seems to be room for a real answer.

"I'm one of the non-believers," I reply simply.

He looks surprised and asks me to explain.

"I just woke up one day, sitting in meditation or prayer, whatever you want to call it, and realized I don't believe in the storyline of being a Mormon. I'm not just a non-practising Mormon; I'm not a Mormon."

Steve nods and asks, "What about God and spirit? What do you think happens to you when you die?"

I didn't expect this response. He isn't trying to corner me; he is just asking me and listening thoughtfully to my answer. No one has ever asked me these questions in this context and been actually curious about what I thought.

The narrative about a white male God who created man in his image and women to be partnered with a man under his priesthood authority, to live a life of tests, to earn up points toward some heavenly reward system, just feels contrived next to my life experience.

Brittany hasn't had much to do with church teachings since she was ten. One day she asked me to explain something to her. She laughed, saying Mormonism sounded like the plot of a video game with all the levels of heaven and points to move up to the next one.

I continue talking to Steve. "I know heaven and hell are the basic storyline of Christianity, so I guess I'm not a Christian either, even though I do love the teachings of Christ. But Christ didn't make the Christian Church. All of that came after him." Even I'm surprised as I confess my musings to Steve, who appears to be genuinely interested.

"Spirit is the consciousness, the inspiration or divine design of nature. We are created in the image of God because God is all things. We are not separate of the earth—we are made of the earth. It is our nature to create, and when we are in balance with nature, with the natural self, destruction and creation are in balance." I continue passionately. "Nature is cyclical, so there is no concept of permanence. Eternity as a long, linear, unchanging, sparkly forever doesn't make any sense to me. And destruction as God punishing dissidence seems just as silly, when destruction is essential to rebirth. Everything that ever was cycles through, is created and destroyed, births and dies and becomes part of the universal creative life force of what is to come next. Consciousness feels like the closest thing to permanence, but it is constantly evolving."

Honestly, I'm surprised he's still listening. In my experience, Mormons shut down long before this part of the conversation. He laughs good-naturedly at my emphatic philosophical monologue. "You sound just like my mother," he says.

"Your mother sounds like a smart lady," I affirm.

He tells me his parents split up when he was eight, so he was raised mostly outside the church, as was his wife. They both converted to fundamentalist Mormonism and each had a testimony, feeling called to live the fullness of celestial marriage in their family.

"So you just have no religion?" he inquires.

"I feel there is lots of value in a group of people sharing a narrative that helps them connect and achieve shared goals. I don't feel threatened by religion or feel there is anything inherently sinister about the narrative of Mormonism, as long as people are wary of manipulation to harm people. But no, I guess I don't have a religion. I have a hunch maybe I'm a Buddhist or a Hindu." I laugh. "I just don't know enough about those religions to know if I'd call them mine."

He continues to nod. He says he has studied many religions and feels that Mormonism has the most consistent information about the creation story and the afterlife.

We discuss the satisfaction of being with like-minded people who share common values. We agree that religion gives a group of people a set of agreed-upon terms, a clear way of helping people feel safe in the world. "Similar to governments," I note. "By this definition governments are a secular form of religion." Steve's eyes narrow. He isn't quite ready to concede this one to me.

By now, some of my sisters have gathered around and those sitting near us have perked up their ears, picking up the pieces of our unusual conversation at a church gathering. I think my family has decided I am strange, but we are getting to a place of more mutual acceptance.

They announce the last waltz and Steve asks me to dance. A handful of teenagers set up some tables and bring out trays of cheese and crackers and fruit with little cups of creamy fruit dip. The hall fills with the tinkle of young laughter.

It's a shared narrative that is holding this gathering together. People have travelled thousands of miles to be here. Whatever it is that pulls us together, human connection is the starting point for community. I personally don't think community and religion are interdependent at all, but religion can be a powerful glue that pulls people together, and community is created naturally through connection.

After my dance with Steve, I sit with my little plate of snacks in the busy church hall. Just a few decades ago, my cousins and I were just a barnyard full of scruffy farm kids. Now my grandfather's direct descendants number well into the thousands. This room of devoted Mormons who cherish our grandfather's faith are a small fraction of his posterity. We have scattered to the four winds, following our dreams and responding to the demands of our lives.

From my mid-thirties, looking back, I can feel that growing up with a constant foreshadowing of destruction and living with the ominous threat of an angry and destructive God who punishes dissidence with the fire and brimstone of hell is abusive to the psychological development of a child. Still, I have compassion for people who believe in heaven and hell.

Realizing I'm not a Mormon has been one of the most helpful experiences of my adult life. With it I also get to accept that my dad doesn't need to be anyone other than just my dad, a human being and a man. I don't need to analyze what he says and how it matches up to this scripture or that prophetic teaching. I don't have to debate which Prophets and leaders were inspired and which ones lost their priesthood connection to God. Dad is a kind man, an inspired man, a creative, talented and hard-working man, but he can also be selfish and shitty. Sometimes dads are like that, and I've learned that women don't have to hate their dads in order to be feminists.

My dad didn't have a dad past the age of seventeen. I often think that in his mind he and his dad would have gotten along perfectly. He thinks his dad would have counselled him kindly, applauded his good works and answered his calls and texts. All I can say is, not if he was anything like my dad.

I watch my dad parenting adult children and I know he's frustrated that we seem lazy and indulgent compared with what his life was like at our age. At the age of seventeen, my dad was helping to raise his own father's half-grown children and run the family farm. He didn't have savings or vacations in Mexico.

These days, my dad and I mostly talk about writing. Few people understand why, on my favourite days, I wake up in the morning and turn on my computer for hours of delicious indulgence. He knows. From the time I was a kid sitting at the big dining room table with my stubby yellow pencil, I've always known I was a lot like my dad.

🐚

The bouncing church social life flows out the double doors. The warm summer air invites me to take the long way home around "the block" before I walk over the hill to my cabin. The familiar smells of summer hit me in waves as I walk under the street lights in the dark down the Long Road, past the willows in the swamp, and the dogwoods' fragrant blossoms instantly take me back to riding my bike down this road as a kid.

Tonight I'm pondering God as I walk. When I was a little girl kneeling beside my bed, God was a close companion. On my journey, it was remembering God, not faith, that kept me going in my darkest and loneliest days. From every corner of the planet I've travelled to, I've prayed with men and women who know God.

I believe in people. I believe in community, and I believe in nature.

I dream of a world peace where we live in balance, creativity and abundance. I believe nature, not religion, is the best expression of God.

PROTECTING THE SACRED

My friend Anthony is picking me up at the Vancouver airport. He insisted it was no problem when I told him I would take the train. My brown leather boots clip on the shiny floor and the wheels on the bag make that I've-got-places-to-be airport sound. My floral frock and red felt hat make for a sassy getup.

I could hear his smile on the phone when he called me two weeks earlier. "An international Indigenous leaders' spiritual gathering—it seems just like something you would be into," he said. A group of friends are taking a trip through Whistler and have an extra spot in the car. I'm also excited for a visit to the city and the beaches near Kitsilano.

"Protecting the Sacred" feels like a fitting theme for this gathering in the steep winding valleys of the Fraser River. We meet on the traditional territories of the St'át'imc Nation. This is the fifth year the St'át'imc have invited guests to their ancestral home, with elders representing from Peru and Africa for four days of ceremonies, feasting, healing and speakers.

The elders open a circle and invite all to stand and receive the pipes and blessings of the Sun Dance warriors to send healing prayers to the sky while the drums and singers pray in unison with the heartbeat of the earth. "We cannot fight each other," the elder says, "or we have already lost." A prayer of healing is offered for all the survivors of the residential schools and for all of humanity to come together in healing and a time of peace.

Connected to Mother Earth in this sacred ancient way, I imagine such a circle of my cousins and aunties and uncles standing together. My community and family have experienced so much brokenness in these last two decades and I pray also for our healing.

Tears run down my face. Gratitude overwhelms me. I'm thankful for leaders who have the courage and inspiration to take their suffering and heal and use their voices to call up the world to do the same. I watch the men and women who have invited the descendants of their perpetrators into their homes, sharing their food and their sacred ceremonies. Uncle Phil Lane Jr. speaks of fulfilling the prophecies of the four nations coming together to unite the world on Turtle Island, as the First Peoples call North America. He retells the prophecy of the white buffalo that will bring "peace, harmony and balance for all those living in the Mother Earth.

We are all indigenous to Mother Earth," he reminds us.

Sitting in the shade of a large pine tree, I strike up a conversation with an elder. He's a broad-shouldered man wearing a cowboy-style shirt with pearled snaps and a cowboy hat with a feather stuck into the hatband. He sits on the school board and reminds me very much of my Uncle Rich, who was one of my favourite teachers. When I introduce myself, he responds, "Blackmore? Any chance you know Winston Blackmore?"

He is thrilled to hear I am Winston Blackmore's daughter. He tells those around us about the time when they were doing the Unity Ride across Canada. The goal was to work with local First Nations all across the country to provide horses, shelter and food for the riders as they carried the ceremonial staff from coast to coast. When they reached the Kootenays, the local band was not able to provide what they needed. Dad heard about their call for support and rounded up fresh horses and trucks, trailers and feed to transport and care for the tired horses and riders. My father as well as some of my uncles and brothers joined in for large stretches of the ride. The elder finishes his story and nods in my direction. "When you see your father, tell him George said to say hello. He'll remember me."

✤

Through the gathering, I find myself most challenged listening to the elders speak of the traditional roles of men and women, as well as trying to suspend my judgment of their emphasis on modesty in women wearing skirts that reach below their knees and covering their shoulders so as to not be a distraction to the men who are in ceremony. Modesty and strict rules about types and styles of dress were so pressed on me growing up. Girls had the moral responsibility to cover our bodies to protect the minds of men from immoral thoughts. I've struggled feeling that distinctly separated gender roles reduce the role of men to simply breadwinners and authority, rather than being part of a team to contribute to community and family in a meaningful way.

Each night with our small band of ceremony goers, Anthony and I sit with the others in a circle and pass a talking stick, sharing what has come up for us while listening to the speakers and in ceremony. During my stay in Lillooet, with the focus on protecting the sacred and honouring our elders, my grandmother has been constantly on my mind. She taught me to love service and be proud of my skills to run an efficient, economical home. She taught me to garden, cook, clean, sew and never waste our precious resources. At an early age I developed pride at being a clean and spiritual woman with a good work ethic and a positive, pleasant disposition.

As I've sat in the intense heat of the sweat ceremonies each day, I've been surprised how the layers of my struggles have come up for me to process. Suddenly I'm remembering how later in my marriage, as I went to university and learned more about the world, I began to challenge traditional gender roles and my role in my own life. I began to see my skills not as my own power but as enabling the men around me to be complacent. It seemed to me that industrious women enable men to become secondary in their role in the family. Men in power rarely seem to be proactive in using their power and influence to improve the world around them. When my own marriage was crumbling and I was struggling to find my place in the world as a woman, my mind somehow diminished my wise and capable grandmother into a simple and oppressed polygamist woman.

✸

Three days of deep soul-searching and prayer have brought a tangible humility over the gathering. The final ceremony brings Bear Dancers enrobed in exquisite silver-tipped grizzly bear regalia. "Get up and dance with your grandmothers," the elders encourage us. "Be with them. Dance with them. Touch them. Offer your prayers."

I dance in the sacred ancient rhythm of the ancestors who speak the language of this land and whose prayers pass through the trees like the wind. My feet pound the earth and my heartbeat takes the rhythm of the drums that washes over this circle like ocean waves. I dance as if in a dream, moving through and around the dancers circling our prayers.

I can feel emotions rising in my body; tears pull at my eyes. The breath catches in my throat as waves of shame and guilt and judgment and confusion crash over my body. A thick fog threatens my mind and blurs my vision.

My feet continue to dance. The sacred drumbeat is all that is holding me.

I feel my young, my flesh and blood, trusting me to guide them.

I must keep them safe. I must find a place we can go. We need to get away. I force the panic from my brain. I should know what to do. I stumble with the realization that we can't run anymore.

I feel a firm guidance direct me. "Turn to face the enemy."

I take a determined breath and stand my ground. If I can't run, I will fight. I will stand as protector of what is sacred. Blood may fall. Terror blurs my vision. My body is trembling.

There it looms above me. A tremendous grizzly sow, three times my height. A huge paw that could wipe me out with a single blow. I am dwarfed by her strength and size.

"Look at her eyes." I move with the guidance. "Look her in the eyes."

With great effort, I try to look up and up. I am looking as though through a haze of smoke, searching for the feared and hated eyes of my enemy.

Suddenly the eyes are clear. In astonishment, I gasp and step back. I look into the eyes of my grandmother, gentle, patient, knowing.

"Grandma?" My body sags. Confusion and relief splash over me and melt into a waterfall of tears.

For the moment I hold the eyes of my beloved grandmother, realization washes over my trembling body like a splash of cold water. "Grandma. Why am I so afraid of you?"

My feet stop and hold me gently on the earth.

This day, I feel my heart open. I let the layer upon layer of programming I've been wearing, the costumes of my culture and my womanhood, fall to the ground.

"Teach me, Grandma," I breathe. "Show me."

Slowly my feet begin to shuffle. I can feel my beautiful Grams dancing with me, our bare feet padding the soft ground. Tears of gratitude flood my eyes. I put my fingers into the long silver of my beautiful grandmother's hair in the silver fur of the grizzly regalia before me. I offer a prayer for my own humility, that I may be open to receive her wisdom.

Travelling home, I roll out my bedroll on the sand under a canopy of sparkling stars cradled between the mountains next to Kootenay Lake. School is starting soon. I smile, thinking about cooking pancakes for my sleepy, almost adult children as they drag themselves from their beds before driving themselves to school. I think of the many pairs of skates I'll tie and the determined faces as I'm strapping mismatched, second-hand hockey gear onto little eager hockey players that I drive to the after-school hockey program. My heart warms thinking of the smiles of my nieces and nephews in my tiptoeing tiny ballerina class after school on Tuesdays. I think of their concentration as we twirl and leap together across the stage in the school auditorium.

As the waves gently lap against the rocks in the warm late-summer breeze, I strum my guitar softly in the dark. I'm filled with gratitude knowing dozens of kids have fallen in love with the treasure of music because of my fundraising and driving to Calgary to load my hatchback with guitars for a class set. I feel gratitude to have a life in which sharing the wonders of nature and respect for the planet and humanity with the next generation is what I do to sustain my life. These days my social life consists of board meetings and work bees; rubbing elbows with volunteers is a good way to meet great people who, like my grandmother, understand the joy in a life of service.

Tonight I'll rest one more night with the gods before I step back into the clamour of my big full life. A warm wind blows off the water; the night has barely cooled from the late-August heat. Soft, silver-green tendrils of light begin to dance from the north, where the mountains crease and the lake is born of the glacial melt of the Macbeth Icefield.

I sit in the stillness and hold my prayers gently. Maybe it is God or maybe it is my grandmother speaking to me in my dreams, but even the clouds hold their breath. In the stillness, the fierce guardian of my grandmother returns to sit with me in my Kootenay valley home and her wisdom breathes across the still water.

"Your family is not the enemy. There is no enemy."

EPILOGUE

It's still April and my sunflower seeds are now buried safely in the soil along the fence in front of the Cabin. The world is settling into the new normal of COVID-19, social distancing and staying home to save lives.

I pause and reflect on the last few years, which have been hard ones for us. It's been eleven years since I moved home to help my dad, teach school and raise my family. It's already been twenty years since my marriage and almost ten years since Sam and I divorced. Almost ten years since we lost Grams.

Finally seeing the end of Dad's pervading legal fight over polygamy, I imagined we would get a season of peace. I dreamed the media would go home and shut up, and we would stop fighting. I hoped for a while we could just be.

Back in the fall of 2017, while in the midst of Dad's court battle, another kind of enemy showed up in my family. This one also threatened our kids. My niece's twenty-year-old husband, Josh, was diagnosed with bone cancer. A few months later, our little Jenn—of the Starla, Stella and Jenna musketeers—was diagnosed with a rare childhood cancer only months before she turned sixteen. Within six months, the vicious bone cancer took Josh. So brutal, so merciless, so final.

Jenna fought through a year of a million surgeries and chemotherapy, which in her own words took her body "from a beautiful curvaceous teenager" and turned her into a "skinny alien."

Then, just as spring was turning into summer, my uncle's son lost his life to suicide. He was a popular boy who played minor hockey with my son and the cousins and was in my daughter's class at school. Her classmates reeled from the loss, friend groups polarizing and fracturing and mourning in their messy, teenage, human ways. More than a few times I burst through my friend Amber's front door and curled up on her couch to cry my face off.

To spend more time together as a family in Starla's last year of school, Chaz moved into the Cabin with me and my kids.

Finally a ray of hope passes into our world. After the longest twelve months of chemotherapy, Jenna was pronounced cancer-free.

It was grad year for our girls, an exciting milestone to celebrate their transition into womanhood. Starla had sent her application to go to nursing college. Stella was engaged to get married in the summer and Jenna and her boyfriend, Will, were planning to open a store together. To celebrate our daughters and somehow make up for lost time, I organized a grad trip to Mexico. Getting everything together was like herding cats but with Mom, Linda, Jenna's mom Treena and my sister Katie, we piled on an airplane with sixteen beautiful young women bursting with life and dreams. We basked in ten glowing days of Puerto Vallarta beachy sunsets and the hopeful energy of youth.

Only weeks after we got back and after her eighteenth birthday in April, we got news that Jenna's cancer had returned.

Even now, as I dig in my garden, my body stiffens and tears come to my eyes when I reflect on these last two years. I think about Jenna and how these two years changed our enormous family forever. Our family and community teamed up to fight together to help her beat cancer. While she was fighting for her life, we watched as our sassy teenager matured into a fiery and insightful woman. She connected people from every corner of our family. She was always direct and honest and would be the first one to tell you when what you were doing didn't make any sense. She didn't mince words about how backwards she thought a lot of the conservative ways of our family were. She loved tattoos and she even got Grandpa Winston to go get a little tattoo with her. She beamed at the knowledge that no one else could have done that. She loved makeup and fashion and was outright blunt in response to anyone's comments about needing to dress more modestly or conservatively. She was clear in saying that family was much more important than religion and when religion isn't about family, then it is missing the point.

Jenna's care took a team; fortunately we were able to spell each other off to give Mom and Treena breaks. She was finally able to get approved to purchase legal cannabis because she needed to use it for nausea and pain management. She educated herself and actively shared what she knew about the medicinal and healing properties of what she felt was a very important plant. Her cousins and classmates were avid supporters of her efforts to normalize conversations about marijuana and to ensure people had access to quality information to educate themselves.

One sleepless night at two in the morning, I sat with her on the porch, bundled in blankets, while she set up her smoking ritual with her beautifully sculpted glass bong. She rambled on about her adoration for her amazing boyfriend, Will, and that he had given it to her. In her haze of pain and medication she took a few puffs to settle into some relief. Then she handed me her bong with a cheesy grin on her face. "Oh, I don't know, Jenn. I don't even know how to run it," I said, laughing.

She showed me how to light it, suck smoke into the chamber and then release the bowl while inhaling the smoke. She laughed at my coughing and I didn't even realize until the next day when my kids told me they saw a video of me on Snapchat that she'd had her camera. Jenna and I figured we might have found the secret to solving the world's problems, and I reckon she was right about marijuana being an important medicine. It got us both through some really hard days and nights.

It was on one of those nights with her that I understood she was leaving us soon. Yet in the few hours a day when her pain was managed, the vibrant young woman in her got to shine through her sickness. She would start digging around the kitchen bebopping along to her favourite songs and putting savoury things into the frying pan. Starla was taking classes at the college and Jenna eagerly asked her about which classes she liked the best and the boys she liked.

"Mare," Jenna said to me one night in a rare hour of relief, "I've decided I just need to take a college class online. I just need to get my brain to think better. There are so many things I want to learn." We talked for an hour about what classes she should take and her passion for doing research and development for medical marijuana products. Listening to her hope and desires crushed my soul. She steamed up a beautiful plate of food, then she asked me to get her heat packs and her meds, tuck her blankets around her and rub the hard lump on her foot. She picked at her food until she fell asleep. I gently lay down beside her, stroked her soft curls and let all the tears just flow. "Of course you want to go to college, baby girl. You are eighteen."

That fall, only six months since our trip to Mexico, Jenna went to the hospital for the last time. They said draining her lungs again wasn't an option. We called everyone who could make it to come see her in the hospital.

If love and prayers alone could have been enough to keep her with us, she would have stayed. Family spilled into the halls and extra room and gathered at her bedside. She wanted to see everyone, then she sent people out. Then she asked for people again. Will stayed by her side and she stayed as long as she could. She never said goodbye to anyone; she just couldn't stay any longer, and then she left us and finally her pain was over.

If there was still colour in the leaves that last week of October, I didn't notice. I watched Jake and Treena bury their baby girl. I saw my tired mother and how she and Jenna had forged a forever bond through a million hours of bedside care. I thought of how determined Jenna was to live and how much courage she had to dream of teaming up with her ambitious Will to take on the world. I watched our kids. The cruelty of this reality was sinking in. There is a shattering of innocence that comes with witnessing death like this, but I saw the way they supported each other and their ability to feel and share their emotions. She'd have been proud that Grandpa and the dads came to the fire to light floating lanterns, and that this was a church-approved gathering down at the new Old Barn and people were drinking beer.

🖙

Dad's year of probation ended at midnight on Christmas night. He served his time. He's now a free man.

A few days before the new year, Brittany gave birth to the most perfect baby girl and named her Suzie Jayne. Just saying her name feels hopeful. "Now Aunt Susie has to come home," Starla announced, saying what we were all feeling but didn't say. "She will want so badly to see baby Suzie."

As we rang in the new year, 2020 held such promise. This, I thought, would be a year of release and healing and, ultimately, new beginnings. The little kids banged pots and pans and Linda brought out the floating paper lanterns. Groups gathered in clusters of four or five to create the magic of putting burning lanterns into the sky. Kayden and the other big boys worked to light a bright blue lantern, shadows flickering across their smiling faces. Starla helped Linda and I set one up together, both of us reaching around to hold it, laughing as we fumbled with gas lighters. Mir came to assist us with a small blowtorch, which lit the resin in a matter of seconds. We held out the delicate paper as the burning wick filled the bright paper sock with hot air.

Before we let it fly, I held a moment of prayer and with all my will and intention I made a declaration for 2020. "Twenty years is long enough. Twenty twenty is the year of healing." Linda joined her voice with mine and we shouted it to the sky. "The Split is over! We are all family and community! This is the year for coming together. This is the year for healing!"

Near us, Pete was helping his five-year-old twin boys hold the thin paper while they lit the square of resin wick. He smiled at our dramatic declarations for peace.

"And this is the year we will go find Sue," he added. "We get to have her back now. It's time for Sue to come home."

❧

January let us know 2020 was not messing around. I had just arrived home after an intense meeting at work when my phone rang. My mother's weepy voice caught me. "Aunt Debbie died," she said. "They think it was a heart attack." I connected with the pitiful remorse in her voice. Aunt Debbie had been sick for about six months, but with Jenna's illness and passing, neither sister had been able to travel. "Her life has been so hard. But it was getting so much better," Mother sobbed. "She was going to retire and spend time with her children. No! I just wanted it to get easier for her. I was so hopeful that she would get this next season of time to be with family and friends. All she has ever wanted was to help people and connect. She had such a big heart."

One night, after a long day of planning and organizing her funeral, my mother curled up on the bed beside me in Aunt Debbie's house and I broke down in tears, releasing to her the intense anger that was bursting out of me. These last years my Aunt Debbie and I shared many nights of talking into the wee hours. We are both deep thinkers and justice warriors. We both recognized in the other a call to protect the innocent. I have lived close to her story, even when I didn't have her personally in my life. But this week, with the cousins going through her books and photos and reflecting on her work and mission to liberate the young women of Bountiful, I could not rationalize away the silent, festering anger welling up inside me.

"Mother, I love her and I miss her, but I'm so angry at her," I sobbed. It's hard to put this confusing emotion into words. "I know she had a hard life. I know she carried so much trauma and that wasn't fair. But she made my life way harder than it needed to be."

I thought about being afraid of the police as a child and finding the courage to face the world in college as a young woman. I could feel that I carried a deep resentment that my aunt couldn't see what effect her mission to rescue women from polygamy had on me and my life, and the lives of so many of my sisters and cousins. Finally, I realized I wished that in her crusade Aunt Debbie had taken the time to get to know me as a young woman and understand me in my life rather than viewing it always through the traumatic lens of hers. There were many times in my life when I needed help but not one of the do-good feminists who'd proclaimed themselves my saviours had ever asked me what it was that I needed.

My mother circled her arms around me, ever my witness. "I know, sweetie. She made my life way harder than it needed to be too." I think only my mother and her children could really know what this statement meant. Since their mother's passing when they were still just children, Mother took to quiet fierceness and Aunt Debbie the opposite. They each carried a burden of questions and heartache. Both sisters committed their lives to the service of their families and women. Aunt Debbie had left with her children thirty years ago and mother had stayed. While they knew they had an ally in each other, much of the time they felt the other sister didn't understand.

Later that afternoon, Aunt Debbie's close family gathered, Grandma Joanne's children and grandchildren, and we followed the hearse to the crematorium. We stood together to hold each other and to say our farewells to her.

There was still something I needed to say to my aunt before I said goodbye. I hadn't been able to find a spot for these words as they kept coming up. Standing next to her and the fire that would release her physical form, I said it silently to this woman who had been such an impactful part of my life even though she wasn't present for most of it.

"Aunt Debbie, I want to apologize to you for so much pain and suffering that you have carried. I'm sorry on behalf of adults who didn't protect you when they should have and who added to your pain as a child. I'm sorry for the men and the religion that in the name of God abused your body and your mind. I'm sorry that your efforts to share your story and stop the violence were sensationalized and manipulated by a media and society that didn't know your heart and intent. I'm sorry for all the times you didn't feel belonging, safe and loved.

"Aunt Debbie, I see you. I love you. Goodbye, my dear one."

Now, I feel certain Aunt Debbie's sudden passing must have been a catalyst or at least a sign for this shift toward healing. She talked so often of healing and family coming back together. I imagine wherever she is, she is somehow conspiring for this energetic move toward peace unfolding in our family. She loved fairies and butterflies and I imagine she could return in the hummingbirds that flit around my comfrey patch as the purple flowers begin opening in the spring rain.

✸

Leaving Starla in college and Kayden to explore some independence, with Grandma Jane checking in on him, Katie, Linda and I departed on a long-anticipated trip to India. I was thinking of Aunt Debbie, my family, Jenna and peace. I stepped onto the airplane and envisioned stepping into a portal, activating this energetic shift of completion and new beginnings. My travels were a pilgrimage of sorts. I would offer puja at every temple to pray for healing for my family. I would go to the city of Lord Shiva and bathe in the Ganges River. "It's good for you," I was assured by bright, earnest Indian men. "This is very good for you and your family. Wash away all of your bad karma, from all of your ancestors too."

India was a wild dream of colour, delicious food, intense smells, beautiful faces and adventure. And then, as the world was shutting down, fear of the virus became the collective anxiety tightening around the world like that feeling before a sneeze. When we touched back on Canadian soil and were finally home with our families, we had a little relief, but even then I could feel that the world had changed forever.

Now, as I dig in the good clean dirt with all the smells of spring, it feels so comforting having my mountain standing guardian over my family in these troubled times. My sunflowers are barely warming in the rich soil. Free from my post-travel quarantine, I manage through the grocery store with the arrows pointing me the correct way down the isles. I purchase food for my family through a window of Plexiglas.

⍩

The bright blue of the sky holds the promise of spring. I want to be hopeful. When I hear my sister's voice on the phone, my breath stops and I sag to the floor. My twenty-year-old brother Jared died by suicide at 2:00 a.m.

My heart breaks and I go numb. I let my hands get busy preparing the memorial and meals. Jake, Hyrum, Peter and I work through the details of organizing an intimate family memorial. I spend most of a day and a half going back and forth with health officials and answering emails from counsellors working out how to support a family of 150 children and 100 grandchildren to grieve while meeting the guidelines of COVID-19 and these pandemic circumstances. Divided by a border in lockdown times, many are not able to attend.

The next four days feel like an echo. It's all so familiar, rallying in times of crisis with my family. I'm explaining and defending my family's right to grieve to officials in faraway offices who are trying to enforce regulations that have no room for how interconnected and complex my family ties are. I'm asking for consideration for the bizarre enormity of a family that the world is offended even exists.

After the intimate graveside memorial and after most have dispersed, a group of close siblings sit around the deep rectangular hole, letting our legs dangle against the clay walls of Jared's tomb. Our brother Warren plays the guitar and we sing the most pitiful farewell to Jared: "So, before you go, was there something I could have said to make it all stop hurting? It kills me that your mind can make you feel so worthless. So, before you go …" Barely an arm's length away, our Jenna is buried next to him in the cemetery that doubled as a field for games like capture the flag and British bulldog when we were kids. We bury our brother on Saturday, Jenna's nineteenth birthday. The next day is Jared's twenty-first birthday.

"There's gonna be a party in heaven tonight; Jenna's finally legal to party!" Jeron, Jenna's twin brother from another mother, howls. He makes us smile, remembering the cute sibling relationship they shared. The same group of friends, cousins and close siblings hang around the graveside that evening, blowing bubbles and telling stories of Jenna and Jared, who had both been infamous mischievous rascals in our family.

I smile at these almost adult kids as they pull out well-rolled marijuana cigarettes, light them up and pass them around. When it comes to me, I hold it, watching the smoke rise in delicate curls, remembering Jenna talking about this important medicine. I puff up the clouds for Jenna and breathe a tribute to my little brother who lived fast and loud, filling the world with music. Maybe cannabis is good medicine for broken hearts.

ꙮ

I'm thankful in my spare minutes when my house is quiet to escape to my garden. I'm thankful to pick up a shovel and for the physical work of moving dirt in my wheelbarrow from the pile of soil Pete brought over with the tractor from the cow pen. I dig and stir to prepare the dirt, which has been my sanctuary this past month. I'm thankful for my professional training and for the kindness I've felt from the larger community of the Creston Valley these past weeks as I've tried to best support my family as we fumble through the messiness of grief and the hundred layers of regret that I've learned are close companions of suicide.

These last months with my family, I watched my community change. For weeks we had nowhere else to go. Work was shut down. Schools were closed. The community was bustling with life, and for the first time in my memory we all just stayed home. Kids were home all day and the sun was out. Moms were home. Dads were home. The big boys and young men were home. There was nowhere to go, so all the teenagers just stayed home. Everyone was out working in their gardens and building projects in their yards. People were cleaning up junk piles that had been sitting for years. The barnyard was full of kids riding horses. Everyone was out hiking the mountain and pushing to reach their fitness goals. I watched my brothers relax a little and take the time with their families that they rarely could before. Each evening families sat around campfires roasting marshmallows and the adults drank beers.

🔊

A rainy spring has warmed into a vibrant, green summer. On my social media, I can feel that COVID has changed the world too. Borders remain closed and social distancing is now part of our everyday lives, but something else has shifted. Collectively we've had time to reflect, and there is no way we are going to let the world go back to the way it was before. Globally people are standing up against institutionalized racism, police brutality and abusive systems of control. Collectively the world is saying, "This is enough!"

I can feel this restlessness in my body as I sit in mediation each morning. I feel into the spaces between the rules and the programming that are every day loosening control over my thoughts. When I listen, God reminds me to bravely peel away my layers of identity; I can trust and connect with my desires—the voice of my spirit—to be the guide for my life. I've sat with the flood of emotions and sadness that have overwhelmed me, and I let the tears flow freely as I grieve the passing of this season of my youth and the hopes and dreams that I lay to rest as I close this chapter of my life.

A long time ago, I set out to live a life as a faithful and obedient Mormon, a committed daughter, wife and mother. I set out to live a life as an educated and feminist mentor, teacher and friend. I set out to be good and helpful and forgiving.

I set out to be a woman.

My mind swirls with the stories of my mothers and grandmothers who live on in the DNA of my body and in my memories. They carried their babies across the plains. They buried children and they loved until their hearts broke. They worked until their backs curled, and their anger with injustice made them bitter too.

I think of how many sickbeds and birthing beds it takes to turn your long hair white.

Today, I hold young Mary Jayne with compassion. From a place of my deepest love I hold my story, and for me, today, this means I hold my womanhood with a grace I've never known. Today, for the first time, I am committing to me first. Not as someone's daughter, not as someone's wife, not as someone's mother, or girlfriend, or friend, or partner or lover. Today, I'm proclaiming this body to be my own for the joy and experience of my spirit's expression.

On this warm July day, against the backdrop of the Skimmerhorn mountains, the first smiling faces of my sunflowers are beginning to open to the blue sky. The barnyard is quiet. Kayden is gone kayaking with his cousins, and Starla is in Cranbrook doing a serving shift at the Fire Hall, the restaurant that my little sisters, Nesta and Niki, opened with their husbands. My orange cat, Leo, perches on a big rock shaded by draping comfrey leaves, and my dog, Raisin, stretches in the grass beside me.

Hummingbirds and bumblebees visit the purple blossoms hanging from the heavy green foliage of my grandfather's comfrey, which has turned my yard into a jungle.

Today I take a deep breath. Finding solace in gardens feels like an ancient way for women to find peace.

ACKNOWLEDGEMENTS

My first thank you is to my hero, my mom, Jane Blackmore, who is the woman I esteem the most in the world.

From the bottom of my heart I thank my Dad, Winston Blackmore, for sharing his love of writing and storytelling and for enthusiastically reading my stories and poems in his good preacher voice when I was a kid.

With gratitude and honouring, I thank my aunties, mothers and grandmothers, who have influenced the woman I am: Anna Mae Blackmore "Grams," Memory Oler "Grandma Mem," Elene Quinton "Granny," Alaire Oler, Marlene Palmer, Miriam Palmer, LaRee Blackmore, Debbie Palmer, Mary Ann Blackmore, Freyja Inanna, Leona Blackmore, and many more women I've looked up to and aspired to emulate in my life.

I thank my beloved Linda and Brittany Blackmore and the badass women who have walked a million miles with me and are my inspiration each day, especially Miriam Chatwin, Amanda Oler-Gipman and Katie Cooke.

A big thank you to my family, the multitude of cousins and siblings who have coloured my life with so much texture and flavour and who have become the dynamic characters in my memories and storytelling, and to our parents who raised us with music, animals, gardens, and a sturdy work ethic. The most sincere thank you to my big brothers Jake, Hyrum and Pete and my crew of talented little brothers and sisters. Some of us are sporting a few silvers in our hair now, but adventures with you guys still make me feel like a kid.

A special thank you to my niece Kristi who, when she was in my English class in grade nine, started asking me to tell the stories about the old days in Bountiful when we were kids. The stories slowly came alive as I would tell them to my students. In the evenings, I'd start plunking them into my computer. As the book has taken shape, telling this story for Kristi and our youth has been my reminder for why I am writing.

A special thanks to Luanne Armstrong who gave me the right amount of encouragement and the right amount of sympathy when I approached her after one of her own book readings and told her I was writing a book about my family. Also I thank her for being the right kind of no-nonsense gal who could say, "just send it to me," and who had the courage to wade into the wilderness of a mountain of words and the skill to start shaping the book.

An enormous thank you to my soul sister, Amber McGregor, for the walks and the talks and hashing out the fine points of feminism, for the careful and articulate unraveling of ideas. For encouragement, for goal setting, for showing up at Mormon functions and falling in love with my family. For the Tiny Room to curl up in and blankets that soak up tears, for cuss words, camping, wine, endless laughter and bulldogs, and for introducing me to Deryn Collier.

A profound thank you to Deryn Collier for reading, for work-shopping my book, for use of the sweet little studio, for being my really cool writer friend I get to go see in Nelson, and for introducing me to the talented community of women of the Kootenay writers.

A big high-five to my editor Ruth Daniell for getting down and dirty with me through the messy process of editing a story as it is still being lived out, and for being an example of a modern feminist motherhood career woman working from home with toddlers and killing it!

Thank you to Vici Johnstone, Monica Miller and Sarah Corsie at Caitlin Press for the work they do helping to birth books.

Extending my biggest love and blessings to my two Suzies—my sister and beloved childhood playmate, who was my shoulder to cry on and a sturdy rock in one of the hardest years of my life. And, my little baby Suzie—the brightest ray of sunshine who showed up in our lives just in time to beam her light all the way through the chaos of this crazy year 2020.

Finally, I thank Starla and Kayden, the two people on the planet who have taught me the most and who've witnessed the book being born in the background of their lives, weekend after weekend, summer after summer. These two are both finding their way out on their own just as the book is finding its way into the world, leaving me suddenly with an empty nest!

ABOUT THE AUTHOR

MARY JAYNE BLACKMORE was born and grew up in the polygamist community of Bountiful in rural British Columbia. She is the fifth child of Winston Blackmore's one hundred and fifty children and had a church-assigned marriage four days before her seventeenth birthday. She gave birth to her two children before she was twenty years old, and started college at twenty-one. The young family moved frequently for her husband's work and her studies, but their goal was always to return home to raise their children within the Bountiful community. After eleven years of marriage, Blackmore and her husband went their separate ways.

Mary Jayne has spent the last decade raising her children and raising a few eyebrows attending Burning Man and Shambhala. She enjoys backpacking and snowboarding. Passionate about understanding culture and women, she connects with the men and women in her travels to places like Turkey and India. She is engaged in political and environmental activism and ran for Mayor of the Town of Creston in 2018. She is an active member in the Bountiful community where she grew up and currently plants her garden and proudly calls herself a feminist.